AF541097

# Chanakya Today

# Chanakya Today

Kautilya Arthashastra
Chanakya Sutra
Chanakya Niti

**Dipavali Sen**

Publisher
UNICORN BOOKS

F-2/16, Ansari Road, Daryaganj, New Delhi-110002
☎ 011-23275434, 23262683, 23250704 • *Fax:* 011-23257790
*E-mail:* info@unicornbooks.in • *Website:* www.unicornbooks.in

**Branch : Mumbai**
23-25, Zaoba Wadi, Thakurdwar, Mumbai-400002
☎ 022-22010941, 022-22053387
*E-mail:* rapidex@bom5.vsnl.net.in

© **Copyright:** *Unicorn Books*

ISBN 978-81-7806-393-5

Edition: 2018

The Copyright of this book rests with UNICORN BOOKS. No part of this publication may be reproduced, stored in a retrieval system or transmitted, in any form or by any means, electronic, mechanical, photocopying, recording or otherwise, without the prior permission in writing from the Publisher. Anybody doing so shall face legal action and will be liable for damages.

***Printed at :*** Param Offsetters, Okhla, New Delhi-110020.

## *Dedication:*

***Anjali Sen, my mother,***
***who could recite Chanakya***
***even in her seventies***

# Contents

# Preface

About 2300 years ago, there lived in India a man who was nothing short of a phenomenon.

A middle-aged Brahmana scholar named variously as Chanakya (चाणक्य) Kautilya (कौटिल्य) and Vishnugupta (विष्णुगुप्त), he literally `made history' by deposing the reigning king of Magadha in central India and putting on it a rival claimant named Chandragupta whom he had groomed for the purpose. He taught Chandragupta how to oust the invading Greeks and to integrate various parts of India as the Mauryan Empire. Then he resigned his post as Chandragupta's minister and penned down his proven principles of political economy and civil society as:

- *Kautilya Arthashastra* कौटिल्य अर्थशास्त्र
- *Chanakya Niti* चाणक्य नीति, *and*
- *Chanakya Sutra* चाणक्य सूत्र.

Customarily, the first body of work is referred to as *Kautilya Arthashastra* whereas the other two works are associated with the name of Chanakya rather than Kautilya although Chanakya and Kautilya are one and the same person. Of the three, the *Arthashastra* deals with statecraft, the *Niti* and the *Sutra* are more general in nature.

The sections are thematic in the *Arthashastra* but more or less random in the *Niti* and the *Sutra*. There is some overlap between the two.

Right from his own times, Chanakya's works have been cited, studied and discussed. In *pathashala*s and *gurukul*s as well as many households, children were made to learn Chanakya's tenets by heart. My own mother used to say that in her childhood (the 1930s), all the children in their joint family', would be reciting some Chanakya-*shloka*s together every morning. (She could recollect a few right up to the age of 80.) But the tradition is clearly on the wane.

In order that we, the people of India, go on reading Chanakya, we need a readable presentation of Chanakya in an international language.

The available presentations, in diverse forms, textual, graphic, celluloid as well as digital, are either overburdened with interpretations or too scholarly to be readable. Sometimes they are oversimplified, distorted, and not exactly what Chanakya had said. But in this era of liberalization and globalization, every one everywhere has the right to make his or her own acquaintance with Chanakya, to know what exactly he said – and what he did not.

What this book does is to address that need.

It provides simple but faithful English translations of all three of Chanakya's works. While *Niti* and *Sutra* are presented in full, the *Arthashastra* has been abridged. Only authentic texts endorsed by scholars have been used as source material.

In this book, the readers will get a comprehensive idea of what Chanakya's writings actually contain. No other book, to the best of my knowledge, provides such faithful yet summary information on the *Arthashastra*. It should encourage readers, especially young ones, to get to the actual sources and the scholarly works. The References and the Glossary at the end are meant to aid that process.

❐

# 1

# Chanakya, Kautilya or Vishnugupta

## The Man and the Myth – the Enigma

To get an idea of the man before we plunge into his works, we string together the generally accepted information on Chanakya, Kautilya or Vishnugupta.

The actual *Arthashastra* text came to light only in early 20th century but some references to Chanakya can be found in ancient texts. The *Panchatantra* by Vishnusharma begins by paying respects to makers of *Niti/Nyaya shastra*, which includes Chanakya: " ....*Chanakyaya namah*."

The *Vishnu Purana* too refers to Chanakya dethroning Dhana Nanda.

In the first half of the 7th century, Banabhatta (the author of the romantic Sanskrit novel *Kadambari*) too had mentioned him, although critically. "Is there anything that is righteous for those for whom the science of Kautilya, merciless in its precepts, rich in cruelty, is an authority?" (*Chanakya*, MH Syed, p 77)

*Mahavamsa* and its commentary *Vamsatthappakasini* (in Pali) provides a Buddhist version. *Parisistaparvan* by Hemachandra provides the Jain version. The Kashmiri version is provided by *Kathasaritsagara* by Somadeva and *Brihat-Katha-Manjari* by Kshemendra. There is also a Sanskrit play by Vishakhadatta named *Mudrarakshasa* (Signet Ring of Minister Rakshasa), dated between the 4th and the 8th centuries.

It has been said that there is "little written material" on Chanakya who therefore remains an enigmatic character (*CHANAKYA The Master Statesman*, Roopa Pai, p 5). I would rather say that there is too much written on him, but we do not know how authentic it is.

Personally, I had gathered my first impressions of Chanakya from *Chandragupta*, once a most popular Bengali play by noted playwright Dwijendra Lal Roy. Masterly in conception and execution, the play had presented Chanakya as a genius, a maker of history, but lonely and unhappy.

Later, as a student of Economics, I had fingered available translations of the *Arthashastra*, and come across related articles. Did I get the same man?

Well, if a man becomes a myth, why not see him as man and myth together? Let us fit fact and fiction and work out a jigsaw puzzle: the enigmatic face of Chanakya.

## Early Life

Although there are claims that Chanakya belonged to the southern parts of India, specifically Kerala, the consensus is that he belonged to the northern parts and was born in Magadha (मगध) in the ancient kingdom of Gandhara. This was about 2300 years ago, the third century BC.

Chanaka was a Brahmana scholar of Magadha, so reputed as to be called Rishi (sage) Chanaka. When he had a son born to him, Chanaka found him born with a full set of teeth!

"That's the mark of a king and so, a Kshatriya – but I am a Brahmana scholar!" A worried Chanaka got the baby's teeth uprooted. Instead of a king, he became a king-maker, the real power behind the throne of Magadha.

The child was named Vishnugupta but came to be better known as Chanakya (son of Chanaka). His other name was Kautilya (derived ungrammatically from the word *kutila* ( not straight, that is, devious and/or diplomatic).

Although Chanakya did not have good looks, he was brilliant and mastered all the four Vedas while he was still very young. To encourage him, Chanaka sent him to Takshashila (तक्षशिला,Taxila, now in Rawalpindi, Pakistan) for higher studies.

When Chanakya first came to the University of Takshashila, tired and unkempt, he sought shelter with an *acharya* or preceptor named Pundarikaksha. After getting some rest there, he went with Pundarikaksha to seek admission from Shatananda, the registrar of the university.

Being a Magadhi (one from Magadha), he was an outsider to Takshashila. After an interview, he was admitted on condition that, for the first year, his upkeep would be Pundarikaksha's responsibility.

In spite of being teased by his fellow-students for his clothes and appearance, he won a scholarship the very next year, absorbed all the learning that Takshashila could give him, and then went on to be a professor there. He came to be called *upacharya* (vice-preceptor).

He was much respected by students, two of whom were named Bhadrabhatta and Purushadutta. But as he told *acharya* Pundarikaksha, he felt bitter about being teased for his looks. He got married and had a daughter. But he lost his wife and, on a stormy night, found his hut robbed even of his baby daughter.

Around this time, Alexander the Great from Macedonia in Greece had invaded India and defeated King Puru (Porus). Although Alexander's tired soldiers did not allow him to make further inroads, he left the provinces he had conquered under able generals. One of them was Seleucus I Nicator, who had a beautiful daughter named Helen.

After the Greek invasion, Takshashila was getting flooded by refugees from the kingdom of Puru. In the city of Pataliputra (पाटलिपुत्र), there ruled a king of Nandavamsha (नंदवंश, Nanda dynasty) who was named Maha Nanda (Nanda the Great).

He cared little for his impoverished subjects. Thus the country was under threat, internally as well as externally. Sensing this, an already embittered Chanakya moved away from Takshashila with two students Bhadrabhatta and Purushadutta.

## Conflict with Dhana Nanda

After some wanderings, Chanakya came to Pataliputra.

By then it was King Dhana Nanda of Nandavamsha who on the throne of Pataliputra. Rishi Chanaka had passed away, pierced badly in the foot by the razor-sharp blades of Kusha grass. Chanakya developed a terrible hatred for Kusha grass, although it was used in many puja rituals. (In another version of Chanakya's life, it is Chanakya himself who had been hurt by Kusha grass.) Every day he would go to the fields, pluck out Kusha grass by the roots and pour sugar syrup into the holes.

One day as Chanakya was performing this strange activity, a man named Katyayana came up to him.

Chanakya took no notice of him but went on plucking the Kusha grass and pouring syrup into the ground.

When the man asked him to explain, Chanakya said: "I am getting rid for ever of one who was insolent to a Brahmana. Ants eat up the syrup and, in the process, eat up the roots of the Kusha grass which thus cannot take root again."

What a subtle and devious mind Chanakya had, marveled Katyayana.

Basically a grammarian and scholar, Katyayana had been minister of King Dhana Nanda. But then Dhana Nanda had unjustly thrown him into prison, along with his seven sons.

The sons had died of starvation and Katyayana had helplessly watched them die, one by one. Dhana Nanda had later released Katyayana and made him the chief minister. However Katyayana secretly wanted to take revenge upon Dhana Nanda and overthrow him.

On seeing Chanakya tackle the Kusha grass with sugar syrup, Katyayana knew he was the right person to help him.

He told Chanakya that Dhana Nanda had invited him to the palace to conduct a ceremony and attend a feast. Chanakya was not keen to go but Katyayana persuaded him to do so. However, when he arrived at the palace, he was subjected to insults by Dhana Nanda's brother-in-law. In one version of his life, Chanakya was ridiculed for his looks. In another version, he had incurred displeasure because of his haughty behaviour. A feast had been laid out at Dhana Nanda's palace. Plantain leaves had been spread out on the ground in rows. People were seated on the ground to eat out of the plantain leaves. There was also a throne nearby, meant for someone high-up. Perhaps because he was a Brahmana, and highly reputed, Chanakya had walked up to the throne and sat down on it, instead of sitting down on the ground with the others. The king's brother-in-law had resented this and taunted Chanakya badly. The king had done nothing to reproach his brother-in-law. Rather, he had ordered: "Throw this stupid Brahmana out!" Chanakya was manhandled. His *shikha* (the tuft of hair in a Brahmana's otherwise shaved head) got untied.

Outraged, Chanakya vowed to dethrone Dhana Nanda and destroy the Nanda dynasty completely." Till the time I pluck you out at the roots like I did the Kusha grass, I will not tie my *shikha.*"

Katyayana was happy because this was why he had got Chanakya invited to the palace - to set Chanakya against Dhana Nanda , the king who had tortured Katyayana.

## Bringing Dhana Nanda Down

Wandering along the Ganga, one day Chanakya came to Peeppalli Kanan, a grove of Peepul trees (now the village Pipra near Champaran).

He saw a boy – a sturdy youth – sitting on a rock and playing a game with village lads who were minding the cattle. He was acting the part of a king, making the other kids soldiers and spies, and ordering them about.

As Chanakya came up, the boy asked, "What gift of charity may I grant you, O learned Brahmana?"

His manner was exactly like that of a king granting favours.

Amused, Chanakya played his part in the pretend-game.

"O king! Grant me some cows so that I can give my pupils a drink of milk."

"Here!" the boy called out to one of the cowherds playing with him. "Grant this Brahmana a hundred cows from the State."

Playing the game, Chanakya asked: "Have you taken the permission of your guardians before granting me this gift of charity?"

"A king does not need to take anybody's permission for making his decisions", the boy replied haughtily.

Chanakya admired his royal style. In the lines of his forehead, he read the possibility of his becoming a king in the future. Still, he wanted to read the boy's palm.

"Where are your parents?" he inquired

"I do not have a father and my mother Moora (मुरा) lives over there". From his rocky throne, the boy indicated a nearby village with his hand, giving Chanakya an opportunity to read his palm. There, too, Chanakya read a royal future.

He went over to the village and found the boy's mother out.

"Hand over your son to me", he said to her. "I will make a king of him."

Moora happened to be a wife of the former king Maha Nanda and a wet-nurse to his son and heir, the present king Dhana Nanda. (Elsewhere, Maha Nanda is called Sarvarthasiddhi and has two wives Sunanda and Moora. From Sunanda were born several sons known as the Nandas and from Moora, one – the youth Chanakya had chanced upon.)

Moora had been thrown out later by the Nanda brothers while she was still expecting. Going to her kinsmen, she brought up the son born to her as a village-lad. Thus the boy Chanakya had spotted was really a co-brother of Dhana Nanda and therefore a rival claimant to the throne. Moora belonged to the Shudra *varna* and the boy was not of pure Kshatriya blood. But if Dhana Nanda could be dethroned, the boy had a right to become king.

He also had the spirited and commanding attitude of a king. Chanakya wanted to groom him further.

The whole night he reasoned with Moora and her son (who had by now come in from his game).Mother and son did not want to part. But in the end Chanakya could convince them about the great possibilities that the boy could have under his guidance.

Moora let him go. "Forever will your name be associated with your son", said Chanakya. "I name him Chandragupta Maurya. The royal dynasty he sets up will be known as Maurya-*vamsha* rather than Nanda-*vamsha*."

In a slightly different version of the above story, Chandragupta is a little older and himself aware of his claim to the throne. With this end in mind, he had himself been observing/studying the Greek army in Takshashila so as to use its techniques for future use.

He had even been caught doing so and taken for a spy. But when Alexander had heard Chandragupta's story, he said that he would let him go ... on condition that they would have a drinking match. If Chandragupta could hold his drink while Alexander succumbed to it, he would be free to go. Chandragupta, even though he had not tasted liquor before, kept his head. Alexander, who had a weakness for wines, sunk into a drunken stupor and Chandragupta walked out of his tent free! If he did so remembering Chanakya's principles of self-control, that would mean that he had already met him. No one can be sure of the order of events.

Yet another version says that Chandragupta was a tribal lad with the peacock or *mayur/mor* as its totem. Chandragupta also loved to eat peacock meat. That would explain his epithet Maurya.

Chanakya wanted Chandragupta to pick up all that a good ruler would require: warfare as well as statecraft. He got him admitted to the University of Takshashila. The university education developed his reading, writing and taught him martial arts, and also political principles and diplomatic tactics.

Chanakya now felt that the time had come to overthrow Dhana Nanda. He was already unpopular with his subjects because of the high taxes he imposed on them to pay for his personal luxuries, and because of his inertia in protecting the country from external aggression. The country held together because of Amatya Rakshasa, the loyal and wise chief minister that Dhana Nanda had.

Chanakya gathered villages and communities together and spoke to them. Sometimes his platforms were only the hillocks in the countryside.

He made the people see that in spite of the large army that Pataliputra had, the kingdom would fall because of a lack of leadership. Nanda was no protection against the *mlechchha* (a derogatory term for foreigners). "Unite against Dhana Nanda! Rise in revolt!"

The second plank of his argument was that Chandragupta would be a better option for them than the avaricious and decadent Nanda or his brothers.

"Make Chandragupta your new king."

The people began to get convinced. Villagers and mercenary communities enlisted as soldiers.

Soon Chanakya had raised an army for Chandragupta to command.

Under Chanakya's guidance Chandragupta began attacking the Nanda kingdom at its heart, Pataliputra. But every time he did so, he was defeated. Chanakya felt worried. Was it Amatya Rakshasa's guidance or the sheer right of Nanda's army, or was it some mistake that he, Chanakya, was making?

One day, while worrying over the matter, he came upon a child crying because he had scalded his lips in eating steaming hot food from the centre of the dish.

His mother was comforting him but reproaching him at the same time.

"How often have I told you to eat from the edges where it is cooler and not from the centre where it is hottest! "

Chanakya felt that the lady had taught him a big lesson. The core or central area was naturally the most powerful. It would be the edges which would be weaker. Now he had to change the battle strategy and make Chandragupta attack at the edges rather than Pataliputra itself.

Conquering the bordering villages helped Chanakya and Chandragupta get more soldiers for army.

But Chanakya realized that they needed some royal assistance as well.

Chanakya sought and won the friendship of the Himalayan king Parvataka (Parvatesha, Parvateshwara) who brought his strong hill-tribe soldiers to support Chanakya's cause. Himalayan prince Chandraketu became Chandragupta's friend and princess Chhaya even fell in love with him.

Because Alexander's troops were tired and did not want to proceed further into India, he had withdrawn, leaving a governor (*kshatrapa,* later called *satrap*) in charge of every territory that he had conquered. The governors often faced rebellions and the Indian ones themselves wanted to be free of a distant foreign rule. One of them, named Philip, was killed. Others lost control, Alexander was far away and died mysteriously in Babylon in 323 BC. One by one, territories or provinces in northern India came under Chandragupta who was being guided by Chanakya.

However often the people of the conquered areas often wanted to be free of Chandragupta's authority, and rebelled as soon as his troops marched onward, and so, had to be conquered all over again. Chanakya advised Chandragupta to place some of his troops on the conquered territories while he moved on to the others. That solved the problem.

Nearly the whole kingdom came gradually under Chandragupta's control and then Chanakya advised him to attack Pataliputra.

This is what he had learned from the mother teaching her son. Hot stuff should be attacked from the outer ring rather than the centre.

Amatya Rakshasa started preparing the royal army to face Chandragupta's onslaught. To keep abreast of his plans, Chanakya cleverly planted his spies in the enemy camp.

It was a formidable battle. Though Chandragupta's army was smaller, it was very well-organized. It attacked the palace of Dhana Nanda and took him prisoner.

Chandragupta felt like sparing Dhana Nanda's life.

His mother Moora, who had been Dhana Nanda's wet-nurse (later thrown out and insulted), also softened towards him.

But Chanakya knew that like Kusha grass, the enemy had to be destroyed at the very roots -- completely and irrevocably. He got all Dhana Nanda's brothers killed and by reminding Katyayana of how Dhana Nanda had starved his sons to death, stirred him up so that he chopped off Dhana Nanda's head.

The Nanda dynasty was finished. Chandragupta's claim to the throne was absolutely clear. He became the new king, called Chandragupta Maurya.

Chanakya felt that he had fulfilled all his vows. He now tied up his *shikha.*

## With Chandragupta on the Throne

But his concern for Chandragupta and the country was not over.

He continued to be at Pataliputra and protect the new, inexperienced king. However, he went on living in his ramshackle hut and did not take up quarters in the palace.

The boundaries of the kingdom were extended and Chanakya's dream of building up a powerful empire under Chandragupta began to come true.

Chandragupta confronted Seleucus I Nicator, the governor of the eastern territories conquered by Alexander under whom he had once served as a general.

Faring badly in the confrontation with Chandragupta, Seleucus conceded large areas and in a diplomatic exchange of gifts, gave his daughter Helen's hand to Chandragupta in marriage. (Chhaya was also taken as a wife. And there was another wife named Durdha.)

Seleucus also sent a Greek ambassador to Chandragupta's court. He was Megasthenes from whose account we get to know a lot about India in Mauryan times.

The story goes that Megasthenes was shocked to find the prime minister of Magadha living in a hut.

"It is because the prime minister of Magadha lives in a hut", Chanakya told him, "that people in Magadha live in mansions."

Living frugally, Chanakya spent all his time fiercely guarding the interests of the kingdom. He tried to protect Chandragupta in every way he could, even physically. So much so, that every day he mixed small doses of poison with Chandragupta's food so that he would develop immunity to it and escape any attempt to poison him.

However, this led to a tragic mishap. Queen Durdha, who was expecting, once partook of Chandragupta's food by chance. As she had no immunity built up within her, she died. But Chanakya operated upon her and took the baby out while it was still alive. A drop (*bindu*) of poison had gone inside (*sara*) him and so he came to be known as Bindusara.

Chanakya kept track also of what Nanda's loyal minister Rakshasa was doing now for revenge. Amatya Rakshasa was, in fact, trying to make secret attempts upon the Chandragupta. After averting a few such attempts, he realized that the best way to stop such attempts was to win Rakshasa over.

Chanakya put Rakshasa's friend Chandanadasa into prison. Out of loyalty to his friend, Rakshasa surrendered to Chanakya and asked for Chanadanadasa to be freed in return. Chanakya agreed, on condition that Rakshasa became Chandragupta's chief minister and, for the sake of the kingdom, worked for and not against Chandragupta. Rakshasa agreed.

Thus Chanakya gave up his own power and position to ensure the safety and integrity of the kingdom.

A different version is that, after a while, Chandragupta became tired of Chanakya's guidance and came to see it as domination. He wanted to enjoy himself with dancing girls and other palace luxuries. He began to disregard Chanakya's advice and even made slighting remarks to him. When he came back after conquering the Deccan, he wanted a grand reception with victory arches set up in the capital to welcome him. But Chanakya called off the celebrations.

"Why? Upon whose orders?" Chandragupta asked Malayaketu.

"Upon Chanakya's orders, my friend", said Malayaketu.

"Who is the king, Chandragupta or Chanakya?" demanded Chandragupta. "And remember that friendship is among equals."

Malayaketu, very hurt at this remark, was banished from Pataliputra. Chanakya was asked for an explanation. Chanakya smiled but refused to give one.

Soon Chandragupta realized that the remnants of Dhana Nanda's men had been plotting to kill him on his return. It was no time for celebration and that is why Chanakya had put off the celebrations. Dhana Nanda's brother-in-law had got an underground tunnel built secretly for 25 men to go and kill Chandragupta in a newly-built apartment. Chanakya's spies had revealed this plot to him and he had posted men to kill the brother-in-law as soon as he emerged from the tunnel. In one version, it was not a tunnel but niches in the wall cleverly hidden behind mirrors and portraits that Chanakya spotted at once as suspicious. Further, Seleucus I Nicator had crossed the river and was approaching Pataliputra with his army. Katyayana was his advisor.

Katyayana knew that Chandragupta was in difficulties, having alienated Malayaketu and Chanakya. This was the time for attack, he advised Seleucus.

But Chanakya negotiated with Seleucus and prevented a showdown. He drafted a treaty that Chandragupta would give 500 elephants to Seleucus and marry his daughter Helen while Seleucus would yield some conquered territories to Chandragupta and retreat. Moora wanted Chhaya to be her daughter-in-law but Chanakya explained that diplomatically it was much more important that Helen became Chandragupta's wife. However Helen was generous enough to marry Chandragupta as well as accept Chhaya as a co-wife, and so this issue was amicably settled.

After this, persuading Katyayana to be an advisor to his one-time ward the proud Chanakya withdrew from the scene.

There are variations in the prevalent stories. In one, Parvateshwara, the Himalayan king whose support Chanakya had enlisted for Chandragupta, had intended to get a share of the territories under Nanda once he was defeated by their coalition. But Chanakya is supposed to have killed him through a *vishakanya* or poisonous woman. (These were women who either actually poisoned the man they were sent out to kill or carried some lethal disease which spread to him through physical contact). Parvateshwara's son and successor Malayaketu (Chandraketu) joined up with Rakshasa, demanding all the old territories of the Nanda and hatching a plot to kill Chandragupta.

Chanakya fabricated evidence to show Malayaketu that Rakshasa was willing to betray him and cross over to Chandragupta's side. He used a *mudra* or signet ring found by a spy to stamp a fake letter apparently sent from Rakshasa to Chandragupta. This drew in a wedge between Malayaketu and Rakshasa.

Chanakya forced Rakshasa to become Chandragupta's minister. This he achieved by announcing death penalty for Rakshasa's old friend Chandanadasa and withdrawing it only on condition that Rakshasa took over as Chandragupta's minister.

At this juncture, Chanakya's long-lost daughter too was restored to him. Her kidnapper had got blinded and taken to begging, using the now-grown-up baby as singer. By chance they came singing near Chanakya's hut. Recognizing his daughter's voice, Chanakya rushed out and was re-united with her. The hardness in his heart melted down and he lost interest in actual governance.

He gave up his position in the Magadha court and resumed the life of a Brahmana *pandit*. Away from court life, he wrote down his observations and prescriptions on statecraft, economic policy, military strategy and even ways of everyday living.

**The Last Days**

In course of time, Emperor Chandragupta turned to Jainism. Once Bindusara had grown up, Chandragupta relinquished the throne to him. Following Jain saint Bhadrabahu, he went to a cave in Shravana Belagola in Karnataka. In the tradition of Jain ascetics, he abstained totally from food and drink and gave himself up to death.

As the new emperor, Bindusara had many ministers. One of them, a detractor of Chanakya named Subandhu revealed to him the story of his birth which had so far been unknown to Bindusara. He added the twist that it was Chanakya who had really killed his mother.

Seeking out nurses who had attended upon his mother at his birth, Bindusara asked: "Is it true that Chanakya had slit open my mother's belly upon which she had died?"

"Yes" answered the nurses and Bindusara rushed out seething with anger at Chanakya.

When the story of Bindusara's wrath reached Chanakya, he gave away all his money in charity and went and sat on a pile of dried-up dung, neither eating nor drinking. In the mean time, Bindusara came to hear the true story of his mother's death. He had realized that Chanakya had really salvaged the situation as best as he could. With the best interests of the country and the king, he had saved the heir to the throne – which was Bindusara himself.

Bindusara now hurried to the pile of dung and pleaded with Chanakya to come down.

Chanakya sent him back, saying, "I have lived enough and been hurt enough".

Bindusara went back and, in his fury, took Subandhu's life.

Chanakya, king-maker, no, emperor-maker, and author of *Arthashastra*, *Chanakya Niti* and *Chanakya Sutra*, starved himself to death on the dung-hill.

In another version, Bindusara did go back and unleash his fury on Subandhu. The wily fellow pretended that he would himself go and get Chanakya back to the court. He went and made a show of arranging a reception as Chanakya would get down from the dung-heap. But as the process started, Subandhu cleverly flung a live coal upon to the heap of dried dung which immediately went up in flames. Chanakya was thus burnt to death.

It was only then that Subandhu himself was killed by the king.

According to Jain texts, this took place around 275 BC.

Bindusara ruled on, maintaining cordial relations with governors remaining in India and Egypt. His son was none other than Samrat Ashoka.

## Continued Influence

The empire under Ashoka owed a lot to the economic and administrative principles of Chanakya as applied by Chandragupta. But ultimately, Ashoka gave up warfare and espionage in favour of the peace-loving ways of Buddhism. In this sense, he rejected the military and diplomatic ideas of the *Arthashastra*.

However, the ideas continued to influence household life as well as wider socio-political life in India even after the times of Ashoka. Today, it is more relevant as ever as India is – to use Chanakya's term a *Vijigeeshu* or Aspirant-Conqueror of the globalized world—not in terms of territory but in terms of economic development.

❐

# 2

# Chanakya Reviewed

## Chanakya and Krishna

In the *Mahabharata*, Krishna was the advisor of the Pandavas right from the time of Draupadi's *swayamvara*. While Duryodhana enjoyed the comforts of Hastinapura, the Pandavas went about in forests in disguise, and Krishna advised them about their moves and especially befriended Arjuna. On the other hand, Duryodhana's counsel Shakuni gambled on behalf on Duryodhana but never trained or groomed him. Krishna encouraged Yudhishtthira to perform the Rajasuya *yajna*, and Arjuna to get training from the gods in divine weaponry. He acted as the negotiator from the Pandava side but when the Kurukshetra War started, urged Arjuna to forget that he was fighting his relatives, teachers and friends. Krishna advised Arjuna when to attack and when to withdraw, what weapons to use on whom, and occasionally used his own super powers to save the situation. Once the Pandavas won, Krishna remained their well-wisher but stayed largely at Dwaraka.

There are parallels with Chanakya raising Chandragupta to Dhana Nanda's position and then retiring. If Krishna gave us the *Gita*, Chanakya gave us the *Arthashastra*.

And this is not surprising because Chanakya was a follower of Vishnu, the Preserver, of whom Krishna was an incarnation. Vishnu being the Preserver (rather than the Creator and the Destroyer), his work is aimed at *sthiti*, preservation or maintenance (in this case. of northern India). But it is not just political or administrative preservation but the preservation of correct principles (*niti*). Krishna had said that Vishnu/Narayana gets reborn from time to time for re-establishing Dharma ("*dharmasamsthapanarthaya*").Or, for example, "*Swadharme nidhanam shreyo paradharma bhayabaha*"

The *Arthashastra* begins by Chanakya's bowing to the great godhead Vishnu. His actual name too was Vishnugupta. Chanakya's lifetime achievement must be seen in this tradition of preservation rather than restructuring. In *Trayisthapana*, *Arthashastra*, he says that *Swadharma* or adherence to one's own *Varna* and *Ashrama* is the way to heaven and so, a king should not allow the transgression of *Swadharma*.

## Chanakya and Machiavelli

Chanakya has often been compared to Machiavelli.

To quote Jawaharlal Nehru in the *Discovery of India*, "Chanakya has been called the Indian Machiavelli and to some extent the comparison is justified.." (M.H. Syed, P 78).

Henry Kissinger too has compared Chanakya to Richelieu and Clausewitz.

Well, who were these people?

Machiavelli (1469-1527) was an Italian official in the Republic of Florence. During1498-1512, when the Medici were out of power, he was most powerful but once they regained power, Machiavelli withdrew from active politics and wrote *The Prince*, a pioneering work of political science, highlighting the virtues of a strong , unscrupulous and ruthless ruler. Machiavellianism has come to be synonymous with deviousness and immorality in statecraft.

Richelieu (1585-1642) was a French bishop and statesman who was chief minister to King Louis XIII. He curbed the nobility , consolidated the king's powers and made state powers more centralized.

Clausewitz (1780-1831) was a Prussian general and military theorist writing on moral and psychological aspects of warcraft in the famous but incomplete *Vom Knege* (On War).

To quote Kissinger :

"Kautilya wrote about an India comparable in structure to Europe before the Peace of Westphalia. He describes a collection of states potentially in permanent conflict with each other. Like Machiavelli's, his is an analysis of the world as he found it; it offers a practical, not a normative, guide to action. And its moral basis is identical with that of Richelieu, who lived nearly two thousand years later: the state is a fragile organization, and the statesman does not have the moral right to risk its survival on ethical restraint.

...... For Kautilya, power was the dominant reality. It was multidimensional, and its factors were interdependent. All elements in a given situation were relevant, calculable, and amenable to manipulation toward a leader's strategic aims. Geography, finance, military strength, diplomacy, espionage, law, agriculture, cultural traditions, morale and popular opinion, rumors and legends, and men's vices and weaknesses needed to be shaped as a unit by a wise king to strengthen and expand his realm — much as a modern orchestra conductor shapes the instruments in his charge into a coherent tune. It was a combination of Machiavelli and Clausewitz.

...... The *Arthashastra*'s exhaustive and matter-of-fact catalogue of the imperatives of success led the distinguished 20th-century political theorist Max Weber to conclude that the *Arthashastra* exemplified "truly radical 'Machiavellianism' . . . compared to it, Machiavelli's *The Prince* is harmless." (*TOI*, November 21, 2014)

Nehru's stand was sensible. "..But he (Chanakya) was a much bigger person (than Machiavelli) in every way, greater in intellect and action. He was no mere follower of a king, a humble adviser of an all-powerful Emperor. A picture of him emerges from an old Indian play, "The Mudra Rakshasa" which deals with this period. Bold and scheming, proud and revengeful, never forgetting a slight, never forgetting his purpose, availing himself of every device to delude and defeat the enemy, he sat with the reigns of empire in his hands and looked upon the emperor more as a loved pupil than as a master…" (Nehru, quoted by M.H. Syed, p78)

G. Harihar Shastri wrote: "… (The *Arthashastra*) when compared to *The Prince* of Machiavelli, is on many grounds far superior in quality and far larger in content" (*Social Philosophers, p 46*)

Recently Roopa Pai, Jaideep Prabhu and Sourav Roy too have contrasted Chanakya with Machiavelli.

Pavan Varma, accredited IFS officer and author, has called the *Arthashastra* "one of the world's most incisive treatises on statecraft" and urged that Chanakya was not the Machiavelli of medieval Europe who, in any case, wrote 1800 years later. He was more. He never wanted the king or his men to deviate from rectitude, become corrupt and unjust. He just wanted them not to be fools.

Impractical idealism was no part of Chanakya's thinking. Not that he was too much of a cynic to believe in a just society, but Chanakya believed in practical ways and means to achieve it in a focused way. That is how he re-built a Bharatvarsha that was reeling under foreign invasion and falling apart through internal strife. This is the lesson to be learnt from Chandragupta's guru now.

## Chanakya's works are empirical rather than theoretical

Although the word *shastra* is attached to his work, Chanakya was not a philosopher who had his head in the clouds. Chanakya's writings are not theories but tested and proven observations. Only after overthrowing Nanda and securing Chandragupta's position did Chanakya retire to pen down his ideas on governance and statecraft. He is thus an empirical economist and policy-maker, not a theoretical one. He does not make assumptions and make conclusions. He gives out rules, diktats or prescriptions that have worked.

Henry Kissinger would agree. In the *Times of India*, 21.11.2014, he has written:

"….his (Kautilya's) is an analysis of the world as he found it; it offers a practical, not a normative, guide to action. And its moral basis is identical with that of Richelieu, who lived nearly two thousand years later: the state is a fragile organization, and the statesman does not have the moral right to risk its survival on ethical restraint………The Arthashastra sets out, with dispassionate clarity, a vision of how to establish and guard a state while neutralizing, subverting, and (when opportune conditions have been established) conquering its neighbors. The Arthashastra encompasses a world of practical statecraft, not philosophical disputation."

## Chanakya attaches great importance to wealth and prosperity.

Although he lived the austere life of a scholarly Brahmana, Chanakya's works extolled the pursuit of *Artha.* He who has none of the four virtues of righteousness, material wealth, physical fulfilment and spirituality (*dharma*, *artha*, *kama* and *moksha*) is condemned to die again and again in one birth after another ( *Niti* 3.20).

A home is empty without the son, all the quarters are empty without friends. The heart is empty without intelligence and everything is empty without wealth (*Niti* 4.14).

Dharma has to be protected by wealth (*Niti* 5.9). It is the one with money/wealth who has friends and allies, enjoys life and is considered an important man (*Niti* 7.15). Allies forsake one without wealth. So do wives, servants and well-wishers. The purport of this is that wealth is the true friend in this world (*Niti* 15.5).

**But he also makes it clear that learning is more important.**

Chanakya is, first and foremost, a guru, a teacher, an educationist and placed the greatest emphasis on learning and honing up one's intelligence.

Just a few quotes will illustrate this point:

Even the learned man (*pandit*) tires of advising a stupid pupil (*Niti* 1.4)

Wise men should put their sons into various ways of improving their minds. Principled and cultured sons are the ones revered in the family (*Niti* 2.10).

Parents who do not get their sons educated are, in fact, their enemies. In a gathering of enlightened men, an ignorant one is a crane among swans – a misfit (*Niti* 2.11).

Fools are biped beasts and to be rejected. They prick like unseen thorns (*Niti* 3.7).

Like flowers without fragrance are men without education even if they have youth, good looks and noble birth (*Niti* 3.8).

Even without a fire the following six burn the body: living in an uncongenial place, serving people without a worthy lineage, bad food, a cantankerous wife, an uneducated son and a widowed daughter (*Niti* 4.8.)

What are you going to do with cattle which yield neither milk nor calves? What is the use of a son who is neither educated nor respectful? (*Niti* 4.9)

In an alien country, a man's learning is his friend. (*Niti* 5 15)

One who has no wealth is not really impoverished. If he has determination/conviction, he is a rich man. But one who is bereft of the gem that is learning, he is impoverished in every way. (*Niti* 10.1)

A noble king should enhance popularity through expenditure of wealth. Out of *Dharma*, *Artha* and *Kama*, *Artha* is the most important. *Dharma* and *Kama* are rooted in *Artha. (Arthashastra, Prakarana 3, Rajarshi vrittam)*

## Chanakya's Military Doctrine

"Kautilya's *Arthashastra* had a profound influence on the further development of military doctrine and practical conduct of battles in ancient India", writes Major General G.S. Sandhu in *A Military History of Ancient India* (p 288-9). Its influence was strong and pervasive, and persisted even when modernizing forces had rendered much of it (e.g., its passages on the chariot arm) irrelevant. It is not Kautilya's fault, Sandhu hastens to say, that the art of war developed but slowly in India. Military science formed only about one-fifth of his work and reveals "a lack of practical experience of the actual handling of troops". What is more, Kautilya tended to deduce results from specified actions rather than encourage "inspired generalship which accepts risks in war in order to make greater gains".

## Chanakya and Indian Diplomacy

**Actually, Chanakya is a diplomat, preferring alliances to open combat.** He may have said a lot on warfare and military organization but his main weapon is brainpower. His message is on the following lines:

The huge elephant is controlled by the small probe (*ankusha*). The deep darkness is dispelled by the flame of a lamp (*Niti* 11.3).

The king who aspires to be a conqueror (*Vijigeeshu* or Aspirant-Conqueror) should be well-versed in *Niti-shastra* or Political Principles A king with an adjoining/contiguous territory is an enemy or rival. The king who has a kingdom adjoining that of the enemy king becomes an ally. It is because of some reason that enmities and alliances get created. A king who is getting weaker should make an alliance (go for peace). Strength/power is the reason for making alliances. The strong should have a war (battle/combat) with the weak and not go for alliance. One should not have a war with the equally strong or stronger king (*Chanakya Sutra* 1.55-56).

According to a few, this idea of Kautilya's encouraged infighting among the neighbouring kings of India, and made India vulnerable to foreign invasion, as early as the 12th century.

Scientists from the Defence Research and Development Organization, Bangalore, along with University of Pune, and the National Institute of Virology, have combined in a project to study the *Arthashastra* for 'effective stealth warfare techniques that would give Indian military troops an edge over their enemies" (p 63, Chapter 6, `The Relevance of Chanakya Today', *CHANAKYA The Master Statesman*, by Roopa Pai). According to her, it is Chanakya's consistently amoral tone and unembarrassed pragmatism" that makes him "enormously relevant in a twenty-first century world reluctant to engage in large-scale conflicts" (p 65).

Pavan Varma has related Mahatma Gandhi's *ahimsa* to Chanakya's diplomacy. He has called *ahimsa* "a conscious policy choice elaborated upon and implemented with dramatic efficacy by Mahatma Gandhi" which brought us freedom. "The choice of ahimsa against a much stronger military enemy was, when shorn of the genuine idealism animating the Mahatma, a Chanakyan stratagem" (Pavan Varma, *Chanakya's New Manifesto To Resolve The Crisis Within India*, pp 9, 167, 173, 175, 194-6).

However, Varma feels that, having won freedom in the tradition of Chanakya, India has not taken it forward in the clear-cut way shown long ago by Chanakya. From the 1948 Pakistani aggression of Kashmir Valley to the Kargil War of 1999, India has displayed a "timidity" that is "baffling and disappointing. (http://associationdiplomats.org/publications/ifaj/Vol1/ecodiplomacy.htm)

On the lines of Chanakya, Pavan Varma has drawn up a comprehensive blueprint for India's reconstruction (rather than destruction). For, he strongly feels that even if Chanakya's administrative prescriptions are outdated, his philosophy and good sense are not.

In my own article `Economic Diplomacy-The Making and Unmaking of India', *World Focus* April 2015, I too have linked Chanakya with India's current diplomatic policies.

*Prakarana* 176 *Labdhaprashamanam* (Assuaging What is Acquired) says that When a territory is newly annexed, the conqueror must respect the traditions of the conquered people.

तस्मात्समानशीलवेषभाषाचारतामुपगच्छेत्।
देशदैवतसमाजोत्सवविहारेषु च भक्तिमानुवर्तेत।।

In modern times, this can be interpreted as a recommendation to preserve cultural diversity even in a global world.

## Chanakya is an economist in his own right.

The *Arthashastra* is not a treatise on Economics in the accepted and essentially Western sense though the word often gets translated as Arthashastra or Arthaniti. Hardly any university would include Kautilya's work in the syllabus for Economics, but many do it, at least in parts, in that for Political Science.

But Chanakya was no less an economist than a political scientist.

With respect to wealth, he took a view akin to that of **Physiocrat** economists. In Europe in the Mercantilist era ($16^{th}$ century to the late $18^{th}$), Bullionism prevailed. It was then the prevalent thought in Europe that a nation's wealth depended largely on its stock of gold, silver and other precious metals. Later the Physiocrats ($18^{th}$ century) came to hold that a nation's wealth came from its agriculture. The yield of Land was the basic constituent of its prosperity. Feudalism was the prevailing economic system and this idea was perfectly in tune with it. But as urbanization and industrialization proceeded in the $18^{th}$ and $19^{th}$ centuries, and Capitalism became the prevailing economic system, new ideas were born. Adam Smith, writing in 1776, found the wealth of nations to be based on Production on the principles of Specialization or Division of Labour. David Ricardo became worried about the Diminishing Returns from Land. Thomas Robert Malthus made gloomy predictions about population outstripping food supply, i.e., the returns from Land. Chanakya had also laid down the tenet that anticipates division of labour : One should be employed/engaged in the work in which one is efficient ( *Sutra* 2.25) This is tune with his belief in the Varnas. Isn't it also in tune with the Classical economists' faith in Specialization ?

Chanakya may even be called a **Keynesian**! As is well-known, after the Depression of the 1930s, John Maynard Keynes emphasized boosting up (rather than cutting down) expenditure to give income generation a boost. " It is letting go of wealth which is its protection"(Sutra 4.28).To protect income that one is earning , one should spend off wealth that is already accumulated just as to take in fresh water into a lake, its standing waters should be made to flow out (*Niti* 7.14).

Chanakya clearly recognized the importance of spiritual and sensual aspects of life, not just the pursuit of material gains. He meant his work to be for *Dharma*, *Artha* as well as *Kama*.

This implies that Chanakya envisaged a strong and active role of the State in the socio-economic life of the nation. The Capitalism that emerged in Britain and spread to Europe and the rest of the world is firmly rooted in this maintenance of law and order. Market mechanism or price mechanism works only if the country has a strong legal system. Adam Smith, the great pioneer of Classical economics referred to this as The Invisible Hand. He said that if every individual goes about his business of maximizing his own welfare, then the Invisible Hand will work to ensure that social welfare is maximized.

On the other hand, Chanakya had certain similarities with Karl **Marx**, also a thinker of Classical times but with a most original outlook. Marx developed the theory of Dialectical Materialism and was concerned with material aspects of human society such as production and distribution. 'Artha' was what *Das Kapital* is all about. People function for the sake of material welfare/ means of livelihood (*Niti*). This is the Materialistic perception of Marx.

But Marx totally denied spiritual aspects, saying that religion was the `opiate' of mankind. He envisaged a public take-over of economic activities and a Socialistic state, where all property would be socially owned. Further, he envisaged that in the ultimate stage of Communism, the State itself shall `wither away'.

This is totally different from Chanakya's conception of the feudalistic kingdom with its strong network of espionage and dominant role of the minister – a *Brahmana*.

Nevertheless, it is interesting to note that the Russian emperor Czar Nicholas II was overthrown in 1917 by Marxist ideology (as developed by the Bolshevik and Menshevik Parties). Lenin certainly had Marx as his guru. Stalin too ruled USSR with a highly advanced system of espionage (KGB) and centralized economic planning (GOSPLAN).The Marxian `withering away of the State' never arrived at the USSR (or anywhere in the world as yet).

## Chanakya as Management guru

Not just householders but corporate personnel would also benefit from Chanakya's advice on what today would be called `time management'. Chanakya wrote: He who knows the right time for a job succeeds at it. Exceeding the time for a task leads to time itself consuming up its results. Not for a moment should one waste time. One should begin a task after analyzing its appropriate place and possible consequences (*Sutra* 5-18).

Radhakrishnan Pillai, an authority on the *Arthashastra*, has called Chanakya `leadership guru *par excellence'*, providing principles on how to identify leaders and groom them to govern a country. In *Corporate Chanakya: Successful Management The Chanakya Way*, he has picked up Kautilya's principles and pointed out their applicability in the contemporary corporate world.

Rajshekar Krishan has presented Chanakya as the complete management guru with the first ten sutras of his forming what he calls a Virtuous Circle.

Senior Human Resource professional Challa S.S.J. Ram Phani too has pointed out how today's managers can learn human resource management and marketing strategy from Chanakya. The *Arthashastra* has tips on recruitment, promotion and control of employees that are relevant even today.

Swami Yoga Bharati calls the *Arthashastra* "a classic in the science of polity" and "..on the basis of this teaching, we can examine the modern-day approach to artha and determine where it fails in following these ancient ideals. One can write a very detailed thesis to discuss this approach to modern problems in the business and the political world."

## Chanakya had the essential management skill of talent-spotting or identifying leadership quality.

Dr R.K.Mukherji in *The Foundation of the Mauryan Empire* had said: "..The country had hardly recovered from the shock of Alexander's victorious march througn it…The battle of India's independence…called for a leader of exceptional ability and vision who would infuse new life and enthusiasm into the dropping spirits of a defeated people…Fortunately the country produced such a leader in young Chandragupta who had already been prepared in advance for his great mission in life by the Brahmin Chanakya, better known as Kautilya. Chanakya's superior vision and insight led him to discover in this youth the disciple who would be able, under his direction, to free the fatherland of foreign rule." (*Chanakya*, Ed.Syed, pp 77-78)

## Was Chanakya speaking only to powers-that-could-be?

Chanakya's principles are all addressed to kings or prospective kings, not the ordinary householder, Brahmana or non-Brahmana. This is perfectly in line with the *Gita* and the *Panchatantra/ Hitopadesha*. Krishna was addressing a prince fighting for his elder brother, the crown prince, and Vishnusharma was telling his stories to young princes. The commoners were to be ruled over by the royalty acting on those principles. Specifically, the *Arthashastra* is addressed to a *Vijigeeshu*, a king who wants to conquer the *mandala* or circle of the kingdoms around him.

Amartya Sen, Nobel Prize winning economist and a pioneer of the Human Development Index, has also drawn attention to this prescriptive tone in Chanakya.

He has pointed out that social scientists have long investigated how the concerns of a society's members can be reflected in one way or another in its collective decisions, even if the society is not fully democratic. For example, in the 4th century BC, Aristotle in Greece and Kautilya in India explored various possibilities of social choice in their classic books, Politics and Economics, respectively. The Sanskrit title of Kautilya's *Arthashastra*, translates literally as "the discipline of material wellbeing".

In his book *The Idea of Justice* (2008), Amartya Sen has referred to the idea of justice in Kautilya's *Arthashastra*. He has pointed out that in Sanskrit literature, both the words *nyaya* and *niti* are used in the sense of justice. But *niti* stands for organizational propriety while *nyaya* for a comprehensive concept of realized justice. According to him, Chanakya did not have faith in the people making decisions for themselves and had a more prescriptive format of justice than exhibited later by Ashoka and Akbar.

## Chanakya and the Welfare State

One tenet of Chanakya's anticipates the Welfare State that emerged in Britain only around the Second World War. The king also has the responsibility of providing maintenance to children, to the aged, sick, endangered and orphaned, the childless and the widowed and even their children(*Arthashastra Adhikarana 2*)

## Chanakya on Disabilities

Chanakya regarded it a *Vakparushyam* or punishable act of Verbal Violence to jeer at a disabled physically challenged person *(Vakparushyam, Dharmasthiya, Arthashastra, Adhikarana 3)*. Spies also disguised themselves as dumb, deaf and deformed persons (*Prakarana 7 Gudhapurushapranidhi, Arthashastra*).

## Chanakya's Advice to the Bureaucracy

Chanakya's advice to government officials is relevant even today. For example, in *Prakarana* 92, *Anujeebivrittam* (Behaviour of Followers)

Adhyaya 4, he advises that they should attach themselves to powerful kings with lots of able ministers around him. For example, once appointed by the king, one should do only the work for which one has been appointed and stay neither too far away from the king nor too close. One should not say anything reproachful, sarcastic, incredible or false before the king. One should not wink or curl one's lips, interrupt the king when he is speaking, or keep repeating oneself. If the king laughs, one should not maintain a wooden silence but one should not laugh uproariously either!

आत्मरक्षा हि सततं पूर्वं कार्या विजानता।
अग्राविव हि सम्प्रोक्ता वृत्ती राजोपजीविनाम।
एकादेशं दहेदग्निः शरीरं परंगतः।
सपुत्रदारं राजा तु घातयेत् वर्धयेत वा।।

The wise government official should first think of protecting himself because the condition of those dependent on the king has been said to be more dangerous than that of those who play with fire. Fire burns part or whole of the body but the king can make or mar the entire family.

## Did Chanakya have a Gender Bias ?

Chanakya did not have a high opinion of women. He wrote: Women eat twice as men, are four times as clever as men, are six times as courageous and eight times as amorous (*Niti* 1.17)

One should not trust clawed, horned and armed creatures, rivers, royal families and women. The natural faults of women are falsehood, boldness, guile (*maya*), stupidity, excessive greed, lack of cleanliness and kindness/alertness (*Niti* 2.1).Women should not be trusted at all. They do not have conscience or the idea how to behave in public (*Sutra* 5.67)

At the same time, Chanakya wrote approvingly of a woman in the role of a wife:

That man is already in heaven who has an obedient son, a wife who walks in the rhythm he sets her, and contentment in whatever wealth he has (*Niti* 2.3).She who is clean and pleasant of appearance, dedicated to her husband and content with him, she who is honest and truthful, is a worthy wife (*Niti* 4.13). Of course, she had to bear her husband a son! Wives are (made) for (the purpose of having) sons (*Sutra* 6.20,6.24). He was harsh upon unworthy ones. He wrote: It is undoubtedly deadly to have a wife who is unworthy (*Niti* 1.5) Allies forsake one without wealth. So do wives, servants and well-wishers (*Niti* 15.5).One should protect one's assets for coming calamities. One should protect one's wives even at the cost of one's assets. But one's own self is to be protected at the cost of both one's wives and one's assets (*Niti* 1.6). Note that Chanakya talks of *wives* rather than *a wife*. Polygamy was a usual practice then.

The wife is a chain that is not made of iron. Mischievous/unfaithful wives wear intellectual men down (*Sutra* 5.62, 5.64)

Chanakya respected motherhood, writing: Among gurus, the mother is the greatest (*Sutra* 5.68).

But he also declared: Even a mother should be discarded if she is contaminated (Sutra 4.14).

At the same time, there is a remarkably modern view in the *Arthashastra:* If a courtesan was unwilling and yet forced, the man would get punished (*Adikarana* 2,27,*Ganikadhyaksha* (Superintendent of Courtesans).

## Chanakya – narrow-minded or ritualistic ?

Chanakya certainly was a staunch believer in the Brahmanical tradition. But he was not a narrow-minded ritualistic person. He wrote:

Without rituals before the fire, the knowledge of the Vedas is incomplete. Without charity, a sacrificial ceremony is incomplete. Without genuine feelings, there is no success. Feelings are the basis of everything. If one serves any icon made of wood, stone or metal with genuine feelings, it succeeds in pleasing Vishnu. The deity dwells in neither wood nor stone nor earth. He dwells in genuine feelings which are the basis of everything (*Niti* 8.10-12).There is no enemy like a sacrificial ceremony. It burns up a nation deficient in food grains, a priest deficient in the knowledge of sacred chants, and a performer of sacrifice who is deficient in his donations (*Niti* 8.22)

## Chanakya- a Poet ?

Chanakya's style is terse and tight. His couplets show exemplary economy of words. But some of his quartets use similes and metaphors of striking beauty.

For example,

A single sweet-smelling flowering tree makes the entire forest fragrant, just as a single worthy scion glorifies the entire family-line.

A single dried-up tree, when it goes up in flames, makes the entire forest catch fire, just as an unworthy son ruins the entire family.

A single moon lights up the entire night. So does a good son, honest and well-educated, illuminate entire family-line (*Niti* 3.14-16).

One wonders, with such mastery of words, what if Chanakya had tuned to poetry instead of state-craft ? Perhaps in gaining great insights in Political Economy, we have lost great literature?

❒

# 3

# *Arthashastra*, Translated and Abridged

## The Structure of the *Arthashastra*

The *Arthashastra* is in 15 sections of unequal length containing prose passages as well as couplets and quartets. The sections are called *Adhikarana*s, so-called because, as the *Adhikarana* 15.3 says, the topics or subjects in each section are presented with the force, the strength, the right of conviction (*adhikara*).

1. *Vinayadhikarika*, the first section, deals with Kingship - matters such as the conduct of kings, the tasks of rulers and administrators, the appointment of secret agents/intelligence, the work of ministers.
2. *Adhyaksha-vichara*, the second, deals with Civil Administration - the considerations of a minister or advisor to the king, the treatment of corruption and scams, the principles of punishment and reward.
3. The third section, *Dharmasthiya* relates to Civil Law and teaches men conduct, character and discipline. The Dharmasthas were ministers and officers carrying on the administration of justice.
4. The fourth section, *Kantaka-shodhana*, relates to Criminal and Personal Law, or simply, Penal Law. It deals with the correction (*shodhana*) of those who are thorns (*kantaka*) or impediments to society – social miscreants as well as any government officers, tax-collectors, businessmen and workmen who pester the common people. It relates to the day-to-day administration, especially to craft guilds and artisans' groups. Kautilya made a clear distinction between *Dharmasthiya* and *Kantaka-shodhana*.
5. *Yoga-vritta*, the fifth section, is on the duty and treatment of royal retainers - the service-conditions and maintenance of employee.

6. *Mandala-yoni*, the sixth section, is on seven important aspects of the Circle (*mandala*) – the nature and functions of the seven Constituent Elements (*prakriti*) of State.
7. *Shad-gunya*, the seventh section, describes six ways of dealing with foreign policy.
8. *Vyasana-adhikarika*, the eighth, is on how to deal with adversities or calamities.
9. *Abhiyasyakarma*, the ninth section, is on how to advance or march forward in external and internal troubles.
10. *Sangagramika*, the tenth section, is on war – on battle techniques and strategies.
11. *Samghavritta*, the eleventh and the shortest of sections, is on policies towards oligarchies or the rule of a group rather than of an individual.
12. *Abaliyasa*, the twelfth section, and also a short one, is on strategy relating to a weaker or smaller king being attacked by a bigger and more powerful king.
13. *Durga-lambhopaya*, the thirteenth section, is about how the king can capture a fort and control subjects, officials, businessmen and rivals.
14. *Oupanishadika*, the fourteenth and the last-but-one section, is on secret strategies of attack and defence of the kingdom.
15. *Tantra-yukti*, the fifteenth and the last section, is on the scientific method used in the *Arthashastra* – the grammar and logic of terms and phrases used in the treatise.

Each *Adhikarana* (section) consists of *Prakarana*s (sub-sections), ranging in number from thirty-nine (as in *Shad-gunya*, the seventh section) to just one (as in *Tantra-yukti*, the last section).

## Early Texts

The written text of the *Arthashastra* lay scattered in various parts of India, e.g. a fragmentary palm-leaf manuscript in Devanagari characters was found in a Jain Bhandar in Patan of North Gujarat.

But the first book in English on the *Arthashastra* is R.Shama Shastri's *Arthashastra of Kautilya* (Mysore, 1923, reprinted in 1924 and 1951). It was based on a palm-leaf manuscript in Grantha characters, preserved in Mysore Government Oriental Library. Noted political scholar Radhakrishna Chaudhari has called it a `discovery' (*Kautilya's Political Ideas and Institutions*, Chowkhamba Publication, Varanasi, 1971, p 15).

Soon after, there followed *Arthashastra of Kautilya* edited by T.Ganapati (Trivandrum, 1924-25) and *Arthashastra* by J. Jolly and R Schmidt followed (Lahore 1924). J.J, Meyer's *Arthashastra of Kautilya* was published in Leipzig in 1926. Kaliyanov's Russian translation from Moscow appeared in 1959.

From Bombay in 1960-65 came R.P.Kangle's seminal work *Arthashastra*.

## The Definition of the term `*Arthashastra*'

It is in the last section of the treatise, viz., *Tantra-yukti*, that Kautilya explains what he means by the term `Arthashastra'.

`*Artha*' means the income-yielding activity or occupation (*vritti*) of man. It also means land (*bhoomi*) associated with people. The subject (*shastra*) that studies the ways and means (*upaya*) of nurturing (*palana*) the profit (*labha*) from the earth (*prithivi*) is called *Arthashastra*.

Human beings work upon Nature and generate income. This income (generated by man working on Nature) can be protected as well as further enhanced. How to do that is the subject-matter of *Arthashastra*. (15.1)

Kautilya further says that the *Arthashastra* is a guide to *dharma*, *artha* and *kama* as well, protects them who follow it and destroys the *adharma* that opposes *artha*.

Kautilya then establishes his authorship by saying:

The *Arthashastra* is prepared by Chanakya, also called Vishnugupta, who by his righteous anger rescued the scriptures, the weapons and the land that had gone under King Nanda. Observing the difference of opinion among composers of tenets and their commentators, Chanakya himself has prepared both its tenets and its commentaries.

## A Flowering of Earlier Traditions

It is important to note this last sentence. Kautilya here himself says that his *Arthashastra* is rooted in earlier works by others rather than being a first-of-its-kind. Indian political thought had existed before Kautilya. "The *Arthashastra* of Kautilya represents a definite stage in the history of political thought. It has rightly been called the flower of Indian political thought and statecraft….Kautilya calls it a compendium of all the *Arthashastra*s and a book on statecraft for all time to come……his ideas represented the quintessence of Indian political wisdom. The *Arthashastra* was the most scientific and authoritative interpretation of the older traditions of similar literature." (Chaudhary, pp 7-10)

## The Arthashastra Text

### *Adhikarana 1:Vinayadhikarika*

## The Section On the Discipline of Learning

*Prakarana* 1: *Vidyasamuddesha Anvikshakeesthapana*

**The Purpose of Learning and the Establishment of Philosophy**

There are four types of learning (*vidya*): logic, philosophy or metaphysics (*anveeshakeee*), the threesome (*trayee*) of the Vedas, agricultural techniques (*varta*) and administrative and judicial principles (*dandaniti*).

In other words, one should study philosophy, scriptures, economics and governance.

Contrary to Manu, Brihaspati and Shukra, Kautilya attached great importance to philosophy.

प्रदीपः सर्वविद्यानामुपायः सर्वकर्मणाम्।
आश्रयः सर्वधर्माणाम् शश्वदानवीक्षकी मता।।

Philosophy is the lamp that illumines all arts, supports all activities and protects all *dharma*.

Having said this, Kautilya proceeds to *Trayisthapana* or establishing (*sthapana*) the threesome (*trayee*).

*Sama Veda, Rig Veda* and *Yajur Veda* constitute the three *Veda*s. The *Atharva Veda* and the *Itihasa*s (such as epics and *Purana*s) are also included in them. *Shiksha, Kalpa, Vyakarana, Nirukta, Chhandas, Vichitti* and *Jyotisha* are *Vedanga*s (limbs or auxiliary subjects).

The three *Veda*s help establish the natural or characteristic duties (*swadharma*) of the four *Varna*s and *Ashrama*s.

The *Varna*s are four.

The natural duties of a *Brahmana* are to study, perform rituals prescribed for a *Brahmana*, perform rituals on behalf of others, perform acts of charity and accept gifts of charity.

The *Kshatriya*'s natural duty is to study, perform prescribed rituals, live by the use of weapons and protect everybody.

The *Vaishya* should study, observe the due rituals and perform the activities of agriculture, animal husbandry and trade. The *Shudra* should serve the three higher *Varna*s, perform activities of agriculture, animal husbandry, some job involving skill and artisan or entertainment.

The *Ashrama*s are four as well.

The duties of a *Grihastha* (householder) are to earn a living from following a profession, marrying within the *Varna* but not within the *Gotra* (that is, a woman with the same original paternal ancestor), having children conceived (at the right time) by and born of one's own wife, worshipping deities, forefathers and teachers, putting others first and being happy with whatever is left after they have finished.

The *Brahmachari* (student, disciple, not yet a householder) should study his prescribed texts , feed the sacrificial fire, bathe as per rules and keep himself clean, not work for a living but live only by alms, and by devoting himself till death to his guru, his guru's son and other disciples of his guru.

The *Vanaprasthi* (householder who has left for life in the forests) remains without physical enjoyment, sleeps on the bare ground, wears deer skin and does not tend to his hair. He takes ritual baths and makes sacrifices to the fire, worships deities, forefathers and gurus, He does not either earn his living or beg alms but lives on whatever fruits and roots he gathers from the forest.

The *Parivrajaka* (roaming ascetic, *Sannyasi*) controls his senses completely, gives up all occupation, all possessions, all material interest. He lives on charity from here and there and never settles down in one place for long. Clean inside and outside, he lives in the forests.

But (whatever the *Varna* or the *Ashrama*), all are enhanced by Truth, Purity, Lack of Malice, Kindness and Forgiveness.

*Swadharma* or adherence to one's own *Varna* and *Ashrama* is the way to heaven.

तस्मात्स्वधर्मं भूतानां राजा न व्यभिचारयेत्।
स्वधर्मं संदधानो हि प्रेत्य चेह च नन्दति।।

Hence the ruler of men should not allow the transgression of *Swadharma*. He who holds on to it is happy once he leaves the earth.

व्यवस्थितर्यमर्यादाह कृतवर्णाश्रमस्थितिः।
त्रभ्या हि रक्षितो लोकः प्रसीदति न न सीदति।।

One who is protected by the three *Veda*s, adheres to the occupational arrangement and the *Varnashrama*-structure feels satisfied, not sad.

Kautilya next proceeds to establishing *Vartadandaniti.*

*Varta* consists of agriculture, animal husbandry and commercial activity. It yields food crops, animals, gold, copper and other such minerals. With this art, the king gets his Treasury and his army, the means by which he controls his own people as well as those of the enemy.

कृषिपशुपाल्ये वाणिज्या च वार्ता।।
धान्य पशुहिरण्य कुप्यविष्टिप्रदानदौपकारिकी।
तथा स्वपक्षं परपक्षं बशीकरोति कोषदण्डाभ्याम्।।

The prosperity that comes from Philosophy, Vedas and Agriculture all depend upon *Danda* (penalty or punishment, symbolized by the rule of the rod).The principles (*Niti*) that determine the penalties or punishment to be assigned are known as *Dandaniti*.

आन्वीक्षकी त्रयीवार्तानां योगक्षेमसाधनो दण्डः।
तस्य नीतिः दण्डनीतिः।
अलब्धलाभार्था लब्धपरिरक्षणी रक्षित्तविवर्धनी
वृद्धस्य तीर्थेषु प्रतिपादनी च।

It is this *Dandaniti* that leads to the attainment of what has not been attained (*alabdhalabhartha*), the protection of what has been attained (*labdhaparirakshani*), the expansion of what has been protected (*rakshitavivardhini*) and the sharing of what has been expanded among those who qualify for them (*briddhasya teertheshu pratipadanee cha*).

On *Dandaniti* depends all worldly proceedings (*lokayatra*).

According to the preceptors of earlier times, *Danda* or penalty is the only way of controlling people. But Chanakya differs. According to him, a king dealing out penalties that are too harsh makes his subjects tense, and one dealing out penalties that are too mild, makes them disrespectful. Hence the ruler should deal out penalties that are just and fair (*yathartha*). Judicious penalties make the subjects dedicated to *Dharma, Artha and Kama*. Unjust or unfair penalties, whether meted out in anger, greed or ignorance, infuriate people of every stage (*ashrama*) of life. On the other hand, if no penalty is meted out, there prevails the `law of the fish' (*matsyanyaya*) when small fishes get eaten up by the big. Without a well-thought out system of penalties, there is chaos and anarchy. But if the king rules according to a fair and just principle of penalties, even the weaker subjects feel strong.

If the people belonging to the four *Varna*s and *Ashrama*s are nurtured by the king according to *Dandaniti*, they remain engaged in work in their respective spheres.

चतुर्वर्णाश्रमो लोको राजा दण्डेन पालितः ।
स्वधर्मकर्माभिरतो वर्तते स्वेषु वेश्मसु ॥

*Prakarana 2: Vriddha-samyoga*
**Development**

The three types of *Vidya* (also called *Vinaya*) are rooted in a just and fair system of penalties. It is of two types, self-evident or axiomatic (*svabhavika*) and developed or constructed (*kritaka*).It should be imparted only to the deserving, those who are keen, attentive and conscientious. The (male) child should be taught the alphabet after his ritualistic shaving of hair (*mundana*). After the ritual of getting to wear the sacred thread (*upanayana*), he should be taught Philosophy and the *Veda*s by a learned *Brahmana* of good conduct, *Varta* by a responsible person in that area, and *Dandaniti* by an expert in the subject. He should observe the rules of the *Brahmacharya ashrama* till the age of sixteen. After that he should make charitable donations and get married. To enhance his education, he should now associate with a learned and venerable old man. In the first part of the day, he should learn practical skills such as the use of weapons and care of elephants, horses and chariots. In the later part, he should study subjects such as the *Purana*s and the *Arthashastra*. The rest of the time should be spent in acquiring new knowledge and revising knowledge that is already acquired. If he has not understood a subject on hearing about it once, he should hear it again and again. The various *Vidya*s and *Shastra*s develop intelligence and create a taste for *Yoga*, which in turn, develops our inner strength. This is the power of education.

विद्याविनीतो राजा हि प्रजानां विनये रतः।
अनन्याम् पृथिवीम् भुङ्क्ते सर्वभूतहिते रतः।।

It is the enlightened king engaged in promoting the education of his subjects and the welfare of all who enjoys an uncontested reign on earth.

*Prakarana 3: Indriya-jayah Arishadvargatyagah*
**Conquering the Senses and Giving up the Six Enemies**

The five sensory organs (*indriya*s : ear, skin, eyes, tongue and nose) have to be controlled. The six enemies (*ari* or *ripu*), viz., desire (*kama*), anger (*krodha*), avarice (*lobha*), arrogance (*mana*), intoxicants (*mada*) and excitement (*harsha*) have to be conquered.

Kings such as Jamadagni, Ambareesha and Nabhaga, who have conquered the six enemies and kept their senses under control, enjoyed long their reign on earth.

*Prakarana 3: contd.*
*Rajeshvita*
**Activities of a Saintly King**

A noble or saintly king (*rajarshi*) should control his senses, develop his wisdom through association with elderly and mature people, employ spies to gather information, conduct state affairs through his enterprise, see to it that the subjects observe their respective duties, spread education, enhance popularity through expenditure of wealth, and generally take interest in the welfare of his subjects. He should not covet or violate others' wives, and wealth. He should not laze around, lie, insult or keep bad company. It is not that he should not enjoy life. But he should do it without transgressing righteous principles. There should be a balance among the three objectives (*trivarga*) - the spiritual, the material and the physical (*dharma, artha* and *kama*). Excessive service to any one of them leads to great suffering.

Kautilya goes beyond this usual and accepted advice. Where the *Arthashastra* is distinct from all other *shastra*s is the emphasis Kautilya places on the material aspects of life.

अर्थ एव प्रधान इति कौटिल्यः ; अर्थमूलौ हि धर्मकामाविति ।

Out of *Dharma, Artha* and *Kama, Artha* is the most important, says Kautilya. *Dharma* and *Kama* are rooted in *Artha.*

But at the outset Kautilya also makes the point that the king should not function as a dictator or autocrat. He says that it is his advisors and agents who establish the respect accorded to a king. They caution him and prevent him from blunders, sometimes by reminding him of the time or using other checks.

सहायसाध्यं राजत्वं चक्रमेकं न वर्तते।
कुर्वीत सचिवांस्तस्मात् तेषां च शृणुयान्मतम् ।।

Just as a vehicle cannot run on one wheel, a kingdom cannot function without advisors. The king should thus appoint worthy ministers and listen to their advice.

***Prakarana 3:*** ***contd.***
***Amatyaniyukti***
**Appointing Courtiers**

Kautilya discusses the views of other preceptors on the issue of appointing courtiers, ministers or advisors. For example, Bharadvaja has said that courtiers should be chosen out of one's old fellow-students. For then the king will be convinced of their integrity and efficiency. However, Vishalaksha has said that then the king runs the risk of being ridiculed or reprimanded. He should rather choose his courtiers out of those who are assisting him in secret assignments. Kautilya stresses efficacy or efficiency as a quality. The king should not ignore his fellow-students and old friends. But he should appoint his courtiers on the basis of their intelligence, education, courage and other such qualities, and never make them ministers or advisors.

***Prakarana 4:*** ***Mantri-purohitayorniyukti***
**Appointing Ministers and Royal Priests**

The royal advisor/minister should be born of the same country, without bad qualities, a good horse-rider and a man with skills. He should be articulate, a good speaker, enthusiastic, influential, determined, patient, steady, pleasant of appearance and without envy or enmity.

Before appointing the minister, the king should make proper enquiries about him (such as about his residence and solvency, health and general conduct) from his neighbours and acquaintances, and test his abilities through various new assignments.

The royal priest should be high-born, highly educated (learned in the three *Veda*s, *Vedanga*s and *Jyotisha*) and able to treat/counter natural and man-made calamities through ways prescribed by the *Atharva Veda*.

### *Prakarana 5: Upadhabhih Shouchashouchagyanamamatyanam*
### Taking Secret Tests of the Purity of Courtiers

The king, after appointing a new courtier, should secretly try out (*upadha*) of his genuineness (*shouchyashouchya*).For example, the king may order the priest to go and perform a ceremony in the house of a lowly person. If the priest refuses, the king may de-recognize him as the royal priest. The disgruntled priest may seek to stir up a rebellion among the courtiers. If the newly appointed courtier refuses, the king recognizes him to be a loyal person fit for his new position. However, Kautilya thinks that the king should not jeopardize himself or his queen by resorting to such tests. He should use some external means to test his courtiers, or use secret agents (*gudhapurusha*).

### *Prakarana 6: Gudhapurushotpatti*
### Emergence of Secret Agents

After testing out his courtiers, the king should appoint secret agents or spies. There are five types of *Samstha-guddhapurusha* - spies who do their job staying (from the verb *stha*) in one place.

The *Kapatika* dress as students and are good speakers. The *Udasthita* are dressed as mendicants. The *Grihapatika* spies come in the guise of poor farmers, the *Vaidehika* in that of poor traders. The *Tapasa* pretend to do rigorous meditation (*tapasya*) and are either clean-shaven or have matted hair.

*Prakarana 7: Gudhapurushapranidhi*

## Matters relating to Secret Agents

*Bhramansheela* or *Sanchara* spies move about as they do their job, passing on information from one to another.

The *Satrin* are not part of the administration but necessary for it and so maintained by it. They know fortune-telling, hypnotism and can entertain people by singing and dancing.

The *Teekshna* are those who can mix and mingle with one and all to extract information.

The *Rasada* are lazy, venomous, and cruel even to their own relations.

The *Parivrajika* is a widowed, elderly or poor Brahmana lady who enters a household as a mendicant.

The *Munda* is a lady with shaven head, begging for alms.

The *Vrishali* is a spy from the *Vaishya varna.*

For example, A *Teekshna* may serve courtiers and observe their equipment and their use. A *Satrin* may communicate this information to the *Kapatika* and others.

Spies also served as domestic servants e.g.,

*Sooda* (cook), *Aralika* (one who especially cooks meat), *Snapaka* (one who aids bathing) , *Samvahaka* (one who makes the bed), *Kalpaka* (barber), *Prasadhaka* (toiletry assistant), and *Udaka-parichalaka* (water-bearer).Spies also disguised themselves as dumb, deaf and deformed persons, tribal people and jungle-folk, story-tellers and acrobats

Kautilya considers it essential for a ruler to employ spies. If three spies, unknown to one another, bring the same secret information, he should accept it as correct. Sometimes the ruler should pay a salary to a spy who is already in the employ of his enemy king. He should use traders who come to his fort to do business, mendicants who come there to ask for alms, farmers in other parts of the kingdom and even jungle-folk (who can inform him about the coming and going of enemies in the jungle).

Kautilya thus attaches great important to the development of a secret service force.

### *Prakarana 8: Svavishaye Krityakritya-paksharakshanam*
### Protecting Own Subjects Susceptible to Temptation

Once the king had engaged spies upon his ministers, priests and such others, he should also engage them to learn the attitudes of his subjects towards himself, which of them are susceptible to temptation (*kritya*) by rival kings and which are not so treacherous (*akritya*).

Theses spies should go to market places and social gathering, and start up a fight among themselves. One of them should start criticizing the king, and another should counter the criticism. Then they should report the reactions of the citizens to the king.

The king should reward citizens who had supported him by giving them grain, gold and cattle. He should give grain, gold and cattle also to those who are unhappy with his rule. He should make an effort to win them over. But if that does not work, he should make his officials (the police or the tax collector) set them against the rest of the citizens. Once the others turn against them, the king should quietly have them killed or suppressed or even take away their wives and children away from them for mining and such other public work. For, weak, greedy or disgruntled people cross sides easily. Whatever the means, the king who is aware of attitudes towards himself will prevent all his subjects, big or small, successful or otherwise, from moving over to the rival side.

### *Prakarana 9: Paravishaye Krityakrityapakshopagraha*
### Getting Hold of the Rival King's Susceptible Subjects

The king should find out through his spies which people of the enemy country are wavering and vacillating in their loyalties and which are not (*krityakritya*). Such people may be of three categories – those who are angry with the rival king (*kruddhavarga*), those who are scared of him (*bheetavarga*) and those who are covetous because they have had losses under his rule (*lubdhavarga*).The king should seize them and bring them under himself. He should stir up the anger in those who are angry, and assure protection to those who are scared and wealth to those who are covetous.

There is another category – those who are highly positioned and well-respected under the rival king (*maanivarga*). The king should send spies to them and create a split between them and their patron. He should entice them to take shelter under him.

As for the others, the king should penalize them in order to bring them under his control.

*Prakarana 10: Mantradhikarah*

## Ministerial Consultation

*Mantrana* (secret consultation) should be done in absolute secrecy, in a sound-proof room where birds too cannot fly in. Not even by gesture or body-language should the king or his ministers give the consultation/discussion away. None but the king himself should fully know the secret consultation. Only the person initiating the consultation should have an inkling of it and even he should get to know of its conclusion only at the end. The king should not insult anyone while in consultation, not even a junior person. He should consult just one or two ministers and take certain decisions sitting quietly by himself. Manu, Brihaspati and Shukracharya have indicated specific numbers for the council of ministers to have. Kautilya prescribes that the number should be according to the abilities of the persons concerned. Indra had a thousand sages in his court as advisors and so was called Sahasraksha (thousand-eyed). But whatever the number of ministers, each minister should be educated in the *shastra*s. A person who is not well-versed in the *shastra*s is not fit to be a minister to a king.

*Prakarana 11: Dootapranidhi*

## Matters relating to Messengers

Only after secret consultation among minister is over, should a messenger (*doota*) be sent to the enemy territory.

He should be sent with proper arrangements made for his transport and lodging. The messenger should think out what he should say to the enemy king and how.

Even under life-threatening circumstances, he should deliver his master's message exactly as it was entrusted to him. As he delivers his message, he should observe the enemy king's gestures and expressions. If they are welcoming, he has the freedom to make queries of his own. If they indicate displeasure, he should humbly say that he is only a messenger and stay in the enemy territory till given permission to leave. If the enemy king does not let him leave even after his job is done, the messenger has to use his own judgment to meet the situation. For the purpose of serving his master, he can stay on in the enemy territory and pass on information to his own king through spies. The messenger has a whole host of responsibilities, including setting free the princes held by the enemy king as hostage.

*Prakarana12: Rajaputrarakshanam*

**Protection from the Princes**

Only a king well-protected from enemies as well as close relatives can take proper care of his kingdom. The king should first and foremost protect himself from his own queens and sons. Like crabs, princes have a tendency to eat up their fathers. So right from their birth, they should be kept under strict watch and supervision. Citing Bharadvaja (who wanted disrespectful princes to be killed) and a few others, Kautilya prescribes proper value education for the counseling of expecting queens. If the king has an only son who is a rebel, the king should imprison him and try to beget a grandson who is fit for the throne. If he has several sons, all rebellious, he should send them off to border regions or even banish them. If he has several sons but only one of them rebellious, he should send him off to another country and keep him in check. If all the sons are equally dear to the king, the eldest of them should be made the king, or all of them should rule by forming a *kulasamgha* or family-oligarchy. Such a rule is invincible because if one member is in danger, the others can carry on with the governance.

*Prakarana13: Avaruddhavrittam, Avaruddhe Cha Vritti*

**Conduct Of and Towards the Imprisoned (Princes)**

Imprisoned princes should do the tasks their father, the king, orders them to do except in case of danger to their lives. If a prince is incorrigible, his father, the king, should get him killed through secret agents.

*Prakarana14: Rajapranidhi*

## Matters of Attention for Kings

The condition of the king's employees rises and falls with that of the king himself. Hence the king should try always to improve his condition. To conduct state affairs systematically, he should divide up the day and the night each into eight parts, or use the shadow of a man to indicate the time.

**Tasks for the Day**

1. Supervise defense matters and yesterday's expense
2. Supervise actions of citizens
3. Bathe, Lunch, Study (*swadhyaya*)
4. Collect revenue and appoint collectors and officials
5. Consult ministers, send official letters, hear the reports of spies
6. Move about and think on his own
7. Examine horses, elephants, weapons
8. Consult army-chiefs and discuss war strategy

After this the king should do his daily rituals (*sandhya-upsana*).

**Tasks for the Evening**

1. Observe the spies
2. Bathe, Dine, Study (*swadhyaya*)
3. Listen to music and go to sleep

4&5. Sleep

6. Get up to the call of bugle and listen to material/financial matters and tasks to attend to
7. Consult ministers and send off spies
8. Get the blessings of the priests, and talk to physician, chief cook and astrologer, go round a cow having a calf and enter the court.

The king should allow direct access to people who seek him for a purpose, and not let his officials come in between. He should first deal with tasks whose terms are over and prevent their becoming even more difficult. He should regularly perform ceremonies and make donations.

राज्ञो हि व्रतमुत्थानम् यज्ञ:कार्यानुशासनम्।
दक्षिणा वृत्तिमासाम्यं च दीक्षितस्याभिषेचनम् ।।

The king should be enterprising and active in performing administrative duties as well as sacrificial rituals, making donations as well as equitable payments, dealing correctly with friends and foes. The king's happiness and welfare are in those of his subjects. His welfare lies not in doing what he finds pleasant but in doing what pleases his subjects. He should be up-and-doing (*utthita*).This enterprise (*utthanam*) is what brings prosperity to the kingdom.

*Prakarana 15: Nishantapranidhi*

**(Matters regarding the King's Inner Apartments)**

The king has to follow certain instructions regarding the inner apartments of the palace. They should be constructed where the *Vastushastra* experts see fit. They should have walls, moats and gates. The king's own apartment must be constructed so that it is either within a maze, or underground, or detachable in emergencies. By planting certain medicinal trees, the apartments should be protected from snakes, scorpions and other pests.

Behind the inner apartments there should be three separate rooms for expecting, sick and incurably ill ladies. The palace should have gardens and bowers for young princes and princesses.

Beyond this should come the council room, court and office, with guards and ushers duly placed.

When going into the inner apartments to meet the queens, the king should be on his guard against possible betrayals and assassination attacks by the queens and /or her paramours. To keep watch over the queens, he should place old or heterosexual men around the inner apartments. Maids and other servants should remain in appointed places and not mix with people outside. Anything that comes in or goes out of the inner apartments should be checked and entered in a register.

*Prakarana 16: Atmarakshitakam*

**About the King's Self-defence**

The king has to be careful of his own safety right from the time he gets up. While changing clothes he should not take the assistance of foreigners or men whom he had sacked and re-hired. The kitchen supervisor or chief-cook should taste every item himself before presenting it to the king. Rice in which poison has been mixed turns blue in fire. One who mixes poison in food looks tense and wobbles on his legs. An expert on poisons and a physician should always be near the king, When treating the king, the physician should prepare it himself and in front of the king. Personal assistants helping to dress or shave the king should also be tested before being taken. Only after testing a garden by snake-charmers should the king visit it. When pursuing something, should be accompanied by hunters and hunting dogs. Even when meeting an ascetic, he should have a trusted man by his side. He should carry his ruling rod, have guards on either side, and steer clear of crowds.

यथा च योगपुरुषैः अन्यान् राजाऽधितिष्ठेति ।
तथा अयमन्यबादेभ्यो रक्षेदात्मानमत्वान् ।।

Just as a king employs spies to secretly trouble enemy kings, he should protect himself from trouble others may secretly inflict on him.

## *Adhikarana 2:Adhyaksha-prachara*

## Declarationabout Officials/Chiefs

### *Prakarana 17: Janapadanivesha*

### Establishing a Habitation/Settlement

The king should establish new habitations/settlements by inviting people from other countries or by extending the cultivated area of his own country. The land that the king allocates to priests and scholars should be tax-free and permanently given out. Officers, physicians, and trainers (of horses and elephants) would also receive land but not absolutely (i.e., they would not be able to sell or mortgage it).

Land allocated to peasants would be subject to tax (*kara*).The peasants would be tax-payers (*kara-da*). On the death of a peasant registered as the taxpayer for a certain plot of land, the king would retain the choice to allocate it to his son. (The son had no hereditary right to it. The king could take it back and give it to someone else.) But if it was an arid, stony land that the peasant had made arable/fertile by his own efforts, the king should not do so. On the other hand, if a peasant let a cultivable land lie fallow, the king should seize it and assign it to some needy and enterprising fellow. He can even extract compensation from the earlier one. The king should favour/aid (*anugraha*) the peasants by providing them grains, seeds and bullocks (i.e., equipment) and each peasant receiving such aid should gradually return it to the king. The king should also provide a certain amount for the peasant's healthcare and medical treatment, without making too much of a dent upon the Treasury.

The king should arrange market places for extracted minerals, chopped-down sandalwood, elephants and other animals on sale, places for export and import, water and land transport facilities, big storage and marketing facilities.

For irrigation purposes, the king should construct big dams across rivers and collect rain-water in big ponds or tanks. If the people themselves want to do it, the king should aid them by providing land, wood and roadways. The king should also provide land and other material for the construction of temples and gardens. Fishes, ducks and lotus-stalks and other marketable items from pools belong to the king.

The king should duly punish offending servants. The king also has the responsibility of providing maintenance to children, to the aged, sick, endangered and orphaned, the childless and the widowed and even their children.

Family elders should take care of the property of the under-age. Temple-property too should be under the care of village elders.

If a man, even though able, does not take care of his children, his parents, young brother, unmarried or widowed sister, the king should fine him 12 gold coins (*pana*).But if for some reason they have gone astray, the man (except in case of the mother) is not bound to take care of them. The king should penalize a man who relinquishes the world without first making arrangements for his wife or son.

The village should not have theatres and gaming houses. Actors, dancers, musicians and gamblers disturb agricultural activities.

The king should protect his kingdom from enemies, tribals, diseases and famines.

*Prakarana 18: Bhumichhidra-vidhanam*

## Prescription for Land Improvement

Arid land should be converted into pastures for cattle and a sanctuary created for wild animals, local as well as from other areas. The keeper of the sanctuary for elephants should keep count of the number of elephants and their conditions, and accord death penalty to those who kill elephants.

*Prakarana 19: Durga-vidhanam*

### Prescription for Fort-construction

On four directions of the habitation (*janapada*), the king should construct forts (*durga*) which can be in a lake or water body (*oudaka*), on a hill (*parvata*), on arid land (*dhanvana*) and within the forest (*vanadurga*).

Cities should be constructed within the habitation, according to *Vastushastra* principles, on the confluence of rivers and on river-banks. Adequate water-supply should be ensured by constructing tanks on all sides. Arrangement should be made for buying and selling of local products and for entering the city by roadway as well as waterway. Moats should be constructed on all four sides of the city, filled deep with water, lotuses and crocodiles. Detailed instructions are given for constructing city walls, gateways and arches, with construction equipment and materials being transported by waterways.

*Prakarana 20: Durga-nivesha*

### Settling people within the Fort

Three roads running from East to West and three from North to South should be there dividing up the city with its 4 walls and 3x4 gateways. The palace should be on firm, central grounds. Its inner apartments should open out to the East or the West.

ES kitchen, store, stables for elephants

E shops for provisions, chief artisans' quarters

SE Treasury, shops for gold and silver work and of royal items

SW armory and metals works other than gold and silver

SS superintendents of police, Treasury, mining and metallurgical works, army- chiefs, restaurants, meat-shops, courtesans, dancers and merchants

WS sheds for camels and donkeys

WN sheds for palanquins and chariots

W workshops for wool-craft, bamboo-craft, leather-craft, making of weapons NW medicines and royal objects

NE Treasury, cattle-sheds, stables

N deity of the city, family deities, blacksmith, stationery shop keeper, and Brahmanas

Whatever space that is unoccupied, is for washer men, tailors, and peddlers.

The cremation-ground should be to the North or the East of the habitation, and accommodate *Chandala*s (social out-casts who aid in cremation work) and *Pashanda*s (who perform rituals defying usual religious practices).

The king should not let unworthy people to settle down in the city. If they do have to be settled somewhere, it should be in the border regions from where they can be made to pay taxes.

*Prakarana 21: Sannidhatrinichayakarma*

**Activity relating to the Treasury and its Associates**

The Treasurer (*Sannidhata/ Koshadhyaksha*) should get the Treasury (*koshagriha*), royal sales outlet (*panyagriha*), store (*koshtthagara*), store for base metals (*kupyagriha*), armoury (*ayudhagara*) and prison (*bandhanagara*) constructed.

They should be strong and *pucca* buildings made of baked bricks and have moats, wells and bathrooms nearby. The Treasury should be located in a well-protected and sanctified basement (*bhoomigriha*). At one end of the habitation, a special treasure-house (*dhruvanidhi*) should be dug out by men under death sentence (who will not live to divulge the secret way).

Gems, sandalwood and other precious stuff should be tested by experts and sorted as to new and old stock. If a gem is replaced by an imitation of it, both the person who replaced it and the one who made him do so should be punished. If the Treasurer himself steals by means of digging a tunnel into the Treasury, he should be given capital punishment. If any thief enters the Treasury by means of making a hole in the wall, he should be punished by a painful death.

The prison should have separate wings for males and females. It should be very well protected on every side. It should have moats around it as well as wells and baths. To safeguard against use of poisons, it should contain cats and mongooses.

*Prakarana 22: Samahartrisamudayaprasthanam*

## Establishing the Collector's Tasks

The Collector (*Samaharta*) should watch over matters relating to fortified towns, countryside, mines, bridges, forests, pastures and trade routes. He should collect revenue so as to increase income (*aya*) and reduce expenditure (*vyaya*).If income reduces and expenditure increases, he should take measures to remedy the situation.

Income can be of three types: *vartamana* (everyday earnings), *paryushita* (arrears and receipts from other kingdoms) and *anyajata* (other categories such as items forgotten, gifts, items robbed from enemy camps, unclaimed items).

Expenditure can be of four types: *nitya* (regular, daily), *nityodpadika* (extra to regular), *labha* (annual, monthly or fortnightly) and *labhodpadika* (extra to annual, monthly or fortnightly).

What emerges after duly considering income and expenditure is *neevee* or savings. That saving which is already in the Treasury is *prapta* (received).That which is about to be put in is *anuvritta*.

एवं कुर्यात् समुदयम् बृद्धिम् चास्य दर्शयेत्।
ह्रासं व्ययस्यम् च प्राज्ञ: साधयेच्च विपर्ययम्।। .

The Collector (*Samaharta*) should make collections and expenditures and calculation of what savings are being made. If a large expense has to be made for a large future gain, he should make it for generating more income for the kingdom.

*Prakarana 23: Akshapatale Gananikyadhikarah*

## Activities in the Accountant's Office

The Chief Accountant (*Gananikya*) should have an office (*akshapatala*) that is east-facing and partitioned for clerks to sit and ledgers to be kept. It should contain records of the names of different departments, output of mines and workshops, the employment of workers, output kept in storage, salaries and so on. All relevant information should be noted down in the ledger books. Names, addresses and even character reports of employees should be recorded in registers and given to the king (very much like service records of government employees today).

The financial year (*karma-samvatsara*) is taken to consist of 354 days and to end on the full moon night of the month of Ashadha. It is according to this calculation of the year that the officials should be paid their salaries.

The registers should record the reporting of employees for work and also their work performance.

The Chief Accountant should employ spies to collect information about employees in every office of the kingdom, and deal out penalties. Instead of blanket rules for penalties as advised by Manu, Brihaspati and Shukra, Kautilya recommends penalties specific to the offences committed.

The various officers should report to the main or head office at appointed times and submit them there for checking. Any delays should be punished.

The Chief Minister or the Chief Accountant should explain the gains and losses to the subjects.

The accounts must be checked often, at regular intervals. Any re-writing, over-writing, double-counting or fraud in respect of *neevee* should be fined severely.

अपराधम् सहेतालपं तुश्येदल्पे अपि चोदये।
महोपकारम चाध्यक्षं प्रग्रहेणाभिपूजयेत् ॥ .

The king should honour the Accountant who does such a big job for the kingdom, and overlook minor offences that he commits.

### *Prakarana 24: Samudayasya Yuktapahritasya Pratyanayam*

### Bringing Back What has been Used or Stolen from the Treasury

कोषपूर्वाः सर्वारम्भाः । तस्मात् पूर्वं कोषमवेक्षेत।

All activities are dependent on the Treasury or court exchequer. So the first thing the king should take care of is the Treasury.

The way to expand the court exchequer or Treasury is to increase the king's wealth, keep watch over thieves, prevent royal officers from taking bribes, encourage agriculture and other products that can be sold in the market, protect the country from arson and extract appropriate taxes on time.

A superintendent who deliberately overstates expenses and understates income (an act of *parihapana*) should be made to pay four times the amount in question. If he himself consumes (*upabhoga*) it or substitutes (*parivartana*) something else for it, then too he has to be fined appropriately. If the king suspects an officer for some offence, he should separately call up other people associated with him in the discharge of his duties, collect full information and decide the case. No one found guilty should go free. One who takes a bribe and changes his statement should be given death penalty.

*Prakarana 25: Upayuktapariksha*

## Testing the Officials

After engaging an official (*upayukta*), the king should from time to time subject him to tests. If an officer in a high position makes an error in his work, he should be fined twice his salary. If an officer fully discharges his duty and out of his own volition, helps another in his task, he should be promoted and honoured. Clerks and other junior officers should co-operate with one another and the superintendent should, through spies, keep watch over his underlings.

यथा हि अनास्वादयितुं न शक्यम् जिह्वातलस्थं मधु वा विषं वा ।
अर्थस्तथा ह्यर्थचरेण राज्ञप्य : स्वल्पोऽप्यनास्वादयितुं न शक्यः ।।

Just as honey or poison placed on the tongue cannot but get tasted, an officer dealing with money cannot but taste a little of the money he is dealing with.

मत्स्या यथान्तःसलिले चरन्तो ज्ञातुम न शक्याः सलिलं पीवन्तः ।
युक्तास्तथा कार्यविधौ नियुक्ता ज्ञातुम न शक्याः धनमाददानाः ।।

Just as fish in the water do not seem to be drinking, officers dealing with money matters do not seem to be stealing.

अपि शक्या गतिः ज्ञातुम पततां खे पतत्रिणाम्।
न तू प्रच्छन्नभावानां युक्तानां चरतां गतिः।।

The flights of birds in the sky can be traced but not the movements of officers stealing money.

*Prakarana 26: Shashasanadhikara*

## Royal Documents

The commands or resolutions that letters from the king bear are called royal edicts or inscriptions (*shasana*).Kings rely on written documents rather than spoken words, such as declaration of truce.

That is why the writer or scribe of such edicts or inscriptions should be well-qualified, knowledgeable about conventions, quick in composition and should write a good hand of letters. A good edict should have consistency, clarity, completeness, sweetness and dignity, It should be grammatically correct and not contain repetitions. It should begin by stating names and royal pedigree, and end the contents with 'Thus in the words of such and such king titled such and such'. If a royal scribe deliberately writes an edict wrong, he should be fined as well as have his feet cut off!

*Prakarana 27: Koshapraveshyaratnapareeksha*

**Examination of Gems entering the Treasury**

The Treasurer should consult experts while taking gems and other precious stuff into the Treasury. Upon him depends the cutting, shaping, cleaning and preservation of such valuables.

*Prakarana 28: Akarakarmantapravartanam*

**Treatment and Sale of Products from Mines**

The Superintendent of Mines (*Akara-adhyaksha*) should be well-versed in metallurgy and chemistry and in touch with experts and traders dealing with mineral products. If someone steals or illegally sells minerals from mines, he should be caught and put to work as a labourer in the mine. If the tax on workers in mines gets too high, the Superintendent can stagger its payment or reduce it or himself make up the shortfall. The Superintendent should also supervise the sale and purchase of shells, pearls, corals and salt. One-sixth of earnings from export of salt should be paid as tax. If any trader of the royal market imports salt, he has to pay a six per cent tax as well as fines. Sellers of adulterated salt should also be penalized.

आकरप्रभवः कोषः कोषदण्ड:प्रजायते ।
पृथिवी कोषदण्डाभ्याम् प्राप्यते कोषभूषणा ।।

The Treasury is born out of the mines, and the penal power of the kingdom depends on the Treasury. This earth is thus ornamented by the Treasury and can be mastered through these two - Treasury and penal power.

*Prakarana 29: Akshashalayam Suvarnadhyakshah*

**Gold-Superintendent in the Gold-building**

The Gold-Superintendent (*Suvarnadhyaksha*) should get a big building constructed for storing and working on gold. Many qualities and many colours of gold may be distinguished. Silver and copper too should be worked upon in this building. Iron may sometimes have to be mixed with gold to change its colour. Gems and pearls may be set in gold ornaments. Experts in the area should be consulted.

*Prakarana 30: Vishikhayam Souvarnika-prachara*

**Chief Trader in Gold Ornaments in the Highways**

The kingdom's Chief Trader of gold ornaments (*Souvarnika*) should see to it that gold and silver ornaments for the citizens are made in workshops where the craftsmen sit and fashion them. The craftsmen too should do their work on time and lose parts of their salaries if they cannot deliver the items as per order.

*Prakarana 31: Koshtthagaradhyaksha*

**Chief Store-keeper**

The Store-keeper-in-chief (*Koshtthagara*) should acquire information about rice, wheat, jaggery, salt, ghee, curds, dried fish and meat, and various other materials collected as taxes and fines. He should see to it that these materials are collected in clean, whole and pure form. There should be due stores of food for elephants, horses, camels and bullocks. Utensils, weights and measures, brooms and other equipment should be stored as well. The store-workers (who keep store clean, weigh the items, hand them out, lift and carry them) are called *vishti*. Grain should be kept above floor-level, ghee and oil in wooden containers, and salt on some container on the ground.

*Prakarana 32: Panyadhyaksha*

**Superintendent of Consumer Items**

The Superintendent of Consumer Items (*Panyadhyaksha*) should gather information about items produced in land and water, valued high or low, and brought in for sale and purchase. He should know about its various types and their popularity or otherwise, and the best times to release them to the market, or withdraw them from it.

The Superintendent of Consumer Items should collect items that are profusely available, raise their prices through tricks of trade, and then release them on to the market. Items produced locally should be brought together and sold from one place whereas items produced in other countries should be sold from various outlets. If the sale of a commodity brings profits but is harmful for the citizens, it should be stopped. For providing storage facilities, the king is entitled to one-sixth of the value of the items.

If, while trading in another country, the businessman and his possessions are suddenly in danger, he should first protect his gems and his life. If he incurs losses, on coming back he may use some money from the royal Treasury to re-start his business. The borders of the kingdom should be well-guarded. Roadways and waterways should be made safe for business activities.

### *Prakarana 33: Kupyadhyakshah*

### Superintendent of Base Metals and Forest Products

The Superintendent of base metals, i.e., metals other than gold and silver, and forest products (*Kupyadhyaksha*) should gather together woodcutters and craftsmen who make wooden items and employ them with appropriate salaries. They should also collect from jungles and forts on the outskirts materials such as charcoal, copper, lead, metal utensils and containers.

### *Prakarana 34: Ayudhagaradhyaksha*

### Superintendent of Armoury

The Superintendent of the Armoury (*Ayudhagaradhyaksha*) should gather together men who can fashion weapons and armours that can protect the fort and the habitation. He should get them to make such weapons and armours, skilfully and in time, and see to it that they are kept rust-free and safe. Various weapons are now mentioned and categorized. Amulets, flagstaffs, hooked rods to prod horses on, and such associated items are also listed. The Superintendent should be aware of the uses of the items placed in the weaponry, along with their problems.

*Prakarana 35: Tulamanapoutavam*

## Weights and Measures

The Officer of Measure of Weights (*Poutavadhyaksha*) should get weights and scales made correctly and specifically according to the *shastras*. A detailed scheme is provided. Although out-dated, it is interesting. For example, ten grains of *Udad daal* was equivalent to one *mashaka* of gold, and sixteen *mashakas* made up one *karsha*, and four *karshas* made one *pala*. Weighing machines had to be made with precision. They were of two types: (a) a balance with two pans and (b) a movable fulcrum steel-yard. For liquid such as ghee, instead of pans at either end, pots were used.

*Prakarana 36: Deshakalamanam*

## Measure of Distance and Time

The Officer of Measures of Distance and Time (*Manadhyaksha*) should make himself informed in the subject. For example, one chariot wheel particle makes eight *anus*. 32,768 *anus* make an *angula* (1.9cm) and so it goes on till one *yojana* (15 km). So far as time is concerned, there is detailed break-down. The blink of an eyelid= 1 *nimesha*, 5 *nimesha*=1 *kashttha*, 30 *kashttha*=1*kala*, 40 *kala*=1 *nalika*, 5 *nalika*=1 *muhurta* and 15 *muhurta* =1 *divasa* and 1 *ratra*, 15*divasa* and *ratra* = 1 *paksha*, 2 *paksha* =1 *masa*. And so it goes on to the seasons (*ritu*), the vernal equinox (*uttarayana*), autumnal equinox (*dakshinayana*), and the calendar year (*samvatsara*), and the era (*yuga*). The *Arthashastra* shows remarkable precision as to the measure of weight, distance and time.

*Prakarana 37: Shulkadhyaksha*

## Superintendent of Tolls, Taxes and Customs Duties

The Superintendent of Tolls, Taxes and Customs Duties (*Shulkadhyaksha*) should get a big building constructed for the purpose of collecting customs duties and mark its gate by a flag. All traders (*vyaparis*) could collect under the flag and records should be kept of their names, addresses and items, their description and the stamps imprinted on them (*abhigyanamudra*). The stamps should be checked with strictness. If a seller is raising the price because of rivalry, the king should take the extra that he has made this way, or extract double the amount from the buyer. The Superintendent should be fined if he exempts anyone from paying the customs duties because he is a friend or has paid a bribe. Attempts to escape paying the Customs Duties at the gate should be strictly penalized. Poison and other items harmful for citizens should be destroyed by the king.Items such as grain which are much-needed by the subjects, or which are difficult to get, should be exempted from Customs Duties.

*Prakarana 38: Shulkavyavahara*

**Exaction of Customs Duties**

Customs Duties (*shulka*) are of three types:

*Vahya*– on goods produced in own country

*Abhayantara* – on goods produced within the palace

*Atithya* –on goods coming from other countries. This can be of two types:

*Nishkramya* – on goods going out, i.e., exports.

*Praveshya* – on goods entering the city gate, i.e., import duties.

The *Praveshya* (import duty) was usually one-fifth of its value. The duty on flowers, vegetables, rice, dried fish and meat was one-sixth of their value. The duty on gems and precious stuff was to be decided with the help of experts looking at the items concerned. The duty on textiles, leather and woolen stuff was $1/15^{th}$ of their value. The duty on rough textiles, earthenware, ghee, oil, salt and wine varied between $1/20^{th}$ and $1/25^{th}$.

For the welfare of the country, the gate-keeper should extract $1/5^{th}$ of the value of items entering the gate as octroi or toll (*Dvaradeya*) duty.

The product of one's own soil should not be sold there. Sale of flowers and herbs of a garden within the garden itself should be penalized. Similar rules would apply to vegetables.

अतो नवपुराणानां देशजातिचरित्रतः ।
पण्यानाम् स्थापयेत् शुलकमत्यन्तम् चापकारतः ।।

Hence the king should impose duties and penalties upon all saleable items (*panya*), old and new, according to local customs and practices.

*Prakarana 39: Sutradhyaksha*

## Superintendent of Yarn

The Superintendent of Yarn (*Sootradhyaksha*) should get information from experts in spinning and weaving yarn, thread, rope etc. and making amulets and other leather crafts. Only master craftsmen should be employed for fine spinning and weaving. Kautilya specifically mentions women crafts-persons in this context. For the supply of material and collection of finished product, the Superintendent of Yarn should send maids to women who are confined to inner apartments, who have no husbands, or have husbands in distant lands, are unmarried and want to be self-reliant.

*Prakarana 40: Seetadhyaksha*

## Superintendent of Agriculture

The Superintendent of Agriculture (*Seetadhyaksha*) should inform himself about the science of agriculture and botany, and take the help of experts to collect, at appropriate times, seeds (of food crops, fruit, flowers and vegetables). He should then get the seeds planted, by servants and slaves, in land that has been ploughed several times over. He should see to it that lack of equipment and/or bullocks does not hamper timely ploughing and sowing. He should sow crops according to season, soil and water availability. Seeds should be sown in accordance with the rainfall. For example, paddy and wheat should be sown even before the monsoon has arrived whereas pulses should be sown in mid-monsoon, peas and sesame at the end of monsoon. If the fields are irrigated by means of pools dug out by the people's own effort and wealth, one-fifth of the yield should be given to the king. If the water is carried to the field by carrying water-pots on the shoulder, one-fourth of the yield should be given to the king. If the water is conveyed to the fields by constructing channels or tanks, one-third of the yield should be given to the king. The seeds should be sown after a *mantra* is recited to invoke the Earth, the Sun and Brahma the Creator,

प्रजापतये काश्यपाय देवाय नमः सदा।
सीता मे ऋध्यताम् देवी बीजेषु च धनेषु च ।।

O Prajapati! O Sun-god! O Goddess Earth! Let my fields be filled with seeds and then with crops!"

When the sown seeds sprout, they should be given the manure of herbal juices and freshly caught small fishes. Snakes should be smoked out of their holes in the fields. Paddy and wheat are the best crops, plantains are medium and sugarcane is inferior, requiring much effort.

At the right time, the crops should be harvested such that all of it is collected and not even chaff is left on the fields. The sheaves of the harvested crops should be made into a high pile, topped by the same material. The de-husking or threshing should be done on a threshing platform (*khala*) and the grain collected in a circular form (*mandala*). People engaged in threshing should not carry fire with them.

### *Prakarana 41: Suradhyaksha*

**Superintendent of Liquor**

The Superintendent of Liquor (*Suradhyaksha*) should give out the job of making and selling wine for the entire habitation either to a big merchant or to several small ones. But he should discourage manufacture and sale by others who have not got this contract, for example, outside the village, at home or in a crowded spot. Not everybody should have the permission to carry wine home; they had to drink only in bars or pubs. Through spies and contractors, the Superintendent had to keep himself informed about the intentions of the people indulging in drinking, and to take care of their ornaments and money while they were in a drunken state. It is to be noted that Kautilya recommended that, to ferment the wine, the Superintendent should make use of women and child labourers.

सुराकिंवविचयं स्त्रियो बालाः च कुर्युः ।

Without behaving inappropriately, he should exact due taxes from those wine merchants to whom the contract has been given, 1/16$^{th}$ by weight and 1/20$^{th}$ of cash.

### *Prakarana 42: Soonadhyaksha*

**Superintendent of Slaughter-houses and Butcheries**

The Superintendent of Slaughter-houses (*Soonadhyaksha*) should appropriately penalize the killing and catching of animals, fishes and birds from reserved forests, sanctuaries and hermitages,

There is a ban or restriction upon them, with due penalty. Upon royalty however the penalty is a little less severe! There is a (lower) penalty even for killing wild animals (such as tiger) or animals without any master or patron (such as deer not belonging to a hermitage).The killing of cows, bulls and calves are absolutely banned. Butchers have to pay taxes at $1/6^{th}$ for permitted animals not from any reserved forest or sanctuary, fish and birds at $11/60^{th}$.The Superintendent has to prevent the sale of stale fish and rotten meat.

*Prakarana 43: Ganikadhyaksha*

## Superintendent of Courtesans

The Superintendent of Courtesans (*ganika*) should appoint courtesans with beauty, youth and expertise to attend upon the king. This was to be done at the rate of one thousand *pana*. These courtesans were of three categories, junior (*kanishttha*), medium (*madhyama*) and senior (*uttama*) with salaries of one thousand, two. thousand and three thousand *pana*s respectively. When they lost their youth and skills, they were given the position of matrons (*matrika*) or even cooks. They could not lend or sell the ornaments given to them. They had to pay taxes (1/15 of monthly earnings). If any one was unwilling and yet forced, the man would be punished.

गणिकामकामां रुन्धन्तो निष्पातयतो वा ब्रणविदारेन रूपमुपाघ्नतः सहस्रदण्डः।
स्थान विशेषेण वा दण्डवृद्धिरनिष्क्रयद्विगुणात् पणसहस्रम् दण्डः

This is to be appreciated as a remarkably modern view.

The state was to bear the expense of training royal courtesans, such as in singing, playing the flute, the lute and the cymbals, dancing, reciting, acting, mind-reading, stringing garlands, making perfumes, doing the hair, massaging and providing physical pleasure. The state was also to bear the expenses of training the sons of courtesans in organizing plays and dances.

*Prakarana 44: Navadhyaksha*

## Superintendent of Shipping

The Superintendent of Shipping (*Navadhyaksha*) has to collect information about sea, rivers and other navigable water-bodies, and ensure that the people observe the rules associated with transport in boats and ships. People living near rivers, lakes and the seas should regularly pay their taxes and also an extra amount should be given as wages to boatmen operating on those water-bodies. Fishermen using boats should pay one-sixth of their earnings to the king. Those who collect pearls and conch-shells will be under rules laid down by the Superintendent of Mines.

Big governmental vessels should ferry across big rivers, small ones on streams flowing basically in summer. There were rules regarding safety and compensation. If a governmental vessel was sunk or damaged because the boatmen were careless or the equipment was inadequate, the Superintendent of Shipping had to pay compensation to the people affected. The Superintendent was to be a father to people aboard ships that lose their way or encounter storms. He should relax their tax dues. He should see to the destruction of pirate ships or ships violating rules. He should keep ferry service regular and strictly regulated.

*Prakarana 45: Go-adhyaksha*

### Superintendent of Cattle

The Superintendent of Cattle should inform himself about the various aspects of cows, buffaloes and so on, and take care of royal cattle in the charge of milkmen and cowherds. The king could also, upon payment, supervise the cattle of the people. He had to be paid taxes by all cattle-owners. Cattle had to be marked with stamps/seals so that their ownership could be established. Their particulars had to be entered in a register. Arrangements had to be made for cattle which were sick, trapped, hurt, stuck under a tree or struck by lightning. Cattle had to be protected from thefts as well as snake-bites. The Superintendent of Cattle had to be fully informed about them. Bull-fighting was to be penalized.

*Prakarana 46: Ashvadhyaksha*

### Superintendent of Horses

The Superintendent of Horses should keep a detailed account of horses purchased, received as gifts or in exchange, or born in the kingdom, and so on. He should get spacious stables constructed for them and ensure appropriate food, nutrition, and treatment. Old, sick, wounded or incapacitated horses should be given food but only to the extent of preventing them from dying of starvation. Healthy horses which are not fit to be war-horses should me made into studs for breeding horses for the citizens. The best horses are the Arabian ones, the medium are from around Rajasthan, the rest are of indifferent calibre. The horses should be assigned duties (war or general transport) according to their speediness. Horses should be bathed twice every day, garlanded and scented. Horses should be dressed and decorated according to the wishes of the one who tends them. Their diet (for example, when they get too fat or too thin) should be as per the veterinary physician says. They should be given regular check-ups.

In case of delay and other negligence, the stable-keeper will be severely punished.

All this applied to camels, donkeys, goats and sheep as well.

*Prakarana 47: Hastyadhyaksha*

## Superintendent of Elephants

The Superintendent of Elephants (*Hastyadhyaksha*) should take care of all types of elephants, male, female, calves and elephants being trained. He should get big stables constructed for them, with a big platform for them to sit down and slopes at the back of their stands to pass stool and urine. He should provide ample and balanced diet for them and maintain their equipment (such as hooked rods and seats) well. He should employ and supervise their attendants, trainers and doctors. He should get them trained and assigned tasks appropriately. Baby elephants still on their mothers' milk should not be captured from forests, except for playing with them and feeding them in small doses.

*Prakarana 48: Hastyadhyaksha Hastipracharashcha*

## Superintendent of Elephants and Conduct of Elephants

Elephants can be of four categories according as they are judged to be fit for training (*damya*), fit to be war-elephants (*sannahya*), fit to be a mode of transport (*oupavahya*) and to be killers (*vyala*),They are to be treated accordingly. Veterinary doctors for elephants (*gajavaidya*), trainers of elephants (*gajashikshaka*) and other attendants (such as cooks and cleaners) should duly take care of elephants. Neglecting or ill-treating elephants would be penalized.

### *Prakarana 49-50: Rathyadhyaksha, Pattiyadhyaksha, Senapatipracharah*

### Chief of Chariot Corps, Chief of Infantry, and Army-Chief's Conduct

The Chief of Chariot Corps (*Rathyadhyaksha*) should act in consonance with the Superintendent of Horses, get old and broken chariots repaired and new ones built for war as well as festive and daily usage. He should also keep himself informed about craftsmen fashioning and repairing chariots and weapons. He is the one responsible for training all those working under him, and disbursing rations, wages and occasional rewards/honours to them, as well as their fitness in war or times of peace.

The Chief of Infantry (*Pattiyadhyaksha*) has responsibilities similar to that of the Chariot Corps. In addition, he has to be fully informed about:

Soldiers guarding the city (*moula-bala*)
Soldiers on hire (*bhrita-bala*)
Soldiers stationed in different provinces (*shroni-bala*)
Soldiers of allied kingdoms (*mitra-bala*)
Soldiers of enemies (*amitra-bala*)
Soldiers to guard forest area or tribal forces (*atabee-bala*).

The Chief of Infantry should be well-versed in tactics of fighting in open plains, forests, hilly terrains, of fighting in the open or from hiding (guerilla attack), in the day or in the darkness of night.

The Army-Chief (*Senapati*) should keep himself fully informed by the Superintendents of Chariot Corps and Foot-soldiers. He should have knowledge of wielding all kinds of weapons, riding on chariots, horses and elephants, as well as thinking out strategies of attack and defense, devising formations (*vyuha*) of soldiers, destroying enemy forts, and the timing of the fight. He should also know how to direct his army through secret codes and gestures so that the enemy soldiers do not get to understand his moves.

### *Prakarana 51-52: Mudradhyaksha Viveetadhyaksha*

### Superintendent of Seals and Superintendent of Pastures

The Superintendent of Seals had to put his seal or stamp (*mudra*) upon a kind of passport document upon the payment of one measure (*mashaka*) of gold, both for entry to and exit from the habitation. Only with this stamp or seal could anyone enter or leave the habitation. If anyone was caught entering or leaving without the seal, he is to be fined 12 *panas*. There were penalties for using falsified seal.

The Superintendent of Check-posts had to supervise enclosures, pastures or preserves (*viveeta*). For infiltrators as well as those who wanted to leave without the due seal, there were penalties. Hunters and poachers roaming about the countryside had to keep watch over people coming in or going out without the required seal. If they spotted any such ones, they were to climb on trees and shout or beat drums in order to broadcast the information.

### *Prakarana 53-54: Samahartriprachara*

### ***Grihapativaidehakatapasavyanjanah pranidhaya***

### **Collector (of Revenue) and Spies of Three Types**

The Collector of Revenue of the habitation should divide the entire habitation into four and place each part under a local administrative officer (*Sthanika*). He should form units of single, five and ten villages and put each under a chief (*Gopa*) who would systematically maintain registers of the records of rivers, hills, jungles, their demarcations, their arid and arable portions, the number of huts and the number of people ( listed by caste and occupation), their earnings and their taxes paid. The *Gopa*s and the *Sthanika*s should exact taxes from the people and control any bullies disrupting law and order. There should be a *Pradeshta* or officer to pursue taxpayers and extract taxes from them. The Collector should make use of spies to collect information from the general public. These spies may be disguised as householders (*grihapati*), traders (*vaidehaka*) or young ascetics ( *tapasa*).

समाहर्ता जनपदं चिन्तयेदेवमुत्थितः।
चिन्तयेयूश्च संस्थास्थाः संस्थाश्चान्याः स्वयोनयः ।।

Thus should the alert and aware Collector, and the various spies, groups and organizations under him, conduct the administration of the habitation.

*Prakarana 55: Nagaraikapranidhi*

**Matters relating to the Mayor or Chief-Citizen**

The Mayor or Chief Citizen (*Nagarika*) who bears the responsibility of the town (*nagara*) like the Collector bears that of the entire habitation (*janapada*), should divide the town into four parts and appoint local administrative officers (*Sthanika*). Under each *Sthanika*, the *Nagarika* should appoint *Gopa*s to keep the records for units of ten, twenty or forty families. The *Sthanika*s and *Gopa*s should collect relevant facts and figures about those households, e.g., number of males and females and even their relationships. The *Nagarika* has to keep control over guests at charitable lodging houses, regulate the buying and selling at fair prices and prevent dealing in stolen goods. He has to maintain law and order, regulate crowds, ensure precautions against fire. He has to keep the town, including its cremation ground, clean and sanitized. He has to inspect its roads, drains, underground passages and general fortification. He is the in-charge of its prisons and the custodian of stolen property. He also has to keep control over the gatekeepers and guards of the town.

## *Adhikarana 3: Dharmashthiya-Judicial/Civil Matters*

*Prakarana 56-57: Vyavaharasthapana Vivahapadanibandhashcha*

**Arrangements for Making and Revoking Contracts, Marriage Matters**

Three members of the judiciary (*dharmastha*) should sit together at the junction of habitations and prepare (or revoke) business deals/affairs, legal contracts /agreements (*vyavahara*). The judges shall declare as invalid such contracts as are concluded in the absence of any of the parties concerned, within the house, in hiding, at night, in the forest, by fraud or in secrecy.

There were exceptions. For example, even if concluded within the house, a transaction concerning inheritance, marriage, deposits or entrusted objects, would be considered valid if one of the parties was sick or a woman and so unable to go out. Even if conducted at night, a marriage transaction or the implementation of the King's order would be valid. People dwelling or travelling in forests as hermits, cowherds, spies, hunters and merchants could enter into contracts within the forest.

Dependents or unauthorized persons, e.g., disowned son or brother, aged father dependent on son, a woman dependent on her husband, a bonded labourer, one criminally accused, a wandering mendicant, and a disabled person could not make contracts.. Agreements or contracts made when one of the parties is inebriated, insane or under duress, are to be regarded as invalid. In case of several contracts existing on the same subject, the latest one will be regarded as the valid one.

### *Prakarana 58: Vivahasamyuktam Vivahadharmah Streedhanakalpah Aadhivedanikam Cha*
### **Marriage-related Matters: acts of marriage, dowry and women's own property**

Civil matters begin with marriage, the purpose of which is to have sons. There are eight types of marriages, of which the first four are lawful and sacred (*dharmya*). The last four are legal (only) with the approval of the parents of the woman concerned.

In a *Brahma-vivaha*, a father gives away a well-adorned daughter in marriage.

In *Prajapatya-vivaha*, a man and a woman jointly perform sacred duties without the prior consent of the woman's (bride's) father.

In *Aarsha-vivaha*, the husband (bridegroom) regularizes the marriage by presenting two cows to his father-in-law( bride's father).

In *Daiva-vivaha*, the woman (bride) is given away to a priest officiating for the prospective bridegroom inside a temple or some sanctified precincts.

The *Gandharva-vivaha* is a secret marriage of lovers. The *Aasura-vivaha* is giving away the woman for a bride-price.

*Rakshasa-vivaha* is forceful abduction of the woman for the purpose of marriage.

*Paishacha-vivaha* is abduction of a sleeping or inebriated woman.

A first giving of dowry (*shulka*) or voluntary gifts (*preetyaropana*) was permissible in every form of marriage but it had to go to the woman's father or mother or either in the absence of the other. A second giving (as in remarriage) had to go to the woman concerned.

A wife's wealth or property (*streedhana*) could be a stipend (*vritti*) set at the minimum of 2000 *panas*, or it could be tied (*abandha*) as in the form of jewellery. Kautilya specified circumstances under which the wife was permitted to use her *streedhana*, e.g., when her husband has gone away on a long journey without making provision for family upkeep. If the wife allows her husband to use her *streedhana* for more than three years, in *Brahma*, *Prajapatya*, *Aarsha* or *Daiva* marriage, the wife will lose any claim to compensation. In *Gandharva* and *Asura* marriage, the husband will repay both forms (stipend and jewellery) with interest. In *Rakshasa* and *Paishacha* forms, the husband will be regarded as having stolen the *streedhana* and accordingly, pay the penalty.

If the wife dies before the husband, her property shall be divided up on the following lines:

sons and daughters getting equal shares,

daughters getting equal shares if there is no son,

husband getting it all if there are no children.

The dowry and the wedding gifts should go back to those who had given them.

The husband can re-marry with his wife living but only after certain specified years of waiting:

Eight years if the wife does bear any children in that time,

Ten years if during that time she gives birth only to stillborn children,

Twelve years if during that time she has live births but only of daughters.

There are penalties for not observing this rule.

Kautilya states clearly that the purpose of having a wife is to have sons. *Putrartha hi striyah.*

Not having intercourse with a wife in her child-bearing years is a punishable offence. Men should not force women to have intercourse but a women who wants sons can approach her husband even if he is a leper or a lunatic.

Under certain circumstances, the wife is permitted to leave her husband.

नीचत्वं परदेशं व प्रस्थितो राजकील्विषी ।
प्राणाभिहन्ता पतितस्त्याज्यः क्लीबोऽपि वा पतिः ॥

A husband who is vicious, residing abroad, rebelling against the king, a murderer, a fallen or a debauch can be abandoned (*tyajya*) by the wife.

***Prakarana 59: Vivahasamyuktamshushruabharmaparushya-dveshaticharopakaravyavaharapratishedhashcha***

**Marriage-related Matters: disregard of rules, maintenance, cruelty and excesses and their redress**

A female of twelve years and a male of sixteen years is legally an adult.If after this age they disregard (*asushrusha*) royal orders or laws, they can be fined, the young woman twelve *pana*s and the young man its double, i.e., twenty-four *pana*s.

There are clear instructions about the maintenance (*bharmya*) of wives.

If the duration of the maintenance is indefinite, the man should make appropriate arrangement for her food and clothes and expenses (*grasachchadanam adhikam*) or even more as per his own earnings. But if the duration of the maintenance is limited and the woman has refused taking back the dowry and other property, the husband should give back the bound form, that is, jewellery.

The husband is not to be accused if his wife has entered her parents' place or lives separately.

The husband should not call his wife names, shout at her or vilify her. He should try to gently make her understand the problem, and if that fails, strike her back thrice with a bamboo stick or lash her with a rope. If he exceeds this, he will be penalized. A woman who physically abused her husband would also be likewise penalized.

If a wife went outside the marital home for seeking pleasure, she would be penalized.

A wife who hates her husband (*bhartarm dvishatee stree*) refuses to sleep with her husband for seven menstrual periods, she should be made to return to her husband her endowment and her jewellery (presented to her by him) and allow him to sleep with another woman. A husband who hates his wife should permit her to live apart but with some guardian.

आमोक्ष्या भर्तुरकामस्य द्विषती भार्या, भार्यायाश्च भर्ता ।
परस्परं द्वेषान्मोक्षः ।।

Without the husband's consenting to her release, a wife who hated her husband could not get released from the marriage. Correspondingly, without the wife's consent to set him free, a husband who disliked his wife could not get out of it. Release could come only through mutual dislike (leading to both sides letting go of the other).

**Marriage contracts could be revoked** but only under certain circumstances. For the *Brahmana*s, *Kshatriya*s and *Shudra*s, it could be revoked up to the (*panigrahana*) or even later if a sexual impediment came to light (impotency in the man or loss of virginity in the woman). *Shudra*s could revoke marriage agreements even later, up to the actual consummation.

**If the woman had conceived a child by the man concerned, their marriage agreement just could not be revoked.**

### *Prakarana 60: Vivahasamyukta Nishapatanam Patthyanusaranam Hrasvapravaso Deerghapravasashcha*

### Marriage-related Matters: A Wife's Leaving the Marital Home, Accompanying Men Other Than Her Husband, Duration (short and long) of Staying Away from Home

Unless ill-treated by her husband, a wife should not run away from her marital home. Such a wife and the one who gives her shelter shall be subjected to a range of punishments. No man should give shelter to another man's wife unless it is to save her life. However, a wife, ill-treated by her husband could seek shelter in the house of any of the following: a kinsman of the husband (even when there are other males in the household), a trustee, a guardian, the village chief, a female mendicant or her own kinsmen.

It was a punishable offence for a wife to go out of her husband's house and go to a different village. But if she did it to join her husband elsewhere, she would not be regarded as guilty. If she did it to have physical enjoyment on the way or in some jungle or secret place, she could be arrested and punished appropriately.

However, for women who enjoy greater freedom of movement by custom or are wives of people on the move (such as fishermen, hunters, dancers, bards), going on a journey with a man is permissible.

Kautilya considered it wrong to frustrate a woman's fertile period. He provided for the re-marriage of wives, in the case of a short absence (*hrasvapravasa*) as well as a long absence (*deerghapravasa*). A wife could remarry but after a period of waiting (*akangsha*) and the approval of judges. The period of waiting would depend on whether the marriage had been consummated, whether the husband had informed the wife before his departure, and whether he had kept in touch with her during his absence, and had paid the full dowry.

After the due waiting period too, the wife should marry only within her husband's own family, extended family (*sapinda*) and family-line (*kula*). An only brother or immediate elder/young brother would be a good choice. This was a strict rule whose violation was punishable. Not only the wife but anyone who was party to it would be penalized.

*Prakarana 61: Dayavibhage dayakrama*

## Rules of Inheritance

While the parents, or at least the father, is alive, the son cannot be the owner of the (ancestral) property. After the father's death, a partitioning (*dayavibhaga*) can be made. No partition can be made of self-acquired (*swayamarjitam*) property.

In a joint family where sons, grandsons and even great-grandsons live together, all are entitled to a share of the ancestral property, up to the fourth generation and if there is no break in the line of descent.

Those brothers who have not got any share of their father's property, or continue to live and earn with their brothers even after the partitioning of property, can again divide up the property. The brother who has contributed the most to the increase of ancestral property can get two shares.

The property of one who has no son can go to his own brother or (interestingly) companion. The daughters can take some of it but only as much as is needed for their marriages.

Only when the sons are adults, should partitioning of the property be done. The share of a minor should be placed in trust with a relative on the mother's side or with a village elder.

The partitioning should be done openly and announced loudly in the presence of witnesses.

*Prakarana 62: Dayavibhage Angshavibhaga*

## Further Partitioning

**Special Rights according to the Order of Parental Caste**

If a woman has several sons from several husbands who are of different castes, the *Brahmana*'s son should inherit the goats, the *Kshatriya*'s son the horses, the *Vaishya*'s son the cattle and the *Shudra*'s son the sheep. The daughters do not have a share but can take old utensils and ornaments from the mother.

If a man has wives of different castes, the son born of the *Brahmana* wife will have four shares, the son born of the *Kshatriya* wife will have three shares, the one born of the *Vaishya* wife will have two and the one born of the *Shudra* wife will have one.

*Prakarana 63: Dayavibhage Putravibhaga*

## Division of Property by types of Sons

If a man has a son through a woman who is not his wife but another's, who does the son belong to? Some earlier thinkers felt he was the property of the woman concerned. Some others felt that he belonged to the father from whose sperm he was born. Kautilya feels that both of these men should be regarded as his father.

If a husband-and-wife duo of the same caste, taking consecrated water in their hands, gives away their natural-born son to another person then the son becomes the *Datta* (Given) son of that person and becomes heir to his property.

देशस्य जात्याः संघस्य धर्मो ग्रामस्य वापि यः ।
उचितस्तस्य तेनैव दायधर्मप्रकल्पयेत् ।।

The division of property should be done according to whatever is best and according to *Dharma* as well as considerations of the place/country (*desha*), the community (*samgha*), and the village (*grama*).

*Prakarana 64: Vastuke Grihavastukam*

### On the Construction of Residential Buildings

Disputes about residential construction should be settled by village officials. The boundaries of every residual construction should be clearly marked by putting pillars at the corner. One house should not use the wall of another. The roof of a house should be about three inches away from that of another or overlap it. Care should be taken of rainwater drainage. No part of one house should obstruct any part of another. An occupied house should have its doors and windows covered/curtained. Appropriate and specific distances should be maintained between the facilities of neighbouring houses, such as places to park carts, to store water, or to keep the grinding mill. There should be sewage channels running along houses and these should be kept clear and open in monsoon. Sheds, courtyards, toilets, fireplaces and places for pounding grain should be enjoyed in common whereas houses and courtyards would be for private use.

*Prakarana 65: Vastuke Vastuvikrayah*

### On the Sale of Residential Buildings

If a house is to be sold, the owner of the house should first ask his own relatives, then the village chief and the trader/moneylender. Only then should he approach outsiders. The owner of the house property should publicly announce its sale in front of the property and of neighbours. An owner of a field, garden, tank or embankment should proclaim the sale at the boundary of the property and in the presence of the elders of the neighbouring village.

The method or procedure for sale is that the owner has to say three times: "This is the price of the property. Who is willing to buy it at this price?" If within that time, no one challenges the owner's right to sell, the prospective buyers can begin to bid for it. Proxy bidding is not allowed. If there are competing bidders and the sale price is higher than the call price, the Treasury gets the margin along with the tax payable. The tax (on the transaction) is to be paid by the bidder who succeeds in purchasing the property. If the successful bidder fails to pay and take possession within seven days, the property can be auctioned again.

If there is dispute regarding the border of two adjoining villages, it is to be settled between the chiefs or representatives of the two villages or those of five (or ten) neighbouring villages. Dispute regarding the borders of field should be settled by village chiefs or elders. Disputes regarding pasture land and arable land too should be settled at the level of village chief/elders. Other than temple land and land for sacrificial ceremony, all land could be used for cultivation.

Tax exemptions are spelt out, along with procedure relevant for water bodies.

*Prakarana 66: Vastuke Viveetakshetrapathahimsa Samayasyanapakarma cha*

**Obstruction and Damage to Land**

Depending upon the use to which the concerned land is being put, its encroachment, obstruction or damage is a punishable offence. One should take care not to affect the fields of others, else, compensate for it. Adequate arrangements should be provided around every village for cows, buffaloes, goats or camels to graze in and move about. Every peasant should participate in village community works or he can be fined. The king should take care of villagers who build roadside restaurants and lodges and keep the village well-maintained.

*Prakarana 67: Rinadanam*

**On Debts**

At the time of making the loan, the rate of interest should be agreed upon and not be changed during the loan period.

Interest should usually be charged at the rate of 1-and- 1/4$^{th}$ per month (15 per cent p.a.).The interest rate would be higher for commercial transactions, even more so for risky ones such as travel through the forest or on sea. If anyone charged a rate of interest higher than this, he would be fined. Grains lent shall be repaid at harvest time at the rate of 50 per cent. Money lent on stocks of commodities shall be paid yearly and at the rate of 50 per cent per annum. Those who miss an interest payment deliberately or through being away on a journey shall pay interest at the rate of 100 per cent.

*Prakarana 68: Oupanidhikam*

## On Deposits

A person to whom a property is entrusted shall not misappropriate, substitute, sell, mortgage or lose it. But he is exempt from returning it if he himself suffers from some civil strife, flood or fire.

*Prakarana 69: Dasakarmakarakalpam*

## On Slaves and Labourers

Kautilya urged that the king should enforce the laws regarding *Udaradasa*s or, simply, *Dasa*s (slaves and bonded labourers). So while slaves and bonded labourers existed in Chanakya's times, they were treated less cruelly than the slaves of ancient Greece or Rome.

The Mlechhas (non-Aryans) could sell or mortgage their children but a minor child of the *Arya*s, whatever his *varna*, could never be made a slave, that is, sold or mortgaged. This was a punishable offence, the punishment being higher for higher *varna*s.

Slaves could be of four kinds - born in the house, inherited, bought, captured or gifted. A woman slave expecting a child could not be sold or mortgaged without provisions being made for her welfare. Slaves could be freed on receipt of redemption money. A slave's property would pass on to his relatives, if any, or pass on to his master.

A slave or bonded labourer could be (i) one who had mortgaged himself, (ii) was mortgaged by someone else, (iii) was sent in distress to work for someone else in return for maintenance, (iii) was working off a fine, or (iv) had been captured in war. He could be redeemed by paying the amount of the debt or the fine. An *Arya* who had mortgaged himself as a bonded labourer would be entitled to keep what he earns on his own without affecting work for his master. Cheating a bonded labourer of his due wages or rights was a punishable offence. But the bonded labourer could not run away from his master's household. If he did so, he would forfeit the right to redeem himself ever.

A Labourer or Worker (*karmakara*) received wages or salaries (*vetana*). The agreement between a labourer and his employer must be made in public and payment to him paid as per that agreement. If there is no prior agreement, the labourer shall be paid according to the nature of the work and the work-hours. It was customary that cultivators would be paid one-tenth of the crops they had helped produce, cowherds one-tenth of the ghee they had helped make, and merchants one-tenth of the goods they had traded. Wage disputes had to be settled only on the basis of the testimony of witnesses, or on-the-spot enquiry. Denying due wages to the labourer was a punishable offence.

*Prakarana 70: Karmakarakalpah, Sambhuyasamutthanam*

**Contractual Work, Collective Labour**

If, after taking the wage as per the agreement /contract, the employee did not do the work as per contract, he could be fined or even thrown into prison. The employee was obliged to perform his duties as per the contract but if ill or otherwise unable to complete it, he could have his contract annulled or have the work done by someone else.

Some thinkers say that if a labourer who has reported for duty does not do his work, he is still entitled to his wages. But Kautilya does not think so. According to him, wages are given for work done, not for sitting and doing nothing. If the employer makes him work just a little but does not make him do the whole work, then it will be taken that the worker has done the work fully. If the worker does not do the work as per instructions or does the opposite of what he was supposed to do, he will not be taken to have done the work. If the worker does more work than he is supposed to do, that extra work is considered to be futile.

Collective labour is bound by the same conditions as individual labour. A worker sent by the collective labour group shall stay on job for seven days, another will be sent for the next seven days, and so on, till the work concerned is over. The earnings will be divided among workers, either equally or according to some earlier agreement.

*Prakarana 71: Vikritakritanaushaya*

## Disputes of Sale and Purchase

If the seller goes back upon his word after the agreement to sell had been made, he can be penalized. If defects surface in the objects sold, that too is a punishable offence. Fines are imposed also when people or animals sold off as hale and hearty are found to have been diseased. Kautilya treats a wedding as a transaction where the girl's father is in the role of the seller and the boy is in the role of a buyer. The three upper castes (*Brahmana, Kshatriya* and *Vaishya*) cannot go back upon their wedding. They cannot reverse their transactions. The *Shudra*s can. If however a girl has a disease and her father hides it and marries her off, he can be fined and the *shulka* or *streedhana* paid to him can be confiscated. If it is the boy who has the disease and is married off by his father, the father can be fined and the *shulka* or *streedhan* paid by him can be confiscated.

Judges and administrators should see to it that, in case of conflict regarding buying-and-selling and lending-and-borrowing, nobody's interest is hurt.

*Prakarana 72-73: Dattasyanapakarma, Aswamivikrayah, vaswamisambandhah*

## Withholding Donated Property, Selling Un-owned Property, and Acquiring Tenancy Rights

Not to actually part with something that has been donated/gifted (*datta*) is a punishable offence like theft.

To sell something of which one is not the owner is also an offence. If one uses/enjoys something continuously for a long period without being its actual owner, even without any witnesses supporting his claim, he gets the right to it. For example, if a tenant stays on in a house for twenty years with the actual owner ignoring it or overlooking it, the tenant acquires a right to it.

*Prakarana 74: Sahasam Vakparushyam Dandaparushyam cha*

## Violence of three kinds

To openly and violently seize the property of another is a daring act or act of violence (*sahasam*). To surreptitiously take away, waste or not return the property of another, is an act of theft (*steyam*).According to Kautilya, the punishment for daring acts, such as robbing of valuables and durables, is to be commensurate with the offence. One who performs robbery deliberately and /or prior intimation is twice as culpable. One who deliberately instigates another to commit robbery is to be fined severely and several times.

Harshness of speech or verbal abuse is also an act of verbal violence (*vakparushyam*) and therefore a punishable offence. Kautilya distinguishes between five bases of verbal violence: *shareera* (physical defects) –when a physically challenged person is jeered at,

*prakriti* (caste)- when a person's caste is the basis of ridicule,

*shruti* (education) – when the level of a person's education is the basis,

*vritti* (occupation)- when one's occupation or livelihood id ridiculed,

and *desha* (country)- when one's country or village is the butt of ridicule.

स्वदेशग्रामयोः पूर्वं मध्यमं जातिसंघयोः ।
आक्रोशाद्देवाचैत्यानामुत्तमम् दण्डम् अर्हति ।।

To denigrate one's own country or locality is a punishable offence, to denigrate one's own caste or community is a more severe offence, but to denigrate temples and places of worship is the most severe offence.

Punishable physical violence or assault (*dandaparushyam*) is to touch (*sparshanam*), hurt (*avagunam*) or wound (*prahatam*). Touching includes pushing, kicking, throwing things and restricting bodily movements. It is a punishable offence to touch the body below the navel, whether by hand or by throwing dust or dirt at it. Similarly punishable is touching anyone with unclean hands or with one's feet. The penalty is higher if the assault is upon a superior (*vishishta*) person like an elder. If during a scuffle or fight, property is destroyed, that too is punishable.

Kautilya lays down that in case of a physical assault, the evidence of witnesses is what is relevant to the judgement, not whether who has approached the court first. Penalties for damaging public or private property, including plants, are listed in detail.

It is interesting to note that it was a serious offence to tear off leaves and blossoms from shady trees in parks, temple grounds and the roadside, not to speak of chopping down branches.

*Prakarana 75: Dyutasamahvayam, Prakeernani*

### Gambling and its Associated Remainders

Gambling and Betting were not illegal activities but were strictly under State control. There were Controllers of gambling and betting who had to ensure that gambling was conducted under controlled conditions and at fixed appointed places. Playing in places other than the authorized gambling halls was prohibited. The masters of the gambling halls had to provide unloaded dice and other un-doctored equipment. They could charge entrance fees and accept objects for sale in lieu of money if the gamblers finished up their money in course of the game and still wanted to play.

The Chief Controller of Gambling and Betting collected a tax (of 5 %) on all winnings as well as all fines imposed.

## *Adhikarana 4: Kantakashodhanam*

## *Punishing Social Miscreants-Protecting Subjects from Oppressors*

*Prakarana 76: Karukarakshanam*

### Protection of Artisans

There should be three ministers (*amatya*) or commissioners (*pradeshta*) to regulate craftsmen and artisans (*kantaka*) who could be troublesome otherwise.

Among craftsmen or artisans forming a group or guild, only a responsible leader or chief should be allowed to take an article or money from others on trust. In case the person to whom the article was entrusted passes away, the guild has to compensate the person who had entrusted the article in question. The artisans should begin their work only after agreeing upon the time within which the work is to be completed. (If the work to be done is of a special nature, no time limit need be stipulated.)

The artisans should complete their work within the stipulated time and act in a responsible fashion. Those who do not can get fined. The weaver (*tantuvaya*), for example, should turn out eleven *pala*s of cloth every ten *pala*s of yarn supplied. Charges varied among cotton, silk and woolen fabrics. The washer man (*rajaka*) should wash clothes on a clean wooden board or slab of stone. He should not wear, sell, rent out, mortgage, lose or change the clothes given to him by his customers. The tailor and the goldsmith were under similar regulations. The doctors were liable to penalties if they worsened their patients' problems leading to their death or disability. Before performing any risky treatment, they were to inform the authorities. Entertainers, beggars and mendicants often travel from place to place. The stipulation was that they should not do so in the monsoon when lots of field hands were required. If they did, they could be beaten up with an iron rod. An interesting point on the importance of agriculture.

*Prakarana 77: Vaidehakarakshanam*

### Traders Protection

The marketing/trade superintendent (*samsthadhyaksha*) should make appropriate arrangements for the export and import of stocks and examine the scales and measures to ensure that the weighing is accurate. There could be some permitted/tolerated deviations but if the shopkeeper deliberately used short weights for selling and excess weights for buying, they were to be fined severely. Selling adulterated items was also punishable. The trade superintendent should himself check the everyday profit and loss of the various shopkeepers. The shopkeepers would get items from the trade superintendent on a wholesale basis. If a shopkeeper found such terms damaged due to some sudden calamity, the trade superintended could re-issue such material to him. The trade superintendent should issue items to shopkeepers on a wholesale basis. In case of products from other places /counties, the superintendent should use ways and means to get them sold.

*Prakarana 78: Upanipatapratikarah*

### Coping with Calamities

Kautilya is very clear on the role of the State. The ruler has to protect the subjects of his kingdom from eight divine calamities (*daivani*), viz., fire, flood, disease, famine, rodents, wild animals like tiger, snakes and demons. As protection against fire, villagers should in summer do their cooking outside the house and keep fire-fighting equipments at hand. As protection against floodwater, villagers by the riverside should move to higher grounds and keep at hand means such as wooden planks, bamboo and boats. People being carried away by floodwater should be rescued using boats, canoes, tree trunks and even gourds and skin bags. Vedic prayers should be chanted to propitiate the gods.

In case of diseases or epidemics among people, physicians as well as ascetics chanting prayers should make their efforts. In case of disease or epidemics among animals, their sheds should be cleaned and ritually purified.

Famine-related measures listed in Kautilya are relevant even today.

Food and seeds should be distributed to the public from royal stores on concessional terms. Royal food stock should be shared. Food-for-work programmes (building dams and forts) should be undertaken.

Private stocks of food should be made available for sharing. The help of friendly kings should be sought. The people affected should be shifted to a different area. They should be encouraged to migrate (temporarily) to other countries. The entire population, the king with all his courtiers, should relocate to a fertile area free from famines. There should be additional cultivation of grains, vegetables, roots and fruits, more fishing and hunting.

The king should take care of rats and locusts so that food grains produced are not destroyed. For example, cats should be released in areas ridden over by rats. Tigers should be killed by hunters, snakes and demons should be killed on sight as well as remedied by magic chanting.

सर्वत्र चोपहतान् पितेव अनुगृह्णीयात्

Thus on the arrival of calamities, the king should protect his subjects like his own children.

*Prakarana 79: Guddhjeebinam rakhsha*

## Protection of Secret Agents

The Chancellor/Commissioner (*Samaharta*) should employ agents all over the country to report on the honesty or dishonesty of village officials and departmental heads. These agents can be wandering ascetics, roaming minstrels, cart drivers, astrologers, actors, restaurant-owners and so on. They should spy upon anyone suspected of secretly amassing wealth or otherwise leading a dishonest life. Such people should be thrown out of the country or appropriately penalized.

*Prakarana 80: Siddhavyanjanairmanavaprakashanam*

### Control of miscreants by Spies in the guise of Ascetics

Spies disguised as ascetics (*siddha*) should stay in the midst of thieves and miscreants and secretly learn their ways. Then they should get them arrested and make it publicly known how the king is ever-vigilant and all-knowing.

*Prakarana 81: Shankaroopakarmabhigrahah*

### Identification of Doubtful Characters and Thieves

This chapter lists ways of identifying people who seem to be doubtful or shady characters. Examples are: those whose ancestral property is gradually eroding away, those whose salaries are inadequate, those who hang around wealthy houses, those who are too engrossed in women. Stolen goods and thieves too can be identified by questioning around and by employing spies.

*Prakarana 82: Ashumritakapareeksha*

### Examination of Sudden Death

This provides practical guidelines for examining cases of sudden or unnatural death. For example, if the dead body has emptied bowels, swollen limbs, marks on the neck and protruding eyes, the cause of death should be taken as strangulation. If the body is bloodied and broken in places, the person has been beaten to death, and so on. The clothes, and personal effects like umbrella should be traced to the traders who sold them, and the information used to find the murderer out.

*Prakarana 83: Vakyakarmanuyogah*

### Coercive Methods of Eliciting Confession

This chapter discusses under what circumstances coercive methods can be used to make the suspect confess his/her guiit. These methods include strokes of the stick, lashes of the whip, suspension by the arms, tying the right leg to the head, pouring of salt water through the nose, pricking under nails, or slapping 32 times. Only when guilt is strongly suspected, should such methods be used. The following are exempt for such torture: suspects of petty offenses, the old and the very young, the sick and the disabled, the drunk and the insane, those tired after a long journey, hunger, thirst or even over-eating. Women should be subjected only to mild methods of torture and no torture should be meted out to expecting or new mothers.

Various punishments for various offences are listed as well.

A Brahmana was exempt from the death penalty or even corporal punishment. He was to be publicly declared guilty, branded on the forehead and banished or sent to work in the mines.

*Prakarana 84: Sarvadhikaranarakshanam*

### Control over Officials

The General Commissioner or Chancellor (*Samaharta*) and Commissioners (*Pradeshta*) should keep close watch over the various officers under them. If any of them commit theft (of foodstuff, weapons, and other valuables), they should be severely punished. For example, if an officer steals diamonds and other gems from the mines or workshops, he could be given the death penalty. If the jailor let a prisoner escape, he too could be given the death penalty.

एवं अर्थचरान् पूर्वं राजा दण्डेन शोधयेत् ।
शोधयेयुः च शुद्धास्ते पौरजानपदान् दमैः ।।

Thus should the king first correct his own officials through appropriate penalties and then get them correct the general population.

In view of the corruption and scams that prevail today, this is a notable point.

*Prakarana 85: Ekangavadhanishkraya*

### Mutilation

Mutilation was also prescribed for certain minor offences like stealing of poultry or fish. The pilferer could have his nose cut off. Trapping or stealing animals from reserved forests was to be fined.

But punishment had to be given on a judicious, case-by-case basis.

पुरुषं चापराधम् च कारणम् गुरुलाघवम् ।
अनुबन्धम् तदात्मं च देशकालौ समीक्ष्य च
उत्तमावर मद्यत्वंप्रदेष्टा दण्डकर्मणि ।
राज्ञश्च प्रकृतीनां च कल्पयेदान्तरा स्थितः ।।

At the time of dealing out penalties, the Commissioner should take the king and the ministers along with him and examine the nature of the offence, the circumstances of the offender, the situation and the consequences.

*Prakarana 86: Shuddhashchitrashcha Dandakalpah*

### Death Penalty with or without Torture

The death penalty could be *shuddha* (simple, without torture) or *chitra* (complex and torturous).If a man killed another in an open fight following a quarrel, he would be tortured to death. If the man he had hurt died seven days after the quarrel and the fight, there was to be no torture - only execution. For example, a man who had killed another on a sudden or stolen a herd (ten or more) of animals, should be simply put to death. But one who had poisoned another, or broken a dam, should be drowned.

*Prakarana 87: Kanyaprakarma*

### On young, virgin girls who had not reached puberty

Deflowering of a young virgin was a serious offence. If a man deflowered a girl of his own *varna* who had not yet reached puberty, he could have his hands chopped off or fined severely. If his act led to the girl's death, he could even be given the death penalty. If the girl had already reached puberty, the man could have his fingers chopped off or subjected to heavy penalty. One who enjoyed himself with a girl betrothed to another could also have his hands chopped off.

*Prakarana 88: Aticharadanda*

### Penalties for Transgressions

There are varied and specific penalties for transgressions (*atichara*). For example, if a Brahmana or Kshatriya eats and drinks items that are taboo, he should be banished from the country. One who feeds them such taboo items is also to be punished. If due to the walls being weak or the wheels of the vehicle being unsteady, someone causes the death of another, he is to be penalized as per rules. If one uses force against an unwilling prostitute, that is a transgression and subject to penalty.

अदंड्य दण्डेन राज्ञो दण्डस्त्रिंशद्गुणोऽम्मसि
वरुणाय प्रदातव्यो ब्रह्मणेभ्यस्ततः परं ॥
तेन सम्पूयते पापं राज्ञो दण्डपचारजम् ।
शास्ता ही वरुणो राज्ञाम् मिथ्या व्यचरतां नृषु ॥

In case the king extracts penalty from a person who should not be penalized (*adandya*), the subjects should extract thirty times that penalty from him. This monetary penalty (*arthadanda*) should first be offered to sea-god Varuna and then distributed among *Brahmana*s.

Thus while Kautilya provides detailed prescriptions of penalties in every possible case, he states that there should be no undue penalization.

## *Adhikarana 5: Yogavritta - Activities of Yoga*

### *Prakarana 89: Dandakarmikam*

**Correcting those who harm the king and the kingdom**

The king should engage able spies to keep watch over ministers, priests and other government employees who get their salaries from the king but secretly denigrate him or join his enemies. Employees (priests, chiefs) who secretly spread rebellion but cannot be openly decried or exposed should be secretly killed by the king (*upangshuvadha*). Seemingly terrible courses are recommended! In the case of a corrupt or suspect chief minister (*mahamatya*), the king should summon a brother who has not got his due share of ancestral property and arm him with poison or weapons of torture against his brother and so cause a quarrel/rift between them. Once he kills his brother (the corrupt/suspected minister), the king should get him killed upon the offence of fratricide. Of the murdered chief minister, only the son who does not denigrate the king or wants him to avenge his father's death should be punished.

### *Prakarana 90: Koshabhisamharanam*

**Collecting for the Exchequer**

In great and/or unexpected financial difficulties, the king should collect extra/additional revenue by making a single-time levy upon farmers.

(i) A tax of $1/3^{rd}$ or $1/4^{th}$ of the stocks of grain is to be collected from land holdings (big and small) which have abundant crops and are not dependent on rainfall.

(ii) A tax proportional to yield is to be collected from lands which have middling or poor yield.

Once harvest is over, $1/4^{th}$ of the surplus (after deduction of grain for subsistence and seeds) must be acquired for cash.

Ivory and skin should be taxed at 50 %. The tax rate for commodities like silk cotton, lac, vegetable, firewood should be $1/6^{th}$.There should be appropriate levies on merchants, craftsmen and professionals as well as livestock owners and brothel keepers.

If the above does not suffice, the *Sthanika*s and the *Gopa*s (officers under the *Samaharta* or Chancellor) shall make the farmers raise a summer crop in addition to the normal monsoon crop.

If even that is insufficient, the *Samaharta* should ask the public, in cities as well as villages, to make voluntary contributions. Some state activity should be cited as an excuse. The rich should contribute generously. Those who do not, should be denigrated in society through secret agents. Temple wealth should also be cleverly expropriated. The Temple-Chief (*Devatadhyaksha*) should collect together the wealth of the various temples under him, cite some state expenditure that is necessary, and let the collection to be taken away to the Treasury. Further, people may be tricked or scared into making contribution. A miracle can be staged or a building constructed overnight to impress the gullible into making contributions. A death may be shown up as divine wrath to be propitiated by contributions. A secret agent may pose as a trader, coin-examiner or goldsmith, collect money from the people, show it up as stolen and then pass it on to the Treasury.

Another way was to confiscate the property of the wicked or treacherous people.

Note, Chanakya made no secret of the above methods of augmenting the State exchequer and even recommended them.

*Prakarana 91: Bhrityabharaniyam*

### Maintenance of Government Servants

The employment of government servants should be according to the wherewithal of the fort or habitation, and about one-fourth of the State revenue should be spent on it. Able and efficient government servants should be recruited, whatever the appropriate salaries are. But expenditure on them should not exceed the revenue they help generate and the principles of *Dharma* and *Artha* should not be flouted.

If occasionally there was not enough in the exchequer to pay the government servants, they could be paid partly in terms of cattle, land or forest product. Grain could occasionally substitute for coins.

This chapter spells out the salaries of a variety of government employees from priests, generals, teachers, physicians, guards, gatekeepers, charioteers, spies and messengers.

If a government servant died on duty, his salary and food allowance would go to his wife and sons. His minor children as well as aged or disabled relatives would be aided. On important occasions, his family would receive money as well as honorable mention.

एवमेवेक्षितायव्ययः कोषदण्डाव्यसनम् नावाप्नोति।

A king who pays attention thus to his revenue and expenditure does not face any calamity with respect to his army or his exchequer.

*Prakarana 92: Anujeebivrittam*

## Behaviour of Followers

One who is well-acquainted with the ways of the world should follow kings who are themselves able and powerful, have able and powerful ministers or are looking for able and powerful ministers. Once appointed by the king, one should do only the work for which one has been appointed and stay neither too far away from the king nor too close. One should not say anything reproachful, sarcastic, incredible or false before the king. One should not wink or curl one's lips, interrupt the king when he is speaking, or keep repeating oneself. Anything to the king's benefit, one should tell the king then and there. Anything to one's own profit, one should tell the king's ministers or favourites. Anything to the profit of others, one should keep for a suitable time and place. Upon the king's asking, an official should speak out what is pleasant and helpful, and not what is pleasant but harmful. But what is helpful should be spoken out then and there even if it is unpleasant. If scared while giving an explanation, the government officer should fall silent. He should not mix with one whom the king dislikes. If the king laughs, one should not maintain a wooden silence but one should not laugh uproariously either. If a terrible news has to be broken to the king, one should not say it directly but leave it to another. But if one just has to do it himself, one must face the consequences with the tolerance of the earth(*kshamaban prithibeesamah*).

आत्मरक्षा हि सततं पूर्वं कार्या विजानता ।
अग्नाविव ही सम्प्रोक्ता वृत्ती राजोपजीविनाम् ।।

एकदेशं दहेदाग्नि:शरीरं वा परंगतः ।
सपुत्रदारं राजा तू घातयेत् वर्धयेत वा ।।

The wise government official should first think of protecting himself because the condition of those dependent on the king has been said to be more dangerous than that of those who play with fire. Fire burns part or whole of the body but the king can make or mar the entire family.

*Prakarana 93: Samayacharikam*

### Timely Conduct on the part of Government Officials

The government officials should show the king their net incomes (*vyayavishuddham udayam*), deducting expenditure from the gross. They should report all that is happening in and around the fort and register their reports in a ledger. If the king gets addicted to hunting, gambling or womanizing, they should go along with him but try to wean the king away from these dangerous habits. They should protect him from enemy agents trying to cheat or poison him. They should assess his pleasure or displeasure, for example, by observing if he looks happy to see them or listens to them attentively. They should interpret certain signs as those of disfavour, for example, getting cross upon sight, breathing heavily, not offering a seat, changing the topic, or scratching his own body. They should then leave the king's service.

In case of loss of property or respect too, the government officers should leave service (*arthamanvakshepe cha parityagah*).

But if upon considering one's own offence and the king's nature, the government officer does not want to leave the king's service, he should appease the king through relatives, friends and advisors of the king.

*Prakarana 94-95: Rajyapratisandhanamekaishvaryam cha*

### How Officers Should Combat Difficultiesa and Bring Prosperity

The ministers should deal with calamities coming upon the king. For example, if the king is dying, they should consult with his friends and relatives and declare throughout the country that the king would be holding court with suitable intervals. They should station wise and efficient personnel at the border provinces as well as the forts.

Once the king is dead, the officers should find a suitable day to anoint the heir to the throne, as the crown prince (*yuvaraja*).They should then slowly place the responsibilities of the kingdom upon him.

If the king dies in an enemy country, the officers accompanying him should use diplomatic skills and even strike up a false friendship with the enemy king, to come back to their own kingdom. Afterwards they can anoint the king's minor son as the crown prince and tackle the enemies, internal and external. According to Kautilya, this is the way the ministers should establish a united kingdom (*evamekaishvaryamamatyah karayet iti Kautilya*).This is his stand against that of Bharadvaj who had felt that the minister should take this opportunity to make the prince and the dead king's relatives and friends fight among themselves, to quietly get them all killed (*upangshudanda*), and himself become the new king. Kautilya considers this destabilizing for the kingdom and disturbing for its subjects.

The young prince upon the throne should raise the salaries of the ministers and soldiers. The ministers should give them the assurance that later he would raise their salaries further. Instead of making neat packets for themselves, they should see to the provisions for the young prince. When he comes of age, they should assess if he wants them to continue in their service to him. If he does not, they should quietly leave. If not, they should continue to be by his side and help him rule.

## *Adhikarana 6: Mandalayoni - Divisional Groups*

*Prakarana 96: Prakritisampadah*

**Natural Attributes of Power**

Regal power (*rajasampadah*) has seven natural attributes (*prakriti*).

1. The *Swami* or king should be endowed with the qualities of patience, farsightedness, enthusiasm, quickness, valour, wisdom, considerateness, self-control and the ability to control men and horses.
2. The qualities of the *Amatya* or minister have been discussed in the *Adhikarana* named *Vinayadhikarika*.
3. The *Janapada* or habitation should have a fort nearby, have fields nearby where plenty of food crops can be grown and also have forests and hills nearby which the people, when under attack, can resort to. It should have good weather, rivers and other water bodies, and people who are hard-working and good at heart.
4. The qualities of the *Durga* or fort have been discussed in the *Prakarana* named *Durga-vidhana*.
5. The *Kosha* or Treasury/Exchequer should contain stocks of wealth acquired by the king's ancestors, such as gems and precious metals, which can protect all the subjects during famine or some such calamity.
6. The *Danda* (here in the sense of *Sena* or Army) should have soldiers enrolled through generations, obedient, disciplined, fully satisfied with their remuneration, trained and capable of enduring pain. They should mostly be *Kshatriya*s and share the king's fortunes and misfortunes.
7. The *Mitra* or Ally should be a friend through generations, steady and under one's control. There should be no possibility of enmity from him and he should be capable of providing timely help. In contrast, the *Shatru* or Enemy may not be from any pure royal family, but a lowly fellow, greedy, thoughtless and irreverent.

These are the real powers of a king. A king who has these seven powers (*sampada*) is a powerful (*sampanna*). Such a king can empower or uplift ordinary men. But a king who does not have these powers renders even talented and devoted men useless.

*Prakarana 97: Shamavyayamika*

## Active and Passive Policies

The welfare and security of the State is the purpose of Active (*vyayama*) and Passive (*shama*) foreign policies. A Passive, non-interventionist policy (or a policy involving overt intervention) policy helps undisturbed enjoyment of the results of past activities.

An Active policy makes new efforts towards success.

Six qualities determine Active and Passive policies, viz., *sandhi, vigraha, yana, asana, samshraya* and *dvaidheebhava.*

Three outcomes result from the Active and Passive policies, viz., *kshaya* (decline), *sthana* (*status quo*) and *vriddhi* (progress).

Two kinds of activities (*karma*) lead to these three fruits (*phala*), viz., *Manusha* and *Daiva. Naya* and *Apanaya* are *Manusha* while *Aya* and *Anaya* are *Daiva.*

*Manusha* and *Daiva* are two wheels of the life of human beings. All the right and wrong activities that unseen powers make men do are *Daiva* activities. If they lead to the desired fruits, they are *Aya.* If they lead to adverse results, they are *Anaya.*

All the activities that use powers of command, prayer or enthusiasm and apply the qualities of *sandhi*, *vigraha* and so on, are *Manusha-karma.* If they take man to the desired fruits, they are called *Naya.* If they misfire or lead to trouble, they are called *Apanaya.*

Kautilya now coins a crucial term, ***Vijigeeshu*** - Aspirant-to-Victory or Aspirant-Conqueror.

A king who is endowed with personal qualities, material resources, manpower and personnel ( i.e., is *atmadravyaprakritisampanna*) and is the embodiment of justice (*nayasyadhistthana*) is an Aspirant-to-Victory or a Potential Conqueror (*Vijigeeshu*). All the kings around him in a ring (*mangaleebhuta*) and sharing a common border with him are Inimical or Antagonistic in Nature (*Ari-prakriti*). All the kings around them and sharing common borders with them are Friendly or Non-antagonistic in Nature (*Mitra-prakriti*).

A powerful Antagonistic(*Ari*) neighbour is an Enemy (***Shatru***). The Aspirant-to-Victory should attack him when he falls into a situation of calamity (*vyasana*). The Aspirant-to-Victory should also attack a *Shatru* who is shelter-less (*anapashraya*) or weakened (*durbalashraya)*. As for a *Shatru* who is not weak or without shelter, he should be harassed and reduced to a weak position.

Along the path and ahead of the Aspirant-to-Victory there stand 5 kings in the following order:

Enemy (*Shatru*), Ally (*Mitra*), Enemy's Ally (*Arimitra*), Friend of the Ally (*Mitramitra*) and Friend of the Enemy's Ally(*Arimitra-mitra*).

Along his path but behind him stand another 4 kings:

Rear Enemy (*Parshnigraha*), Rear Ally (*Akranda*), Rear Enemy's Ally (*Parshnigrahasara*) and Rear Ally's Friend (*Akrandasara*).

The whole series or sequence of kings ahead of and after the Aspirant-to Victory is called the Royal Circuit or Circle of Kings (***Rajamandala***).

Allies and Enemies can be Natural (*Sahaja*) or Artificial (*Kritrima*). Among kings with contiguous territories, a Natural Enemy is one from the same family as the Aspirant-to-Victory or of equally high birth. An Artificial Enemy is one induced or made to be an enemy. Among kings with contiguous territories, a Natural Ally is one from the same or equally noble family while an Artificial one is befriending the Aspirant-Conqueror intentionally for purposes such as protection and resources.

A Middle (*Madhyama*) king is one whose king is contiguous to the Aspirant's and who supports him as well as his enemy in either *Sandhi* or *Vigraha*.

An Indifferent/Neutral (*Udaseena*) king is one whose kingdom is not contiguous with those of the Aspirant, his Enemy King or the Middle King, who is more powerful than these three and able to help them whether they are united or not and destroy them individually when they are not united.

The Aspirant, the Ally and the Friend of the Ally are the three Natures, elements or basic constituents (*prakriti*). Each has five Natures (*Amatya, Janapada*, *Durga, Kosha* and *Danda*). Together (3 + 3x5) they make up 18 elements of the (first) circuit (*mandalamashtadashakam*). The Enemy, the Middle and the Indifferent kings have a similar circuit of 18 elements or attributes.

Thus there can be 4 Circuits, each of 18 Elements/Attributes.

There are 12 Royal attributes (*dvadasha rajaprakritayah*), 60 (5X12) Material attributes (*shashtirdravyaprakritayah*), making a total of 72(=12+ 60) attributes, each with its own properties (strength and weaknesses).

Kautilya now takes up the issues of Power (*Shakti*) and *Siddhi* (Success). Power is strength (*bala*) and Success is happiness.

Power or strength is of three kinds.

Power from knowledge (*Gyanabala*) yields the success of counsel (*Mantrasiddhi*).

Power from the Treasury and the army (*Koshadandabala*) yields the success of mastery (*Prabhushakti*).

Power from bravery (*Vikramabala*) yields the success of enthusiasm (*Utsahashakti*).

A king who has more of these three kinds of powers (*Gyanabala, Koshadandabala* and *Vikramabala*) will have greater success and be regarded as Superior (*Jyaya*) while the one who has less of them will be regarded as Inferior (*Heena*).Those who have comparable powers will be regarded as Equal (*Sama*).

Thus a king who aspires to be the conqueror should constantly endeavour to increase his powers and so heighten his success, if unable to increase his own powers, he should try to increase the power of the elements (human) that constitute his state, and reduce that of his enemies.

नेमिमेकांतरात् राज्ञ:कृत्वा चानन्तरानरान् ।
नाभिमात्मानमेअच्छेन्नेता प्रकृतिमण्डले ।।
मध्ये हि उपहितः शत्रुर्नेतुमित्रस्य चोमयोः ।
उच्छेद्यः पीडनीयो वा बलवानपि जायते ।।

In the Circuit of Attributes or Circle of Elements (*prakritimandala*), the Aspirant-to-Victory should always place himself in the centre, his Allies at the circumference and neighbouring kings as radius or spokes of the wheel. The enemy who comes in between the Aspirant and the Allies, however powerful, gets either conquered or harassed.

## *Adhikarana 7: Shadgunya - Six Royal Measures relating to Foreign Policy*

### *Prakarana 98-99: Kshayasthanavriddhinishchayasya*

### Determination of Policies for Progress as against Decline and Stagnancy

The Circuit of Attributes or Circle of Elements (*prakritimandala*) is the source /basis of the Six Royal Policies/Measures (*shadgunya*), each for a different set of circumstances.

Making Peace (*Sandhi*) refers to entering into an agreement/treaty with specific conditions. It should be done when the king concerned finds himself in a weak position *vis-à-vis* his enemy.

Waging War (*Vigraha*) refers to attacking, displaying active hostility. It should be done when the king is in a position superior to his enemy.

Taking a sitting position (*Asana*) refers to maintaining *status quo* or remaining quiet. It should be done when neither king can harm the other.

Preparing (*Yana*) refers to improving or strengthening the position for war.

Seeking Support (*Samshraya*) refers to getting the protection of another king when the king concerned finds his resources reduced.

Dual Policy (*Dvaidheebhava*) refers to waging war with one king but making peace with another whose help is essential in winning over the other.

Kautilya now discusses when to use which of the above six foreign policies. Progress can be achieved through all of them. But the appropriate policy should be chosen in the appropriate situation. For example, the king should use *Sandhi* (Making Peace) when (a) he and his enemy both achieve equal progress in equal time, (b) decline equally in equal time, or (c) experience no change in situation in equal time. He may use the time of peace so gained to improve his situation through productive undertakings or destroying his enemy's productive undertakings secretly, or create other problems for him.

He should use *Vigraha* (Waging War) if he is confident of defeating his enemy because of a superior army or a superior defensive position (mountain, forest or river fort) or because the enemy army or position is very weak.

But when neither he nor his enemy are in a position to harm each other much, he should achieve progress by *Asana* (Sitting it Out) or (making sure his own position is not weakening) by *Yana* (Preparing for War).

If the king is unable to harm his enemy or protect himself, he should resort to *Samshraya* (Seeking Protection), and move towards progress under the protection of a stronger king.

If the king can protect and promote his kingdom by waging war with one king while having peace with another, it is this *Dvaiheebhava* (Dual Policy) that he should follow.

एवं षड् भिः गुणैरेतै स्थितः प्रकृतिमण्डले ।
पर्येषेत क्षयात् स्थानं स्थानाद् बृद्धिं कर्मसु ।।

This is how the king, situated in his Circle of Attributes, should aspire for progress judiciously using the Six Policies.

*Prakarana 100: Samshrayavritti*

**Policy of Seeking Protection**

Kautilya was definitely not a war-monger. He says clearly in this chapter that when the degree of progress is the same from pursuing a policy of peace and a policy of war, the policy of peace is to be preferred. War involves losses, expenses, absence from home and such disadvantages.

सन्धिविग्रहयोस्तुल्यायाम् बृद्धौ संधिमुपेयात् ।
विग्रहे हि क्षयव्यय प्रवासप्रत्यवाया भवन्ति ।।

Even a policy of neither peace nor war (*Asana*) or a Dual Policy (*Dvaidheebhava*) is preferable to making preparations for War.

प्रियो यस्य भवेत् यो वाप्रियोऽस्य कतरस्तयोः ।
प्रियो यस्य स तं गच्छेदित्या श्रय गतिः परा ।।

Two people are bound to like each other if one likes the other. So it is best that a king should take the protection of a king who likes him.

### *Prakarana 101-2: Samaheenajyasa Gunabhinvesho Heenasandhayashcha*

### Qualities of Equal, Inferior and Superior kings and Policy of Peace with an inferior king

In general, the Aspirant-to-Victory should make peace with an equally powerful or even stronger king. With a weaker king, he should wage war where he will win like a stone that strikes an earthen pot. However he should never follow this rule without considering the situation, such as that of a powerful king rejecting his offer of peace or that of the weaker king being a very submissive and docile one. Again, a weak king may also make ready for war if he realizes that the enemy has fallen into irremediable trouble. If a king of equal strength does not seem to be interested in making peace, but keep on creating trouble, the Aspirant should make an equal amount of trouble for him. An unheated piece of iron never attaches to another piece of iron.

### *Prakarana 103-7: Vigrihyasanam, Sandhyasanam, Vigrihyayanam, Sandhayayanam, Sambhuyaprayanam cha*

### Various Policies of Inaction

Neither waging war nor making peace but deliberately following a policy of inaction can be of three types.

*Sthana* is a settled position of not actively pursuing preparation for either war or peace.

*Asana* is sitting waiting for jumping up when the right time comes.

*Upekshana* is ignoring one's ability to act.

When the aspirant and his enemy, in spite of wanting to conquer each other, are both incapable of harming each other, they should pause after declaring war or offering peace.

Here Kautilya mentions several economic considerations. For example, if a king finds that his own economy is prosperous while the other king's economy is doing so badly that his subjects are likely to come over to his side in a famine situation, he should declare war and pause.

If a king finds that his own economy is hovering so close to a famine situation that his subjects are likely to go over to his enemy's unless there is a war in which the king permits them to loot and plunder the enemy, he should declare war and pause.

If the king finds that he can prevent the import into his country of the enemy's goods which harm his country, he should declare war and pause. If he finds that declaring war enables him to divert to his own country the valuable goods going to the enemy country by a trade route, he should declare war and pause.

If after declaring war and waiting for a period during which the king has increased his strength, he shall set out on a campaign (*Yana)*, choosing a time when the enemy does not have all its forces fully gathered together (e.g., because of some natural calamity or epidemic).

If the king finds that he cannot set out on an attack single-handedly but that it is necessary to do so, he should join forces with other kings (weaker, equally strong or stronger). Kautilya also mentions how, in such cases, the spoils of war should be shared.

***Prakarana 108-110: Yatavyamitrayorbhigrahachinta, Kshayalobhaviragahetavah, Prakreetinam Samavayikaviparimarshashcha***
**Preparation, Emergence of Loss, Greed or Irritation in the Elements, and Shares of the Kings helping the Aspirant-Conqueror**

If apart from the natural enemy (*amitra*), another (neighbouring) kingdom is in a vulnerable situation and can be attacked, the aspirant king should choose judiciously whom he should attack first. Between two kings equally affected, he should attack the enemy first because he will never help in attacking the other whereas the other may help in attacking the enemy. If the enemy kingdom is more affected than the neighbouring one, it should again be attacked first because then the other kingdom will have a chance of recovering and perhaps coming to help the attacking Aspirant-Conqueror. If there is a just king seriously affected by calamities and an unjust one not so seriously affected but having disloyal or discontented subjects, it is the latter who should be attacked because his subjects would not rally to his support.

The Aspirant-Conqueror should not let any feeling of greed, neglect or irritation arise in the kings of his Circle (*prakritimandala*) who have helped him. In case such feelings develop, he must immediately take care of them. He must pay his associates (*samavayika*) their shares (*amsha*) and bid them farewell with due respect. The kings who have helped the Aspirant-Conqueror should depart immediately if they find him ungrateful or arrogant.

### *Prakarana 111: Samhitaprayanikam Paripanitaparipaniatapasritasandhayashcha* **Treaties and Agreements, Conditional and Unconditional**

Here Kautilya discusses different types of treaties or agreement (*Sandhi*) between kings. *Paripanita* (upon some *pana* or condition) type of *Sandhi* is treaty upon some specific condition (of *desha* or place, *kala* or time and *karya* or purpose). If the Aspirant king is making a treaty with another king saying "You attack this country and I will attack that", he is making a *Paripanita Desha Sandhi*. If he makes a treaty with another king saying "You work till this time and I will work till that", he is making a *Paripanita Kala Sandhi*. If the Aspirant is making a treaty with another king saying, "You do this much or for this purpose, while I will do that much or for that purpose", he is making a *Paripanita Karya Sandhi*.

*Aparipanita Sandhi* (Unconditional treaty) is when the Aspirant makes a treaty with a lazy, hasty or addicted (to wine, women or gambling) king by falsely creating in him a vague trust without any specific conditions being laid out so that he can find out the weaknesses of the unworthy one and then attack him.

The Aspirant should make one neighbouring king fight against another and take advantage of the situation to attack the enemy kingdom.

When a specific time and place is chosen for the onslaught and is so declared, it is *Prakashayuddha* (Open or direct Warfare). When a big show is made of a small army, when the enemy camp is looted and plundered, or when the attack is shifted elsewhere, it is *Kootayuddha* (Indirect or crooked Warfare). When poison, herbal toxicants or spies are used, it is *Tushneemyuddh*a (Silent or quiet Warfare).

*Prakarana 112: Dvaidheebhavikah Sandhivikramshcha*

## Dual Policy and Treaties

Here Kautilya discusses Dual Policy and treaties associated with it. The Aspirant may take the help of an enemy in order to attack another neighbouring king if, for example, there is no danger of an enemy attack from the back or his own army is much larger. When the Aspirant follows a Dual Policy, he should, while fighting the enemy, make peace with one neighbouring king from whom he will try to get armed forces in return of money or supply his own forces for payment. *Samasandhi* (Equal Treaty) is one in which the stronger king gets a greater share, an equally powerful king an equal share and a weaker king a smaller share. In a *Vishamasandhi* (Unequal Treaty), a strong, equal or weak king does not get a share according to his power. *Atisandhi* (Extremely Unequal Treaty) is one in which one party to the agreement gets an exceptionally large share.

Kautilya urges the concerned kings to first get a clear understanding of the treaty being considered.

आदौ बुद्धयेत पणितः पनमानश्च कारणम् ।
ततो वितर्क्योभयतो यतः श्रेयस्ततो व्रजेत ।।

The *panita*-king (one with whom the treaty is being made) and the *panamana*-king (one making the treaty) should first comprehend the reasons for the proposed treaty. Then they should discuss and argue on it, and only then take the best course.

*Prakarana 113-14: Yatavyavrittih, Anugrahyamitravisheshashcha*

## Behaviour of an Attacking Aspirant-Conqueror and his Duties towards Allies

An attacking Aspirant-Conqueror (Yatavya Vijigeeshu) , when calculating the gains (*labha*) from a treaty should take into account immediate as well as potential gains, i.e., take an overall view, sometimes to the extent of foregoing some apparent gains.

For both the Aspirant-Conqueror and the Enemy, who want to do their duties towards their Allies, there are five kinds of Allies to be favoured:

(i) *Shakyarambhi*-one who can complete the task he begins

(ii) *Kalyanarambhi*- one who can do a good job

(iii) *Bhavyarambhi*- one who can do a job that will yield good future results

(iv) *Sthirakarma* - one who steadily works at his job, and

(iv) *Anuraktaprakriti* - one with devoted followers who, even if they are not numerous, will help him complete the task.

Kautilya also provides advice in cases of both the Aspirant and the Enemy giving help to the same neighbour and in doubtful cases

He ends the chapter saying that in case of getting equal gains, a *Sandhi* should be made, or else, *Vigraha* should be resorted to.

*Prakarana 115: Mitrahiranyabhoomikarmasandhayah*

### Treaties and their Objectives - allies, gold and land

The treaty for a joint campaign (*samhitaprayana*) can be made with three successively valuable gains (*labha*) in mind, viz., ally (*mitra*), gold (*hiranya*) and land (*bhoomi*). Kautilya argues that land can buy allies and gold, and gold can buy allies.

Contrary to the older view that an immediate gain is preferable, Kautilya argues for a large gain, even if it is in the future - like the fruit of a small seed.

*Prakarana 116: Bhoomisandhih, Anavasitasandhi, Karmasandhi*

### Land-treaty, Uncertain Treaty, Work-treaty

By Bhoomisandhi the Aspirant-Conqueror who is versed in the *Arthashastra* can, through a joint campaign with another king, attain the earth as well as achieve distinction for himself.

Out of two kings making a joint campaign, he who acquires good-quality land gets the better of the other. Out of two kings acquiring equally good land, the one who acquires it after overcoming the stronger enemy gets the better of the other. If the land acquired is fortified, it is even better. For, a fort enables the king to protect his territory against enemies and tribals of the forest.

When two kings make a treaty to set up a colony or habitation in an empty or virgin land, it is called *Anavasitasandhi* (Uncertain-treaty). Whichever of them can do it, has a lot to gain.

When two kings make a treaty to do some work jointly (e.g., jointly undertake to build a fort, construct a dam, plant trees to create a forest for timber or for elephants to live in, open up mines and trade routes), it is *Karmasandhi* (Work-treaty). The Aspirant-Conqueror can achieve much prosperity by it.

*Prakarana 117: Parshnigrahachinta*

### Thoughts on Attacking from the Rear

`*Parshni*' means rear or back. This chapter thus contains Kautilya's thoughts on the situation when one king fighting another gets attacked by a third king from another direction, or simply, from the back. For example, in the case of an attack from the rear, the king who attacks the more powerful king is better-off because once he deals with him he can tackle better the king who is attacking him from the back. Further, for fighting the attacker-from-the-rear, untrustworthy or inefficient troops should be used. In fighting the attacker-from-the-rear, they will themselves get eroded. A king attacked in the rear should never ignore such an attack.

The older preceptors pointed out that pursuing the enemy led to heavy losses but Kautilya believed otherwise,

सुमहतापि क्षयव्ययेन शत्रुविनाशोऽभ्युपगन्तव्य:

Even at great losses and expenses, an enemy's destruction just had to be accomplished.

*Prakarana 118: Heenashaktipooranam*

### Recouping Strength

Sometimes an Aspirant whose powers are weakened may get attacked by a *samavaya* (co-operative or confederacy) of other kings. Then he needs to sow dissension in the confederacy and recoup his strength. (i) When the confederacy has a leader, the attacked king will offer him both gold (*hiranya*) and himself as an ally (*mitra*). He will persuade the leader that the others in the confederacy may some day leave him or offer him more gold than he can ever get from the confederacy. At the same time, he can use agents to work upon the other kings in the confederacy. When the confederacy gets divided and weakened, the attacking king will build up his strength. (ii) When the confederacy has no particular king as its leader, the attacking king will decide upon one (e.g., the inciter, or the resolute one) and work upon him.

However this needs time. When the Aspirant does not have the time to sow dissent, he shall enter into a treaty with the confederacy offering his financial or military strength and specifying the terms of the treaty (the time, the place and the work).Then he shall take care of his own weaknesses.

If he lacks support, he shall build up a support base from his friends and kinsfolk.

If he lacks fortification, he shall construct a fort.

If he lacks good advisors, he shall gather old and wise men around him.

प्रभावहीनः प्रकृति योगक्षेम सिद्धौ यतेत।
जनपदः सर्वकर्मणाम् योनिः ततः प्रभावः ।।

If he is lacking in influence, he should try to promote the welfare of his people. For, it is people in their habitation who constitute the source of all activities and therefore of all influence.

If he lacks resources, he can either develop them (by building forts, dams, roads, elephant forests, cattle herds) or get them from allies and kinsmen.

If he lacks enthusiastic soldiers, he shall recruit men from bands of robbers, tribals in the forests, *mlechha* or foreigners and mercenaries and secret agents.

The general advice of this chapter is thus the following:

एवं पक्षेण मंत्रेण द्रव्येन च बलेन च ।
सम्पन्नः प्रतिनिर्गच्छेत् प्राबग्रहमात्मनः ।।

In this way, through allies, friends, advisors, material resources and army, the Aspirant-Conqueror should always go forth to remedy enemy oppression.

### *Prakarana 119-120: Balvata Vigrihyoparodhahetavah Dandopanatavrittam Cha*

### The Weak King under Attack

The weak king (*durbalo raja*) as distinct from the Aspirant-Conqueror (*Vijigeeshu*) , if attacked by a strong king, should seek the protection of an even stronger king who cannot be tricked or out-done by the policies of the attacking (and strong) king. If there are two such stronger kings for the weak to choose from, he should choose the one with cleverer ministers and advisors, and/or the better war preparations.

Otherwise, he should join forces with kings who, though less strong (than the attacking king), are upright, energetic and opposed to the attacking king.

If the weak king cannot find any other king to protect or support him, he should get into a fort well-equipped with stocks and men.

According to some thinkers before Kautilya, if the above does not work out, the weak king has only two options: either leave the fort and run away or face the much stronger attacker and die bravely. But Kautilya thinks that if the weak king finds that the circumstances are conducive to peace between him and the attacking king, he should send a messenger asking for peace (or respond positively if the messenger comes from the opposite side). If however the circumstances are not conducive to peace, the weak king shall first fight and then seek peace or protection.

If the weak king is indeed given asylum or protection, he should behave in a courtier-like fashion to the protector. But he should take care that his own ministers, courtiers or servants do not see him in that situation. To his own men, he should always appear as the lord and master. He should merge his army with that of the protector-king, and seek permission before building forts, installing the heir-apparent, dealing with horses and elephants or going on trips.

*Prakarana 121: Dandopanayivrittam*

### Behaviour towards a king who has Surrendered his Army

This chapter discusses how the Conqueror-king should behave towards a king who has surrendered (*upanata*) his army (*danda*). If, for example, the defeated king seems to dishonour the promise of gold made in the treaty, the conqueror should strategically position his army all around the defeated king's country and eventually attack it. Powerful kings should be controlled by creating dissension among them or by army attack. Weak kings should be controlled through peaceful methods or by using money.

If the Conqueror treats the king who has surrendered with dignity, he, along with his descendants, will be his followers. If he hurts or imprisons him and takes away his property and/or his family members, the entire Circle of Kings (*mandala*) may get enraged and the Conqueror's own ministers and officials may get incensed and join them.

*Prakarana 122-123: Sandhikarma, Sandhimokshashcha*

### Making Treaties and Getting Free from Treaties

This chapter relates to treaties backed by hostages (*pratibhu*) or guarantors (*pratigraha*). Kautilya thinks that treaties based on the word of honour or an oath is superior to those based on the giving of hostages and collaterals. The one who breaks the latter type of treaties feels that he has only some earthly consequences to face; the one who breaks the former, feels that he has to face terrible consequences in his after-life. Kautilya discusses the issue of who makes a good hostage, a daughter rather than a son, a dullard son rather than in intelligent one, and even – an illegitimate son rather then a legitimate one. Here occurs a remark which today seems objectionable.

कन्या आदा यादा परेषामेवार्थाय क्लेशाय च ।विपरीतः पुत्रः ।

The daughter cannot inherit, is of use only to others (her in-laws) and a cause for trouble. The son is the opposite.

The chapter also contains suggestions on how the hostage can escape or be helped to escape, how he can avoid recapture, how he should react when captured, and how the treaty-maker (hostage-giver) should deal with the situation. For example, the hostage may be carried out by attendants in a container (say, by a bed-maker in a box of bed linen or he may use a secret weapon to kill his captors and ride out aided by secret agents). The treaty-maker (hostage-giver) may then get out of the treaty by accusing the receiver/keeper of the hostage by displaying a drowned/burnt dead body of another person as murdered by the hostage receiver/keeper. He may use it as an excuse for attack.

*Prakarana 124-6: Madhyamacharitodaseenacharitamandalacharitani*

### Policies towards the Middle king and the Neutral king

The Middle king's friendly elements (*prakriti*) to the Circle of Elements consist of the Aspirant-Conqueror, the Ally and the friend of the Ally. His unfriendly elements are the Enemy, the Enemy's Ally and the Enemy's Ally's Friend. It is in the interest of the

Aspirant-Conqueror not to let the Middle king become too strong. For example, he may give protection to another ambitious king or keep him obligated by granting him land when driven out of his own.

The Neutral king shares no common border with the Aspirant and is relatively remote but even he can be a threat. Between the Middle king and the Neutral king, the Aspirant-conqueror should lean towards the one who is popular in his Circle of kings. He should support the Middle king if he proceeds against the Neutral. But if the Neutral king proceeds against the Middle king, the Aspirant-conqueror shall see to his own advantage.

## *Adhikarana 8: Vyasanadhikarika:*
## *The Section On Calamities*

***Prakarana 127: Prakritivyasanavarga***

### Calamities for Constituent Elements

Calamities, adversities and vices (*vyasana*) to various Constituent Elements (*Prakriti*) are discussed here.

According to Kautilya, the king, his ministers, councilors and government officers, had a duty to protect people from calamities, divine (*daiva*) or man-made (*manusha*). If the ministers *et al* did not take appropriate policies or make appropriate treaties, the resulting calamity is called *Anaya*. If the calamity is due to enemy trouble, it is *Apanaya*.

Earlier thinkers such as Bharadvaja thought that the king whose ministers are affected by calamities was helpless and so calamity occurring to ministers is more serious than calamity occurring to the king. But Kautilya thinks otherwise. For, it is the king who appoints his ministers and if one minister is beset by calamities, he can appoint others. The king being the head of the State, his character influences that of the other Elements.

But a calamity affecting the minister is more serious than that affecting the habitation (*janapada*). Parashara thought that a calamity to the fortified town to be more serious than outside it. But Kautilya thinks that a calamity to the countryside is more so.

जनपदमूला दुर्गकोशदण्डसेतुवार्तारम्भाः ।
शौर्यं स्थैर्यं दाक्ष्यं बाहुल्यं च जनपदेषु ।।

The fort, the Treasury, the army and even the water reservoirs all depend upon the people in the habitation. All economic activity originates in the countryside.

This is more so if the country consists mostly of agriculturists than of soldiers and army men.

Of the fort and the Treasury, Kautilya considers the fort more important because it has multiple uses, including the safety of the Treasury. So a calamity to the fort is more serious.

Of calamity to the army and calamity to the Treasury, circumstances decide which is more serious. As a Treasury has many uses, including that of paying an army, a calamity to the Treasury is more serious than that to the army.

A calamity need not render an Element totally useless. If there is a danger to some parts of an Element, the other parts may be salvaged for use.

*Prakarana 128: Rajarajyayorvyasanachinta*

### Thoughts on Calamities of the King and the Kingdom

The King and the Kingdom summarize the entire Elements. The Kingdom can have two types of anger (*kopa*) against the King, external and internal. Like a snake living inside the household, internal anger is much more dangerous than external (*ahibhayadabhayantarah kopah bahyakopat papeeyan*).To protect himself from the internal anger of his ministers, the Aspirant-Conqueror should therefore keep the Treasury and the army entirely under his control.

*Dvairajya* (Kingdom with Two Kings) as well as *Vairajya* (Kingdom under the rule of a vanquished king) both can have calamities. Contrary to earlier opinion, Kautilya thinks that through the intervention of able ministers, internal friction in Dvairajya can be kept under control.

A king can be *Andhashastra* (one who is ignorant of the scriptures and philosophies) or *Chalitashastra* (one who knows them but ignores them). Contrary to earlier opinion, Kautilya prefers the former who can at least be corrected by good advice. Out of a king who is sick and one is new to the job, which is to be preferred? As distinct from that of the earlier thinkers, Kautilya's preference is for the former. The new king may turn out to be too arrogant to follow the advice of ministers whereas the sick king is likely to be led by them. However, he makes it clear that this applies only to kings sick of usual afflictions, not to diseases like leprosy (in those days regarded as born of one's sins).

Between a high-born king and a low-born one, Kautilya is for the former because, even if he is weak, he commands the allegiance of the constituent Elements.

Suffering due to not being able to sow is less than suffering due to not being able to reap. For that means an utter loss of effort. No rain is worse than too much rain because life, after all, depends on water.

If both the Aspirant-Conqueror and the Enemy face calamities but the calamity is lighter for the Aspirant, he should launch an attack upon the Enemy. If it is the other way round, he should just sit quietly.

*Prakarana 129: Purushavyasanavarga*

### Calamities of Common/Ordinary Men

It is ignorance and indiscipline (*avidyavinaya*) that cause calamities or adversities of common people. An ignorant person does not perceive the evil consequences of calamities. There are three kinds (*trivarga*) of vices from anger (*krodha*) and four kinds (*chaturvarga*) from desire or lust (*kama*). Anger is the more vicious. One hears often of angry kings getting killed by his own ministers or other constituent elements and lustful kings dying of diseases. Bharadvaja had held that anger sometimes motivates proper action like killing one's enemies and desire or lust is necessary for attainment of the fruits of desire. But Kautilya considers them to be unredeemed sources of vice and, out of the two, anger to be a greater evil.

Anger makes one hated, lust makes one humiliated. According to Kautilya, being hated is worse. Anger leads to loss of friends, desire to loss of wealth. According to Kautilya, loss of friends is worse. Anger makes one suffer from vices, desire from bad company. According to Kautilya, it takes much longer to get rid of suffering from vices.

The three vices resulting from anger are *Vakparushya* (causing verbal injury), *Arthadooshana* (causing injury to another's property) and *Dandaparushya* (causing physical injury). According to

Kautilya the second is more vicious than the first because sweet words can make up for harsh words but not for loss of livelihood. He also considers the third to be more vicious than the second because no one would want to lose one's life even for a big sum of money. Hurting or killing someone in anger is worse than robbing him of money or abusing him.

The four vices resulting from lust are *Mrigaya* (hunting), *Dyuta* (gambling), *Stree* (women) and *Panam* (wine). Hunting involves some physical exercise and knowledge of the habits of animals whereas gambling only leads to uncertainty and irregularity of financial as well as mental states leading ultimately to physical problems. Citing the instances of kings like Nala and Yudhishtthira, Kautilya decries any merits of gambling. But he considers lusting after women to be worse than gambling because it is incurable and leads to erroneous ways, drinking, neglecting work and losing political acumen. However, Kautilya considers addiction to drinks worse than addiction to women. It leads to loss of good sense, good health and good company whereas if the womanizing is confined to household women, it can be productive (of children) and protective (of oneself). Between drinking and gambling, Kautilya considers gambling worse. It leads to enmity, formation of factions and destruction of oligarchic forms of government.

असतां प्रग्रहः कामः कोपश्चावग्रहः सताम् ।
व्यसनं दोषवाहुल्यादात्त्यंतमुभयं मतं ।।

Kautilya thus recommends wise kings to keep check on both anger and excessive desire.

Desire and anger are for the entertainment of evil men and abandonment of good. Because of their serious ill effects, they are regarded as adversities.Hence. Kautilya advises that one should pluck out desire and anger from the roots and keep the company of senior, mature men.

### *Prakarana 130-32: Peedanavargah, Stambhavargah, Koshasangavargashcha*

### Oppression, Harassment and Corruption

Calamities that cause oppression and suffering to the kingdom can be of five types: fire, water (flood), disease, famine and epidemic. Kautilya considers flood to be more devastating because its effects are more widespread. Fire can destroy one, or at the most, five villages together. But the force of water can carry away hundreds of villages at one go. Again, he thinks that epidemics and famines are more serious than diseases. A disease affects only part of the kingdom and is curable, but the effects of epidemics and famine affect the entire kingdom and are more difficult to check.

Earlier thinkers had felt that to lose officers of lower rank was more serious because without them the higher officers could hardly function. But Kautilya feels that it is the higher ones who are impossible to replace or substitute and therefore their loss is a more serious calamity. Earlier thinkers had felt that rebellion by another country (*parachakra*) is less serious than an internal rebellion (*swachakra*) which can cause trouble through imposition of penalties and taxes. But Kautilya feels the opposite because internal rebellion can still be controlled through the intervention of able ministers and councilors but external rebellion can cause loot and plunder, arson and other forms of trouble for the entire country.

Earlier thinkers had felt that rebellion in a guild is more difficult to tackle than rebellion by a rebellious chief. But Kautilya feels that a rebellious chief, because of his arrogance and powers, is the more difficult of the two to tackle.

Calamities in the nature of cessation or stalling of work are internal when they are caused by important state officers and external when they are caused by a king who is a friend or by jungle folk.

Calamities of the nature of corruption occur when revenue gets frittered away, wasted or stolen on the way to the state Treasury through big and small officers, vassals or jungle folk.

*Prakarana 133-34: Balavyasanvarga Mitravyasanavargashcha*

### Calamities to the Army and to Friendly Troops belonging to an Ally

Thirty-two different Calamities can adversely affect the capacity of an army (*bala*), e.g., not being honoured, not being paid, getting depleted or exhausted, having no leader. Kautilya discusses them in pairs, stating which of them is a remediable or lesser one. For example, an unhonoured army (*amanita*) will fight if given money as tokens of respect, not so a dishonoured (*bimanita*) army bearing a grudge. An army which has not received its wages and salaries will fight if paid immediately, not so an army whose men are sick. A despondent army will fight if its hopes are fulfilled but not an army whose chief or general has deserted. An army whose chief is dead will fight under a new chief but not without any leader at all.

If the Aspirant-to-Victory fails to help the friendly troops of an Ally (be it out of inability or out of some temptation), he will find it difficult to regain the friendship of such an Ally. If he does not fulfill his promises to the Ally or breaks the condition of the treaty he had made with him, he will find it difficult to get his Ally back.

It is difficult to regain an Ally who has been disregarded and a king who had asked for an alliance but refused because of the Aspirant's inability. It is not so difficult to regain an Ally who has fought very hard for the Aspirant or been ignored by him by mistake. The Aspirant should thus zealously prevent such discord growing between himself and his constituent Elements. He should take care of such issues as soon as they crop up.

## *Adhikarana 9: Abhiyasyakarma*

## *The Act of Advancing*

### *Prakarana 135-6: Shaktideshakalabalagnanam Yatrakalashcha*

### Considerations of Power, Place, Time, and Starting Time

In the section *Abhyasakarma*, Kautilya discusses the activity of setting out or marching out on a military campaign.

In Prakarana 135-6, he begins by stating that the Aspirant-to-Victory should, before starting out, consider the following aspects:

*Shakti* (power), *Desha* (place of operation), *Kala* (time of operation), *Yatrakala* (season for starting out), *Balasamutthanakala* (time of mobilizing various types of forces), *Pashchatkopah* (rebellions in the rear), *Kshayavyaya* (losses and expenses), *Labha* (gains) and *Apada* (possible dangers). If the Aspirant finds himself in an advantageous position after considering these aspects, then and only then should he proceed on the campaign.

Kautilya disagrees with earlier thinkers who have held enthusiasm to be more important than might. He feels that a mighty king can overpower an enthusiastic one by sheer force of his might. He also disagrees with those who hold that might (*prabhava*) is more important than good counsel and judgement (*mantrashakti*). The king who uses wisdom and knowledge as his eyes (*prajnashastrachakshurhi raja*) can easily arrive at his course of action and choice of stratagems.The three components of power, enthusiasm, might and good counsel, are in ascending order of importance.

From the point of view of the Aspirant-Conqueror, the best land (*uttamo deshah*) is that terrain which is best for his own army operations , the worst (*adhamah*) is that which is best for his enemy's army operations, and the medium or average is that which is equally good for both.

From the point of view of the Aspirant-Conqueror, the best time (*uttamah kalah*) is that season which is suitable for his own army operations and unsuitable for his enemy's. The worst is that which is unsuitable for his army operations but suitable for his enemy's. The medium is that which is equally suitable for both.

Power, Place and Time are inter-related factors, says Kautilya. He does not agree with the older opinion that a powerful king can always rise above the disadvantages of terrain and time.

The Aspirant, having satisfied himself about the above considerations, should first leave behind 1/3rd or 1/4th of his army to protect his capital city, his rear, his forest regions and the borders. He should take with him sufficient wealth and forces to help him achieve his end and only then march towards the enemy. He should not wait for some calamity to befall his enemy but proceed whenever he feels he has got sufficient power.

Big tasks take long to accomplish. Sometimes the troops have to cross rough terrain, or encounter rains, or camp in another country for a long time. All these considerations should be considered when setting out on a campaign.

### *Prakarana 137-9: Balopadanakalah Sannahgunah Pratibalakarma cha*

### **Mobilizing Troop, Building Up Army, Combating Enemy Troops**

Kautilya also provides specifics of when the Aspirant should mobilize his various kinds of troops.

*Moulabala* (the basic or standing army) is to be mobilized when, for example, there is a surplus over and above what is required for the defence of the king's own kingdom and its capital.

*Bhritakabala* (the territorial army) is to be mobilized when, for example, it is much larger than the standing army or is most faithful and above enemy instigations.

*Shreyneebala* (the militia) is to be mobilized if there is a large force of militias which could be used both for the defence of the capital and the campaign ahead.

*Mitrabala* (the friendly troop) is to be mobilized if, for example, it is large and strong enough to defend the kingdom and capital as well as go on a campaign.

*Amitrabala* (the alien troop) is to be mobilized if the Aspirant stands to gain even when the troop loses.

Similarly, *Atabeebala* (the jungle troop) is to be mobilized if whether it wins or loses, it benefits the Aspirant. The payment was to be in terms of forest products or a share of the loot.

*Autsahikabala* (the unorganized, unrecognized enthusiasts) is to be mobilized occasionally under certain circumstances.

*Moulabala* is superior to *Bhritakabala* because their constant association with the Aspirant-Conqueror makes them loyal to him. For similar reasons, *Bhritakabala* is superior to *Shreyneebala*, which is again superior to *Mitrabala*. *Mitrabala* is superior to *Amitrabala* and *Amitrabala* to *Atabeebala.*

When the enemy is mobilizing its troops, the Aspirant-Conqueror should try to obstruct him, all the while safeguarding his own soldiers.

An army on elephants is best met with an army on elephants equipped with three-pronged spears and bamboo-poles. An army on elephants equipped with rocks, sticks, and hooked rods should be considered as fit to take on men riding chariots. It should be combated by cavalry. Armoured elephants, armoured horses, armoured chariots and armoured soldiers should be countered by armed men on horses. This is how soldiers should be gathered together for the army after due consideration.

### *Prakarana 140-141: Pashatkopachinta, Bahyabhyantaraprakritikopaprateekarashcha*

### Thoughts on Rebellions at the Back, Resolution of Rebellions from External and Internal Elements

Even though there is the possibility of a big gain at the front, a small uprising at the back is more important than that because, with the Aspirant-Conqueror gone away, it may escalate due to the anger of people, of traitors, enemies and jungle tribes. Proverbially, troubles come looking like the point of a needle (*soocheemukha hyanartha*).The Aspirant-Conqueror should not venture out on a campaign unless the gain ahead is far more than the possible loss due to revolt at the back. Internal Anger (*Abhyantarakopah*) is worse than External Anger (*Bahyakopah*). It is nursing a viper in one's bosom. It may occur in the form of trouble caused by the king's minister, the royal priest, the army-chief or the prince who is the heir-apparent. If it arises due to some fault of the Aspirant-Conqueror, he should assuage it by getting rid of that fault of his. Otherwise, he should apply penalties of money, imprisonment and use even the death-penalty.

When the Aspirant-Conqueror is about to go on an expedition but suspects internal revolt, he should take the person suspected as a hostage. If he suspects a revolt at the frontier, he should take along the wives and sons of the suspects as hostages. He should not venture out on an expedition without suppressing the internal rebellion and made due arrangements for the protection of the capital. Internal revolt by a brother, a son or some other should be strongly dealt with. So should revolt by a minister or an army-chief. In case of revolt by a frontier chief, jungle chief, or a subordinate king seeking independence, the Aspirant-Conqueror should create trouble among them and set one against the other.

It is important for the Aspirant-Conqueror to understand the nature of the rebellion arising or arisen against him and always be on guard against it. In order to counteract it, he should understand the motivation of the instigator of the revolt – whether he is stirring up rebellion for the benefit of others like him or merely for his own personal gain. With the former well-intentioned one (*kalyanabuddhi*), as well as the villainous one (*shattha*), the king should make (and honour) treaties. But the first should be made with the intention to honour it and the second, with the intention to get out of it.

*Prakarana 142: Kshayavyayalabhaviparimarsha*

**Advise on Losses, expenses and Gains**

Losses here refer to the loss of trained men and animals like war-horses and war-elephants. Expenses refer to the wastage of gold coins and food grains. Gains or profits (*labha*) refer to earnings minus losses and expenses.

The Aspirant-Conqueror should march forth on a campaign (only) when gains are expected to be substantially more than losses and expenses.

Kautilya distinguishes the various types of gains (something which has never been done in any Profit Theory in mainstream Economics).

*Adeya labha* is gain that is easily got while *Pratyadeya labha* is gain that is easily retaken.

*Prasadaka* is gain that pleases, for example, gain that a good king makes from a bad one.

*Prakopaka* is gain that angers, for example, gain made out of a bad king which displeases all concerned.

*Hastakala* gain is that which is made in just a little (*hasta*) while (*kala*).

*Tanukshaya* gain is that involves small losses, i.e., is made by clever ideas rather than hard labour or battle.

*Alpavyaya* is that gain which involves little expenditure such as food expenses.

*Mahan* is gain which is substantial yet available instantly.

*Vriddhi-udaya* is gain which assures much greater gain in the future.

*Kalya* is gain which is risk-free or involves no future loss.

*Dharmya* is gain made in a righteous way, such as in an open battle.

*Puroga* is gains made by Ally-kings unconditionally, i.e., without any restrictions upon the Aspirant-Conqueror.

*Kautilya* also lists out possible obstacles to the above gains (*Labhavighna*), such as anger, fear, negligence, too much piousness, over-dependence on astrology. It is interesting to note that Kautilya asks the Aspirant-Conqueror not to be too dependent on stars and what they foretell.

नक्षत्रमतिपृच्छन्तम् बालमर्थोऽतिवर्तते ।
अर्थो हि अर्थस्य नक्षत्रं किं करिष्यन्ति तारकाः ।।

The childish man who overly consults the stars will have wealth slipping out of his hands. Wealth itself is the guiding star of wealth. What can the stars do here!

नाधनाः प्राप्नुवन्ति अर्थान्तरा यत्नशतैरपि ।
अर्थैरर्थाः प्रबध्यन्ते गजा; प्रतिगजैरिव ।।

Without wealth and other means man cannot attain his aim even if tries a hundred times. Wealth has to be caught with wealth just as elephants are to be caught with elephants.

*Prakarana 143: Bahyabhayantashchapadah*

### External and Internal Problems/Dangers

When methods such as *Sandhi* and *Vigraha* are not applied in the right situations, there occurs mis-carriage (*apanaya*) and it is this which creates problems for the Aspirant-Conqueror.

These problems are of four types:

Initiated by external agents but encouraged by internal men like the king's own ministers and priests

Initiated by internal men but encouraged by external agentsInitiated as well as encouraged by external agents

Initiated as well as encouraged by internal agents.

As elsewhere, Kautilya insists that internal problems are more important than external and require earliest attention. He also states that the problem instigated by a powerful enemy agent requires to be attended earlier than that instigated by a weak one.

*Prakarana 144: Dooshyashatrusamyuktah*

### Problems created by the Enemy by himself and by an Enemy with whom friends are conspiring

In case of direct or uncomplicated problem created by the Enemy acting by himself (*shatrushuddha apatti*), the four methods of *Sama, Dana, Danda* and *Bheda* should be used on those vassals who control the Enemy's ministers or subordinates.

In case other kings are conspiring with the Enemy and making the problem complicated (*dooshyashuddha*), it may be risky to use the *Danda* upon such powerful men, and only the three methods (*Sama, Dana, Bheda*) should be used. Spies and secret agents of the Aspirant-Conqueror should be used to create a split between the Enemy and the friend who has become a conspirator with the Enemy. They should make him win over the king at the border of the confederacy, or at the centre, who will then bring the other kings over to the Aspirant-Conqueror's side.

In persuading the Enemy or the conspiring friend, the Aspirant-Conqueror should use personal and family praise, point out earlier history of comradeship, provide security and offer gifts. When choosing whose mind to work upon, the Aspirant-Conqueror should chose one who is already tired and discouraged, has suffered big losses, or, attaches value to former connections.

### *Prakarana 145-6: Arthanarthasamshayayuktah Tasamupayavikalpajah Siddhayashcha*

### Various Problems and Means of Solving Them

Problems caused by human factors is called *Manushi Apatti* and those caused by factors like fire, flood, famines, epidemics are called *Daivee Apatti*.

Talking of human problems, external ones, like enemies from outside, are provoked by the Aspirant-Conqueror's adopting inappropriate policies while internal ones, like the anger of his own subjects, are provoked by his tendency to anger and desire.

*Artha* (risky acquisition), *Anartha* (wrong acquisition) and *Samshaya* (doubt as to whether the acquisition is risky or wrong) may be of benefit to the Aspirant-conqueror as well as his Enemy. So before starting out on a campaign, he should clearly weigh the pros and cons of doing so, and decide resolution (*Siddhi*) the problems likely to arise.

The *Anuloma* way of resolving or tackling *Manushi* problems is according to the natural order of things. It is as follows: In the context of the son, the brother and friends, the method of making treaties and giving gifts (*sama* and *dan*a) should be used. In the context of prominent citizens, giving gifts and promoting dissension should be used(*dana* and *bheda*).In case of vassals and jungle folk, creating dissension as well as doling out penalties (*bheda* and *danda*) should be used. The *Pratiloma* (against the grain) way is its opposite, e.g., using *danda* upon the son or the brother. A combination of the two is called *Vyamishra.*

A means to tackle the problem that is thought to be the only one is called Niyoga. A means to tackle that is thought to have alternatives is called *Vikalpa*. A means that is thought to be successful in combination with another means is called *Samuchchaya.*

Resolution of difficulties achieved by a single means is called *Ekasiddhi*, Resolution achieved by two, three and four methods are called *Dvisiddhi, Trisiddhi and Chatuhsiddhi*.

That resolution of difficulties which yield material gains is called *Sarvarthasiddhi.*

Talking of *Daivee Apatti*, they may be resolved through rituals performed as per the *Atharva Veda* or by sages and learned men.

## *Adhikarana 10: Sangramika-Section Relating to War*

### *Prakarana 147: Skandhavaranivesha*

### Setting up the Base Camp

The army-chief, the carpenter/engineer and the astrologer, in consultation with one another, should set up the Base Camp(*Skandhavar*a).

The superintendent / administrator (*Prashasta*) of the Base Camp should, in fact, march ahead of the others, taking carpenters and labourers with him, and clear the ground, drive away wild beasts, and arrange for water for the approaching Aspirant-Conqueror and his men.

Set up in a shape suited to the terrain, the Base Camp should have four gates (*dvara*) in the four directions and nine divisions (*varga*). It its very centre, there should be the Aspirant-Conqueror's well-guarded living quarters (about 200 x100 sq. meters in area) with inner apartments (*antahpura*) to its west. In its front, there should be a seat for the king. To its right should be the administrative wing and the Treasury, to its left the space for horses and elephants. Trenches and pits should be constructed at some distance from the king's quarters, and filled with thorny creepers, iron nails, logs and such impediments to the enemy crossing over.

There should be guards constantly patrolling the approach to the Base Camp. Spies should be on the look out for information about the enemy camp. Drunken brawls and gambling among soldiers should be stopped immediately. Entry and exit should be checked by passes with seals (*Mudrarakshanam cha*). Soldiers would not be allowed to leave the Base Camp (because they did not want to fight any more) would not be allowed to do so unless they carried a permit from the king.

*Prakarana 148-149: Skandhavaraprayanam Balavyasanavaskan dakalarakshanam cha*

**March from the Base Camp and Protection of the Army during Battle**

Here Kautilya gives instructions as to how the army (*bala*) was to march out to the battle-ground which was naturally some distance from the base Camp.

How much of food and other provisions were to be transported was decided according to how quick the march was to be, for how long the battle was expected to go on, and the likelihood of getting provisions (grains, fodder) on the way.

What route was to be taken was to be decided according to what was most suitable for the Aspirant-Conqueror's own army.

The Major-General(*nayaka*) of the Army should march in front, the king and the women should be in the middle, horses and bodyguards should be on the sides, elephants should travel next and provisions should be transported on various sides. The Generals of the Army should march at the back, each ahead of their troops.

The army-formations (*vyuha*) are also specified. If the attack is expected from the front, soldiers should be arrayed in the Crocodile (*Makara*) formation. If it is expected from the back, they should be arrayed as a Cart (*Shakata*). If the attack is anticipated from the two sides, the formation Thunder (*Vajra*) should be used. If it is expected from all sides, the All-sided (*Sarvatobhadra*) formation is to be used. In case the army has to make way through a narrow passage, the Needle (*Soochi*) formation is appropriate. There are instructions also on the pace of the march and the ways of overcoming impediments. For example, the march should be slowed down if the path is difficult, and if enemy has seized the point at which a river is to be crossed, the army should cross it at another point and then fall upon the enemy army from the back.

Along the way, the army may be affected by lack of drinking water, fuel or fodder, exhaustion or illness. Arrangements should be made beforehand for such possibilities. But if such problems are detected in the enemy army, the Aspirant-Conqueror should take the opportunity to destroy it.

To prevent the enemy from estimating the strength of the marching army from the quantity of food, bedding, weapons, banners and other provisions being carried, they should be kept hidden while being carried.

Before beginning to battle, the Aspirant-Conqueror should keep ready a fort, on a hill or in a jungle, where his army can withdraw and hide or capture the enemy soldiers.

### *Prakarana 150-2: Kootayuddhavikalpah Swasainyotsahanam, Svabalanyabalavyayogashcha*

### Secretive Battle, Encouragement of Own Army, and Application of Armies of one's Own or of Others

Secretive or deceptive methods of battle (*kootayuddha*) are to be used when the conditions of open battle (*prakashayuddha*) are not met, i.e.,

(i) when the Aspirant-Conqueror's army is not superior.

(ii) when he has failed to instigate forces against his enemy in the enemy-camp,

(iii) when he has not been able to take all precautions against danger, and

(iv) when the terrain is not favourable to him.

Kautilya chalks out several ways in which the secretive or deceptive battle can be done.

For example, the Aspirant-Conqueror can entice the enemy on to an unfavourable terrain by pretending that his own army has been thrown into disarray, and then use his elephants upon the enemy.

Or, he can exhibit only a part of his army to attack the enemy at the front, and then finding it struggling, also attack it at the back with elephants and horses. If frontal attack is not yielding good results, an attack must be made from the back, and *vice versa*. If attack from one side is not working out, it should be made also from the other.

The Aspirant-Conqueror may tempt the enemy with cattle to be seized by them and then ambush them. Good places for ambush are: forested, marshy or hilly terrain, deserts, narrow valleys, misty or dark days.

Encouragement of One's Own Army is something the Aspirant-Conqueror has to do. He should gather his troops together and exhort them: "You and I, your king, are both in service to the kingdom. We'll share its wealth between us. Now, come and attack the enemy." Priests and ministers should bolster up this appeal by pointing out how the army was strong and the battle formation rightly chosen. Astrologers should reinforce this by saying that the gods were on the Aspirant's side.

Once the day and hour of the battle had been decided, the Aspirant-Conqueror should observe a feast on the eve of the day, pray to the gods and pay respects to the *Brahmana*s. He should perform fire-worship according to the ways of the *Atharva Veda*, and at night sleep all ready for the battle – beside his weapons and even his chariot. On the day of the battle, he should take his position among the troops that are strong, fresh, loyal and happy at their treatment. Riding on an elephant or a chariot, guarded by horsemen, he should proceed surrounded by brothers, sons and other warrior kinsmen. A man resembling him should ride out at the head of the battle formation … an impersonation!

Bards should sing out in praise of the heaven that awaits the brave in battle. Priests should announce how they have applied charms and spells against the enemy, carpenters and technicians should highlight what machines and equipment they have built for the use of the troops. The Major-General should announce rewards.

At the rear, as the Aspirant-Conqueror rides out, the army should be followed by: well-equipped army doctors, cooks and courtesans. Provisions, cooked food, water and drinks, medicines and surgical instruments, bandages and ointments should be carried as well.

When it came to positioning the troops, Kautilya advised against making them stand facing the south, considered to be an inauspicious direction. Care should be taken that the troops do not face the sun or strong wind.

For the battle formation to be made, there should be some flat or plain land either in front, back or sides. The choice of the formation should be in accordance with the land, flat, uneven or mixed.

The Aspirant-Conqueror should, if the enemy is more powerful then him, first demolish the enemy formation, and then himself request for an agreement or treaty. If the enemy is equal in power, it may be the enemy which makes the request for it. If the enemy is weak, he should be destroyed so effectively and utterly that he can never rise up again to challenge the Aspirant-Conqueror. But if the weak king is at a favourable spot or has despaired of winning, he should be spared his life. A king who is already weak and despondent should not be provoked and troubled.

*Prakarana 153-4: Yuddhabhoomayah, Pattyashvarathahastikar mani cha*

**Appropriate Land for Battle, Tasks of Foot-soldiers and Soldiers on Horses, Chariots and Elephants**

In this section Kautilya emphasizes the importance of the terrain in a battle. For warriors on chariots, smooth and clean plain land is best. It should have some water nearby and a place to take rest. For soldiers on horseback, rough ground with pebbles and shrubs is suitable. It should not have water, mud or mire.

For warriors on elephants, the suitable land is without mud or mire and big trees with long branches. For foot-soldiers (*patti*), the land should not be thorny, too high or too low, and difficult to retreat from.

Certain tasks or activities are easier with certain means. To occupy suitable battleground ahead of the others, to drive back enemy soldiers, to free own soldiers which have been taken captive, to pursue enemy soldiers whose horses are dead….these are some tasks that are easier to do riding on horses and are called *Ashvakarma* (Horse-tasks). To strike fear into enemy soldiers by their very appearance, to scatter away enemy troops, to gauge the depth of rivers, to gather together Aspirant's soldiers who are fleeing , to break down the gates of the enemy camp….these are some of the tasks that are easier and so are called *Hastikarma* (Elephant-tasks). *Rathakarma* (Chariot-tasks) include safeguarding the Aspirant's foot-soldiers, releasing and carrying back those who are captured, gathering one's own troops together and scattering the enemy troops. The foot-soldier's task is to be ready to fight at all seasons and all occasions and keep fit through regular exercise.

Kings who lack horses in sufficient numbers can harness bulls in their place. Those who lack elephants can keep their troops safe between carts pulled by camels and donkeys.

### *Prakarana 155-157: Pakshakakshorasyanam Balagrato Vyuhavibhagah Saraphalgubalavibhagah, Patthyashvarathahastiyuddhani cha* **Classification of Formations, Army Divisions and Battle of Fourfold Troops**

In this section Kautilya advises in detail on how to arrange the forces into battle-formations (*vyuha*).

The best forces should be kept out of sight as reinforcements at a short distance from the battleground. Warriors on horses, chariots and elephants should not fight alone but in units.

A warrior on horseback would have three foot-soldiers in front and three at the back. Of the three in front, the one in the middle would stand a little ahead of the other and of the three at the back, the one in the middle would stand a little behind the other.

```
          *          foot-soldiers

     *         *

          *          horse- rider

     *         *

          *          foot-soldiers
```

That would be the basic unit for cavalrymen.

A warrior on a chariot and one on an elephant would have five men on horseback surrounding them more or less in a circle.

* horse-rider

* *

* man on chariot/elephant

* * horse-rider

*

Arrays or linear arrangements were formed out of these basic units.

*Paksha* would refer to the men in front fighting close to the horse-riders and therefore most important to them, chariot-rider or the elephant-rider as the case may be.

*Kaksha* would be the men in front who were not in so relevant a position.

*Urasya* referred to the men in front who were in the middle.

The forces could be closely packed or loosely packed. Archers would be placed at greater distances than foot-soldiers with swords, spears or lances because they needed more space to wield their bows and arrows.

Arrays for soldiers with swords, spears or lances:

0 0 0 0 0 0 0 0 0 0<br>
0 0 0 0 0 0 0 0 0 0<br>
0 0 0 0 0 0 0 0 0 0<br>
0 0 0 0 0 0 0 0 0

Arrays for archers:

0 0 0<br>
0 0 0<br>
0 0 0

Soldiers were not to be crowded.

The minimum number in an array of chariots or of elephants was 9, arranged in 3 rows of 3 each.

Each chariot/elephant being supported by 5 horse-riders (each horse-rider being supported by 6 foot-soldiers), the minimum formation would be of 9 chariots (or elephants), 9x5= 45 horse-riders and 45 x 6 = 270 foot-soldiers.

This is how Cavalry Units(x) in an Array should be placed:

```
o       o       o

        x
    x       x
o       H       o
    x       x
        x

o       o       o
```

This is how Elephant and/or Chariot Units (Y) in an Array should

```
E       E       E

        Y
    Y       Y
E       H       E
    Y       Y
        Y

E       E       E
```

Kautilya also indicates how the sizes of such formations can be increased.

Formations may be Balanced and Unbalanced. In a *Samavyuha* (Balanced Formation), the arrays are of equal size. When the arrays in the wings and the flanks are a little longer, it is called *Vishamavyuha* (Unbalanced Formation).

Formations may be Pure and Mixed. A Pure (*Shuddha*) formation consists of arrays of only elephants, only horses or only foot-soldiers. A Mixed (*Mishra*) formation is a combination of chariots, horses and foot-soldiers. For example, there may be elephant units at front, chariot units in the middle and horse-riders at the back. Or, if the objective is to break the enemy's centre, the formation may put elephant units in the centre, horses in front and chariots at the back. Various combinations are possible.

The placement should also take note of the quality of the forces. *Sarabala* refers to excellent, time-tested disciplined forces, whether they be foot-soldiers, horse-men, chariot-riders or elephant-riders. *Anusara* and *Trityiasara* are successively less worthy. One-third of the best among foot-soldiers, horse-men, elephant-riders and chariot- riders should be placed in the centre and the other two-thirds in the wings and flanks. The worst among the forces - are described as *Phalgubala* – and they can be placed in the middle. Much of the force of the enemy attack is then vented upon the weakest forces and the better ones are salvaged.

After setting the *vyuha* up, the Aspirant-Conqueror should make the attack with one or two groups in the array, keeping the rest in reserve. He should use a large part of the best troops to attack the weaker part of the enemy forces, and in case he is attacking the best part (or at least the better parts) of the enemy forces, he should take a much greater number of men. He should use horses upon the foot-soldiers, chariots upon horses and elephants upon horses. Kautilya describes various types of movements or forays for each of the four types of forces. For example, in cases of horses, *Abhisrita* means taking the Aspirant-Conqueror's forces towards those of the enemy. *Parisrita* means surrounding them. *Prakeernika* means using several types of movements together. In case of elephants, an important movement is *Unmatthyavadhana* – spreading out, churning up the enemy forces and getting together again.

The Aspirant-Conqueror should always have reinforcements for troops that may be scattering away. He should remain, with the reinforcements, some distance behind the place where the battle actually rages.

*Prakarana 158-9: Dandabhogamandalasamhatavyuhavyuhanam tasya prativyuhasthapanam cha*

**Danda and other Modes of Attack, Formations and Counter-Formations**

Kautilya agrees with earlier scholars of war-craft that there are four natural formations (*Prakritivyuha*) in which the enemy be attacked.

*Danda* (rod) is one where the wing, flank and centre arrays advance keeping abreast of each other, forming a rod-like straight line. *Bhoga* (Curve) is one where they advance in a curved, uneven way. *Mandala* (Circle) is when the wings, flanks and centre approach from all directions, joining and forming a circle. *Asamhata* (Unfocused) is one which they are dispersed and lack cohesion in their approach.

Each formation has various versions or sub-formations. Kautilya lists 32 of them without providing precise instructions as to how they can be formed. A particular formation is often chosen so that it can counter or withstand another (*prativyuhasthapana*). Kautilya feels that *Durjaya vyuha* (Difficult to Conquer) – a compendium of four *Dandavyuha*s set up together - can counter every other formation.

The commander of every ten chariots or elephants will be called *Padika*. The commander of ten *Padika*s will be a *Senapati*. The commander of ten *Senapati*s will be called a *Nayaka*. Every division will have its own distinctive trumpet call, flags and pinions, calling it to unite or disperse, halt or march, advance or retreat. The respective commanders of the various divisions will be responsible for giving out the wages as well as the food rations of the men they command.

The enemy forces have not only to be fought but be given false alarms, provoked and upset, spied upon, teased and troubled. “The astrologer has predicted dire defeat for you”. “Your fort is on fire”, “So-and-so has rebelled against you”...such announcements should be made so as to dampen their spirit.

At the end Kautilya says:

एकं हन्यान्न वा हन्यादिषु: क्षिप्तो धनुष्मता ।
प्राज्ञेन तू मतिः क्षिप्ता हन्याद् गर्भगतानपि ।।

An arrow from the archer’s bow can kill perhaps one person but a wise man’s clever idea can kill even children unborn,

## *Adhikarana 11: Sanghavritta - On Oligarchies*

### ***Prakarana 160-61: Bhedopadani, Upangshudandashcha***
### **Breaking the Oligarchy, Punishing Secretly**

This section, rather, chapter, deals with a State that is not a monarchy but an oligarchy or rule of the few in a group or team or council called *samgha*. This was a form of government by collective leadership, which Kautilya said, was prevalent in Kamboja (north-west India) and Sourashtra (Gujarat).

Out of gaining an oligarchy, an army or an ally, it is best to gain the group because it is strongly focused or united. Enemies cannot break it easily.

To gain and enjoy an oligarchy, the Aspirant-Conqueror king should use *Sama* and *Dana* when it is favourably disposed towards him and through *Bheda* and *Danda* when it is unfavourably disposed towards him.

He should engage secret agents and create disagreement and distrust among the leaders of the oligarchy (*samghamukhya*). Comparing one with the other, offering wine and women, the secret agents should destroy the unity of the oligarchy.

Rivalry among the children, inter-caste conflicts, praise of rivals, damage of property by hired men, even secret assassination (*upangshuvadha*), Kautilya recommends all as methods of splitting the oligarchy. He also suggests putting up a young prince or nobleman as a claimant to the area ruled by the oligarchy (rather than by any monarch), or setting up a false case of taking bribes against one of the oligarchy leaders. Women too can be used to lure the group leaders away from their positions of responsibility. The Aspirant-Conqueror should try to create in-fighting in the oligarchy while the leaders should try to be on guard against attempts to create in-fighting among them.

For the chief of the oligarchy, Kautilya's advice is to always be pleasant and fair to the others in the group, keep them alongside and conduct the administration in collaboration with them.

संघमुख्यश्च संघेषु न्यायवृत्तिर्हितः प्रियः ।
दांतो युक्तजनस्तिष्ठेत् सर्वचित्तानुवर्तकः ॥

Once the oligarchy has broken down, the Aspirant-Conqueror should remove the weaker leaders from their areas and settle them elsewhere (preferably at a distance from one another, so as to prevent them coming together again).

Whether the oligarchy breaks down because of entirely internal reasons or because of secret external attempts, the Aspirant-Conqueror should befriend the weaker member and play them up against the others.

# *Adhikarana 12: Abalyeeyasa*
# ***Section on the Weak King***

## *Prakarana 162: Dootakarmani*
### **The Work of Messengers**

Kautilya does not agree with Bharadvaja that the Weak King (*durbala*) should bend like a reed before the powerful or with Vishaksha that whether he wins or loses, the Weak King should fight to the finish. He feels that by surrendering abjectly, the Weak King will forever live a life of despair like a sheep without his herd whereas by fighting he will be jumping into the ocean without a boat.What he should do is to avail of the protection of a stronger king or resort to a fort that cannot be broken into. In other words, Kautilya advises diplomacy and negotiation rather than either giving up or being stupid.

Three types of conquerors can be distinguished. To the Righteous Conqueror (*Dharmavijayee*), the Weak King should submit because that will satisfy his aggressor as well as get himself some protection. The Avaricious Conqueror (*Lobhavijayee*) wants land, wealth and goods. To him, the Weak King should yield his material possessions. The Demonic Conqueror (*Asuravijayee*) wants everything...land, wealth, goods, wives, sons and even the Weak King' life. To him, the Weak King can yield all but not his life!

When a stronger king attacks, the Weak King should resort to a king who is even stronger and beyond any diplomatic moves of the attacking king.

When there is no king stronger than the attacking king, the Weak King should resort to a king who is at least on par with the attacking king.

When even that is not possible, the Weak King should seek out kings who are less powerful than the attacking king, but genuine persons opposed to the aggressive ways of the attacking king.

When an attack is imminent, the Weak King can (i) make a treaty (*sandhi*) with the attacking king, (ii) use diplomatic tactics (*mantrayuddha*), or (iii) fight in a clandestine manner (*kootayuddha*).He can try winning over the people in the enemy camp who are favourable to him by applying *Sama* and *Dana*, and hold his own men together by applying *Danda* and *Bheda*.

To get the attacking king agree to having a treaty with him, the Weak King may try to weaken him first, by sending spies to apply poison or jungle people to attack his camp, fort or kingdom. He may then send his messenger to the attacking king with offers of wealth, foot soldiers, war horses or elephants, land and so on. Kautilya advises giving inferior stuff as peace offerings. For example, if he is sending horses and elephants, they should be weak and stupid ones, and poison strong ones before sending them. If he is sending soldiers, he should send unreliable ones. But should the situation be an extreme one, the Weak King may make peace by giving up everything other than his capital city.

In respect of the Weak King's averting an open aggression through *Sandhi*, Kautilya's final advice is to offer the coveted stuff as though it is part of the treaty being made. It is more sensible to save life rather than wealth.

यत्प्रसह्य हरेदन्यस्तत्प्रयच्छेषु पायतः।
रक्षेत्स्वदेहं न धनं का ही अनित्ये धन दया ।।

*Prakarana 163: Mantrayuddham*

**Diplomatic Warfare**

If the strong king is bent upon attack and refuses to make a peace treaty, the Weak King should try diplomatic warfare with him. Through his messenger, he should try to persuade him that, in being aggressive, he is being misled by his apparent friends, scaring true allies, furthering enemy interests and jeopardizing his own. If such persuasion does not work, the Weak King has to adopt other means.

He can incite a rebellion among the subjects of the attacking king. He can get him killed in secret ways, using spies and secret assassins. He can entice the chiefs of the jungle force to his side and make them fall upon the attacking king's territory.

He can subvert important officials of the attacking king and make them either fight or betray him.

Wherever possible, the Weak King should use secret or clandestine tactics to avert direct encounter.

*Prakarana 164-5: Senamukhyavadhah Mandalaprotsahanam cha*

**Methods of Killing Army Chiefs, Encouraging the Circle of Kings**

Kautilya suggests several ways of getting the army chiefs of the attacking king. To take just one example: Spies staying with the king and people close to the king should spread the rumour that the king was displeased with the Chiefs of his army. Getting special permission against the night curfew, the spies should then tell the army chiefs that the king wanted to see them immediately. Once the army chiefs had got out, the spies would kill them and then announce that this had been done on the king's orders. The remaining army chiefs then would leave the king by themselves.

Kautilya also suggests how, in this context, how the Weak King could make use of the Circle of Kings.

He could convince the attacker's enemy in the rear into attacking the aggressor in the rear on the grounds that, after destroying the Weak King, the attacker would turn against his enemy in the rear. This king would be told that, in case the attacker attacked him first, the Weak King would provide help by himself attacking, in the rear, the attacker.

The Weak King could persuade the attacker's own allies that they needed the Weak King to be a buffer against the attacking king. They would then jointly ask the attacking king to spare the Weak King.

He could tell all kings, allied or not, that they needed to help him because otherwise it would be their turn next to get attacked.

He could offer his all to Middle King or the Neutral King for the sake of protection.

*Prakarana 166-167: Shastragnirasapranidhayah Veevadhasarprasaravadhashcha*

**Secret Use of Weapons, Fire and Juice, Destruction of Rice, Grass, and Friendly Soldiers, and Grass**

This chapter mentions ways of making use of weapons, fire and poisonous juices in clandestine warfare (*Kootayuddha*).

For example, the Aspirant-Conqueror' spies, acting as guards, milkmen, mendicants and so on in the forts, villages and towns of the Enemy King, will offer some small gifts of their products to the people who can bear a resentment to the Enemy King. The spies can then tempt them with information as to how they can make entries into the weaker portions of the enemy territory. Once the people so tempted send their spies to find out those points of entry, the Aspirant-Conqueror's spies can extract information out of them as to the weaknesses of the Enemy King. In camps and other habitations, vendors can sell drinks laced with poison, snake-charmers can let loose poisonous snakes, blacksmiths and cooks can do arson. Friendly forces (*mitrasara*), along with loads of rice, grass and wood, can be destroyed when they are going through a narrow passage. Enemy soldiers can be washed away by breaking dams open and choked off by throwing making fires smoke with noxious stuff.

### *Prakarana 168-170: Yogatisandhanam Dandatisandhanam Ekavijayashcha*

### **Attaining Victory through False Means and Force**

There are several opportunities of killing the Enemy King when he is on his way to a temple or on a pilgrimage. For example, a heavy rock can be flung on him by some mechanical way just as he is about to enter a temple. He can be anointed with acidic stuff or made to inhale poisonous flowers. Inside, a weapon tied to the image of the deity can be made to fall on him. Below his bed a deep pit can be dug, filled up with spears and arrowheads, and then covered up. As he lies down to rest, a mechanical contraption can make him fall through to his deathbed.

Other ways of harming the enemy include poisoning the water bodies around the enemy camp, setting fire to all the grass and fodder in the vicinity, laying traps such as concealed pits and obstructing the way with thorns.

A tunnel may be dug from the fort of the attacked king to the camp of the attacking king, and used to carry away his provisions, his people and even himself. If it is a tunnel that the enemy king is digging, it should be flooded by deepening the moat of the fort or by digging a well outside the fort walls.

The king who is attacked and inside his fort may send his men across to the attacking king.They would pretend to be betraying him for money or soldiers. Once the attacking king sent in the money and men into the fort, the money would be appropriated and the men killed, without handing the king over.

When the king under attack is utterly exhausted, he can abandon the fort or try a desperate last attempt to break out of the fort at night, or even escape unseen or disguised. If he cannot do that before the fort is taken, he can hide within the fort for a chance to kill the occupying army and perhaps the king who had attacked him. He can hide in a hollow in the flooring or wall or even within an image, with holes made for breathing and some food and drink.

Kautilya states all this in a practical matter-of-fact way. He attaches no moral stigma to adopting such clandestine methods for survival in a war situation.

## *Adhikarana 13: Durgolambhopaya*
## ***Means of Taking a Fort***

*Prakarana 171: Upajapah*

### Psychological Warfare

If the Aspirant-Conqueror wants to conquer the village or town of another of the Enemy, he should try to encourage his men and discourage enemy men by spreading word that he was omniscient and had received divine visitation. Kautilya mentions various tricks by which he can convince credulous people that he has divine powers and favours. Astrologers and soothsayers should be sent out to advertise this with the help of portents such as dreams, meteors and unusual calls of birds and animals. Through messengers and envoys, it should be conveyed to the officials of the enemy that they have nothing to lose should they cross sides. Spies and secret agents should also ask the subjects in famine-stricken and such other suffering areas to seek relief from the Aspirant-Conqueror rather than their own. Once they do so, the Aspirant-Conqueror should indeed provide them food and shelter and win them over. Kautilya calls this a most effective method of psychological warfare (*karyamityedupajapadadbhutam mahad).*

*Prakarana 172: Yogavamanam*

## Tempting the Enemy by False Means

In this section Kautilya suggests several ways of secretly assassinating the Enemy King in stead of in battle.

A spy (of the Aspirant-Conqueror) can stay in a mountain cave in the guise of a sage with many disciples. He can lure the Enemy King to his hermitage with promises of performing miracles on his behalf, and when the king accepts his hospitality, kill him secretly.

He can also take refuge in a frequently-visited temple in the city and perform magic tricks to impress the important officers. Through them he can trick the Enemy King.

A spy can pretend to be a trader in horses and enter the enemy kingdom on the pretext of showing horses for sale. When the Enemy King comes to examine the horses, he can be surrounded by horses and killed and then the men on horses can make an onslaught upon the capital city.

A keeper of elephants under the Aspirant-Conqueror can be used to tempt an Enemy-king who takes an interest in elephants. He can take him into the deep forests on the pretext of showing new elephants, and then kill him or take him prisoner.

An Enemy King with a weakness for women and wealth can be lured to desolate places through them, and then killed.

*Prakarana 173: Apasarpapranidhi*

## Observations on Removal of Aspirant-Conqueror's One's Own Officials

This chapter is on how the Aspirant-Conqueror can make use of his own official by apparently dismissing him or banishing him from his kingdom but really sending him to win the Enemy King's trust and thereby entrapping him.

Once the Aspirant-Conqueror has made a show of throwing him out, the concerned minister or a chief can resort to the Enemy King for protection and by-and-by gather his own men around him. He can then use his spies to attack a treacherous or weak part of the kingdom or, create dissension among the officers of the Enemy King and watch out for some calamity, and then invite the Aspirant-Conqueror to attack the whole kingdom.

The Aspirant-Conqueror can also use the other kings of the Circle of Kingdoms and with the use of armed forces, create a situation where the enemy is invited to come with armed forces to his help.

For example, the Enemy's Enemy (i.e., a friend) may, by secret methods, be made to appear to do harm to the Aspirant-Conqueror, who shall then attack the friend. The Enemy will then be invited to join it in return for a share of the loot.

Alternatively, the Aspirant-Conqueror can make a treaty with the friend for sharing the Enemy's land. When the friend attacks the Enemy, it shall look as though he is doing harm to the Aspirant-Conqueror, who shall then appear to attack the friend and invite the Enemy to join him in return for a share of the land.

If the Enemy trusts the Aspirant-Conqueror and joins him in person, he shall be killed in an ambush or an open battle with the Enemy's Enemy – the supposed target of the battle. If he sends his army but does not come himself, he cannot be killed but it will be tried to destroy his army. Depending upon the way the Enemy reacts, the attempt to defeat or kill him will be made.

There are other alternatives. The Aspirant-Conqueror can pretend to suffer from a calamity and make his ally encourage the Enemy to attack. Then he and his ally can press down upon the Enemy from either side. They may kill him or at least take away his kingdom.

In case the Enemy cannot be harmed in person, his land may be laid to waste and his army decimated.

Kautilya states these in a matter-of-fact way, with no normative nuances.

*Prakarana 174-5: Paryupasanakarma, Avamardashcha*

### The Task of Depletion and Storming the Fort

Before laying a siege on a fort, the Enemy's resources should be depleted (*paryupasana*), for example, by destroying his crops and sowings, stopping his supplies and secretly killing his men or making them desert him. The area around the fort should be made free from fear and people should be encouraged, through promises of tax exemptions and other benefits, to go and live elsewhere. For, there is no habitation without men and no kingdom without habitation.

न हि अजनो जनपदो राज्यमजनपदं वा भवतीति कौटिल्यः ।।

An opportune time for laying a siege is when the Aspirant-Conqueror's troops have got a good stock of supplies, the weather is good for him and the Enemy under siege is at a disadvantage through famine, epidemic or fatigue.

The Aspirant-Conqueror should encircle the fort after making sure that his own base-camp is protected and the route for his supplies is clear. He should get the water supply to the fort contaminated and the moat either emptied of water or filled up with mud. Tunnels should be dug into the fort. Walls should be broken down by armed elephants. Machines as well as men in hiding should be used upon men defending the fort in groups. Horses should chase down men coming out of secret exits of the fort. Fire should not be used as a rule because its effects are incalculable and uncontrollable. But if it is to be used, there are ways such as catching birds and animals of the fort, tying fire-brands to their legs and sending them forth into the fort to spread the fire.

Kautilya suggests several tricks. For example, the Aspirant-Conqueror may seemingly abandon the fort but actually hide in a nearby forest and fall upon the Enemy as he comes out of the fort thinking that the siege is over. He may make use of other kings or even tribal chiefs to pretend to befriend the besieged king but actually mislead him and deliver him into the Aspirant-Conqueror's hands.

Storming the fort (*avamarda*) requires the choice of an appropriate situation and time. An appropriate situation would be when the besieged enemy is ill, his officers are displeased with him, or his fortification is incomplete. An appropriate time would be when the fort has accidentally caught fire , its people are celebrating some festival, quarrelling among themselves, or are tired and sleepy after keeping long watches, or if the soldiers are fatigued and the day rainy or foggy.

When making the final assault, the Aspirant-Conqueror shall first try to divert the besieged king's forces by making an attack upon the fort with troops of his that are less trustworthy and trained.

He should spare those who are wounded, running away, surrendering (and showing it by letting down his hair or throwing away his arms) and not fighting.

He should enter only after seeing to it that the fort has been cleared of the Enemy supporters, including secret attackers or tricks and traps.

उपजापोऽपसर्पो वा वामनं पर्युपासनम् ।
अवमर्दश्च पंचैते दुर्गलम्भस्य हेतवः ।।

Thus *Upajapa, Apasarpa, Vamana, Paryuvasana* and *Avamarda* are the five ways in which a fort can be taken (*durgalambha*).

*Prakarana 176: Labdhaprashamanam*

**Assuaging What is Acquired**

The Aspirant-Conqueror's achievement or acquisition can be extensive),i.e., in terms of land inclusive of forests, or specific forts, villages or cities. The mode of acquisition may be new (*nava*), past (*bhootapurv*a) or inherited (acquisition).

New Acquisition (*navalabha*)**:** In respect of newly acquired land, the Aspirant-Conqueror shall be good where the Enemy had been bad and twice as good where he had been good. He should act as per his own *dharma* and by making donations, granting exemptions and acknowledging services through gifts and marks of honour.

(*Svadharmakarmanugrahapariharadanamanakarmabhishcha). prakritipriyahitanyanuvarteta*).

He should give the promised rewards to those who had betrayed the Enemy, matching the rewards to the efforts made for his sake. For, he who does not keep the promises made to people loses their trust as well as that of others. So does one who goes against the constituent elements.

(*Avishvasyo hi visamvadakah svesham paresham cha bhavati. Prakritivirudhashcha.*)

He should therefore adopt the way of life and conduct, language and dress of the territory conquered and display respect towards its deities and festivities.

(*Tasmatsamanasheelaveshacharatamupagachhet. Deshadaivatasamajotsavavihareshu cha bhaktimanuvarteta.*)

He should appease the heads of the country, towns, castes and associations or guilds of the conquered territory by taking care of their customary rights, security and tax concessions. Secret agents should be employed to often tell the chief citizens of how their former king- the Conqueror's Enemy – used to trouble them and how they are held in high esteem by the present king – the Conqueror.

He should see to it that all temples and hermitages in the kingdom hold their prayer ceremonies regularly. He should reward learned and distinguished men.

He should release prisoners as well as show compassion to the destitute, the orphaned and the sick (*Sarvabandhanamokshanam anugraham deenanathavyadhitanam cha*). Every four months, he should keep a fortnight free of death sentences being given. No death sentence is to be carried out on a day of a coronation or victory.

Female animals and young animals should not be killed and male animals should not be castrated (*Yonibalavadham pumstopa ghatam cha pratishedhayet*).

Practices in accordance with *dharma* should replace all practices, of either the Treasury or the accounts, which violate it. Thieves, foreigners, prominent officials or priests who were supporters of the Enemy should be located and sent off to border areas. Possible conspirators or inimical people should be killed secretly. The positions earlier filled by the Enemy's men should now be filled by the Conqueror's supporters or at least by those who were not supporters of the Enemy.

If there is someone from the Enemy's family who can recover the kingdom or a well-born person from the border areas who can cause trouble, the Conqueror should give him land of inferior quality in return for an enormous tribute. This is so that the noble in question, in trying to get the amount paid through subjects in the countryside, will antagonize them and get killed by them.

An officer who displeases the people will be sacked or given a posting in a remote, perilous area (*apavahihitasthaneshu sthapayet*).

Old Territory Re-Acquired: On re-acquiring territory that he had once owned but lost, the Conqueror should avoid the mistakes he or the constituents of his state had made and which had led to the loss of the territory. He should develop those virtues which had helped him in recovering the lost territory.

Territory Acquired as Inheritance: On inheriting territory from his father, the Conqueror should avoid any mistakes that his father had made and instead develop any virtues that he had had.

Kautilya concluded this section by commenting that the Conqueror should continue with those practices of his conquered territory which are in accordance with dharma and discontinue those which are not so. He should introduce those righteous practices which had so far been lacking there and encourage those people who are engaged in righteous practices.

चरित्रमकृतं धर्म्यं कृतं चान्यैः प्रवर्तयेत् ।
प्रवर्तयेन्न चाधर्म्यम् कृतं चान्यैर्निवर्तयेत् ।।

## *Adhikarana 14: Oupanishadika*
## ***Section on Secret Instructions***

*Prakarana 177: Paraghataprayoga*

### Application of Extra Blows, Further Attacks?

The Aspirant-Conqueror King, in order to protect the four classes (*varnas*), should apply extra or further blows on those who do not follow *dharma*. Snake-poison may be sprinkled on the clothes of spies who go about secretly as disabled. Weapons may be kept among the sports equipments of men and ornaments or perfumes of women. Certain herbs and flowers, certain animals and insects can be crushed together into a most toxic poison. The entrails of lizards can be burnt to produce a smoke that can cause dementia.

*Prakarana 178: Pralumbhane Adbhutotpadanam*

### Achievement through Strange Concoctions

Eating a paste of Shirisha, Udumbara and Shamee trees and ghee prevents hunger for a fortnight. Rubbing a paste of Gunja berries kept in the mouth of a lizard or a black snake causes leprosy. If fireflies are crushed and put in oil, they give out a glow late in the night. Pests feeding on rice mixed with horse urine can break iron chains; so can lodestone (*ayaskantamani*).

Kautilya advises that strange, sometimes harmful concoctions should also be used by the Aspirant-Conqueror to thoroughly pester the enemy. Even though dangerous and disreputable, in inimical situations they have to be resorted to.

*Prakarana 178 contd.: Pralambhane Bhaishajyamantraprayogah*

**Achievement though Applying Medicine and Chanting**

The eyes of cats, camels, pigs, crows, owls and such creatures that can see at night, can be extracted and crushed separately for the left and the right. If the crush from the right eye is applied like kohl to the right eye, and the crush from the left eye to the left, it can give a person the ability to see everything in the dark.

Certain rituals and certain chants (*mantra*) can make a person disappear from the sight of others, lock and unlock door, cut through an arrow-string, make a platter of food never-ending and even call forth fruits in the trees. Kautilya says that the Aspirant-Conqueror should definitely use such *yoga* or *maya* but for the purpose of destroying the Enemy and /or help out his own men.

मन्त्रभैषज्य संयुक्ता योगा माया कृताश्च ये ।
उपहन्यादमित्रांस्तैः स्वजनं चाभिपालयेत् ।।

*Prakarana 179: Svabalopaghatpteekara*

**Remedying Application of such concoctions, medicines and chanting upon the Aspirant-Conqueror's Own Army**

The Aspirant-Conqueror should apply remedies or antidotes of concoctions, medicines and chants directed at his own army. To cure insanity caused by the Enemy, various herbs and barks mixed with the blood of female monkeys, foxes and dogs may be used. The mixture of Priyangu (Saffron) and Naktamala (Karanja) may be used against leprosy. A gold talisman can be used against fainting and poisoning.

एतैः कृत्वा प्रतीकारं स्वसैन्यनामाथात्मनः ।
अमित्रेषु प्रत्युञ्जीत विषधूमाम्बु दूषणान् ।।

## *Adhikarana 15: Tantrayukti*

## *Grammatical and Logistic Principles*

*Prakarana 180: Tantrayuktayah*

**Grammatical and Logistic Principles**

In the concluding section of his work, Kautilya explains certain concepts and expressions used in it.

First, he defines Arthashastra. '*Artha*' means the income-yielding activity or occupation (*vritti*) of man. It also means land (*bhoomi*) associated with people. The subject (*shastra*) that studies the ways and means (*upaya*) of nurturing (*palana*) the profit (*labha*) from the earth (*prithivi*) is called *Arthashastra.*

Human beings work upon Nature and generate income. This income (generated by man working on Nature) can be protected as well as further enhanced. How to do that is the subject-matter of *Arthashastra*.

Secondly, Kautilya lists the thirty-two grammatical-cum-logical devices (*yukti*) used in his vast work.

1. *Adhikarana* (General Topic)
2. *Vidhanam* (Prescription)
3. *Yoga* (Sentence Construction)
4. *Padartha* (Meaning)
5. *Hetvartha* (Original or Rational Meaning)
6. *Uddeshya* (Purpose)
7. *Nirdesha* (Instruction)
8. *Upadesha* (Advice)
9. *Apadesha* (Statement, Mention)
10. *Atidesha* (Extension /Transfer of Attributes)
11. *Pradesha* (Indication)
12. *Upamanam* (Comparison)
13. *Arthapatti* (Implication, Inference from Circumstances)
14. *Samshaya* (Doubtful Statement)
15. *Prasanga* (Parity or Similarity with an Earlier Point)
16. *Viparyaya* (Indication to the Opposite)
17. *Vakyashesha* (Remaining or Uncompleted Part of a Sentence)
18. *Anumata* (Permitted or Uncontested Statement)
19. *Vyakhyan*a (Explanation)
20. *Nirvachana* (Specification of the Meaning of a Term)
21. *Nidarshana* (Clarification with Instance)
22. *Apavarga* (Limitation to a General Rule)
23. *Svasamgna* (Use of Terms as per Others' Indications)
24. *Purvapaksha* (The First Part of an Argument or Reasoning
25. *Uttarapaksh a* (Second Part of an Argument or Reasoning)
26. *Ekanta* (Statement of some Compulsory Action to be taken)
27. *Anagatavekshana* (Future Reference)

28. *Atikrantavekshana* (Already-made or prior Reference)
29. *Niyoga* (Emphatic Instruction)
30. *Vikalpa* (Statement of Alternatives)
31. *Samuchchaya* (Future Options)
32. *Uhya* (Unsaid Inference or Conjecture)

This shows that the *Arthashastra* is an erudite work written in keeping with all the prevalent rules of grammar and logic.

Thirdly, as at the end of all scholarly or epic compositions, the benefits from a study of this work are indicated:

This very *Arthashastra* guides us to *Dharma*, *Artha* and *Kama* as well, protects them and destroys those who oppose them.

Lastly, Kautilya clearly claims his authorship:

It (the *Arthashastra*) is prepared by Chanakya, also called Vishnugupta, who by his righteous anger rescued the scriptures, the weapons and the land that had gone under King Nanda. Observing the difference of opinion among composers of tenets and their commentators, Chanakya himself has prepared both its tenets and its commentaries.

Thus ends Kautilya's *Arthashastra*.

❐

# 4

# Chanakya Niti

***This is in 17 sections, each ranging between 14-22 couplets and quartets. The sections are not according to any particular themes, though.***

### 1

1-3. Vishnu is the lord and master of the three worlds. I bow my head to him and speak of the political principles (*rajaniti*) evolved from various ancient texts (*shastra*). The best of men learn these famous principles of what is right or wrong, suitable or unsuitable, auspicious or inauspicious. Once a man has mastered these maxims, he has mastered all the knowledge in the world. That is the reason why, to benefit humanity, I come forth with them.

प्रणम्य शिरसा विष्णुं त्रैलोक्याधिपतिम् प्रभूम् ।
नाना शास्त्रोद्धृतं वक्ष्ये राजनीति समुच्चयम् ।।1।।

अधीत्येदं यथाशास्त्रं नरो जानाति सत्तमः ।
धर्मोपदेशविख्यातम् कार्याऽकार्य शुभऽशुभम् ।।2।।

तदहं सम्प्रवक्ष्यामि लोकानां हितकाम्यया ।
येन विज्ञान मात्रेण सर्वज्ञत्वं प्रपद्यते ।।3।।

4. Even the learned man tires of advising a stupid pupil, providing maintenance to an unworthy wife, and mixing too much with depressed people.

मूर्खशिष्योपदेशेन दुष्टस्त्रीभरणेन च ।
दुःखितैः संप्रयोगेण पंडितोऽप्यवसीदति ।।4।।

5. It is undoubtedly deadly to have a wife who is unworthy, a friend who is a charlatan, a servant who answers back, and a residence which is snake-infested.

दुष्टा भार्या शठं मित्रं मृत्यश्चोत्तरदायकः ।
ससर्पे च गृहे वासो मृत्युरेव न संशयः ।।5।।

6. One should protect one's assets for coming calamities. One should protect one's wives even at the cost of one's assets. But one's own self is to be protected at the cost of both one's wives and one's assets. (Note, Chanakya talks of wives rather than a wife. Polygamy was usual then.)

आपदर्थे धनं रक्षेद दारान् रक्शेद धनैरपि ।
आत्मानं सततं रक्षेद दारैरपि धनैरपि ॥6॥

7. One's wealth is to be protected for any contingencies. A man blessed by Shri/Lakshmi, the goddess of wealth and prosperity, need not fear contingencies. However, if this volatile goddess moves away, all one's savings too get destroyed.

आपदर्थे धनं रक्षेद श्रीमतां कुत आपदः ।
कदाच्चिलता लक्ष्मीः संचितोऽपि विनश्यति ॥7॥

8. One should abandon a place where one gets no respect/recognition, livelihood, friends or new skills.

यस्मिन् देशे न सम्मानो न वृत्तिर्न च बान्धवाः ।
न च विद्याऽऽगमः कश्चित् तं देशं परिवर्जयेत् ॥8॥

9. Not a day should one stay where these five are not there: a trader, a worker (*shrotriya*), a ruler, a river and a doctor. or.

धनिकः श्रोत्रियो राजा नदी वैद्यस्तु पञ्चमः ।
पंच यंत्र न विद्यन्ते न तत्र दिवसं वसेत् ॥9॥

10. One should not set up one's establishment where the following five are not there: spiritual faith, fear (of the gods), sense of shame (in being indecorous), charitable conduct and the spirit of sacrifice.

लोकयात्रा भयं लज्जा दाक्षिण्यं त्यागशीलता ।
पंच यत्र न विद्यन्ते न कुर्यात् तत्र संस्थितिम् ॥10॥

11. Get to recognize a servant by his conduct during service, a friend by his conduct at the advent of adversity, an ally by his conduct at the time of (unexpected) trouble and a wife by his conduct at the loss of wealth.

जानीयात् प्रेषणे भृत्यान् बान्धवान् व्यसनाऽऽगमे ।
मित्रम् च आपत्तिकालेषु भार्या च विभवक्षये ॥11॥

12. A friend is one who stands by you in times of stress, at the arrival of sudden calamity, food scarcity, hostile situations, at the royal court and in the cremation-ground.

आतुरे व्यसने प्राप्ते दुर्भिक्षे शत्रु-संकटे ।
राजद्वारे श्मशाने च यस्तिष्ठति स बान्धवः ॥12॥

13. He who leaves the steady and secure so as to serve the uncertain, loses whatever was secure, and whatever was uncertain gets lost as well.

यो ध्रुवाणि परित्यज्य अध्रुवं परिषेवते ।
ध्रुवाणि तस्य नश्यन्ति अध्रुवं नष्टमेव च ॥13॥

14. Marriage should always be performed between families on par with each other. A wise man should not take a low-born bride even if she is beautiful but welcome one from a good family even if her looks repel.

वरयेत् कुलजां प्राज्ञो विरूपामपि कन्यकाम् ।
रूपशीला च नीचस्य विवाहः सदृशे कुले ॥14॥

15. One should not put one's trust upon clawed, horned and armed creatures, upon rivers, women and royal families.

नखीनाम् च नदीनाम् च श्रृंगीणाम् शस्त्रपाणिनाम्
विश्वासो नैव कर्तव्यः स्त्रीषु राजकुलेषु च ॥15 ॥

16. Life-giving force should be accepted even if drawn from what is dross or impure. Gold should be accepted even if extracted from impure stuff; skills that are excellent should be picked up even from petty people and a woman of worth should be picked up even if she hails from a disreputable family.

विषादप्यमृतम् ग्राह्यममेध्यादपि कांचनम् ।
नीचादप्युत्तमा विद्या स्त्रीरत्नम् दुष्कुलादपि ॥16॥

17. Women eat twice as men, are four times as clever as men, are six times as courageous and eight times as amorous (or full of material desires).

स्त्रीणां द्विगुणं आहारो बुद्धिस्तासां चतुर्गुणा ।
साहसं षड्गुणम् चैव कामोऽष्टगुण उच्यते ॥17॥

## 2

1. The natural faults of women are falsehood, boldness, guile (*maya*), stupidity, excessive greed, lack of cleanliness and kindness/alertness.

साहसं माया मूर्खत्वं अतिलुब्धता ।
अशौचत्वं निर्दयत्वं स्त्रीणां दोषाः स्वभावजाः ॥1॥

2. Much penance (*tapasya*) is required to get lots of eatables as well as the capacity to eat, a beautiful woman as well as the capacity to enjoy physical pleasures, wealth as well as the capacity to give it away in charity.

भोज्यंभोजनशक्तिश्चरतिषक्तिर्वरांगना।
विभवो दानशक्तिश्च न अल्पस्य तपसः फलं ॥2॥

3. That man is already in heaven who has an obedient son, a wife who walks in the rhythm he sets her, and contentment in whatever wealth he has.

यस्य पुत्रो वशीभूतो भार्या छंदाऽनुगामिनी
विभवे यश्च संतुष्टस्तस्य स्वर्ग इहैव हि ॥3॥

4. They are the true sons, the obedient ones. He is the true father who takes proper care of his sons. The trustworthy friend is the true friend. The wife who is the fulfillment of desires is the true wife.

ते पुत्रा ये पितुर्भक्ताः स पिता यस्तु पोषकः ।
तन्मित्रं यस्य विश्वासः स भार्या यत्र निवृत्तिः ॥4॥

5. Give up the friend who, like a pot of poison topped by cream, is pleasant-spoken in front of you but damages your work behind your back

परोक्षे कार्यहन्तारं प्रत्यक्षे प्रियवादिनं ।
वर्जयेतादृशं मित्रं विषकुम्भं पयोमुखम् ॥5॥

6. Do not repose your trust upon an unworthy friend. No, do not repose your trust upon any friend at all. If a trusted friend happens to get angry with you, he can expose all your secrets.

न विश्वसेत् कुमित्रे च मित्रे च अपि न विश्वसेत्।
कदाचित् कुपितम् मनसा चिन्तितं कार्यं वाचा नैव प्रकाशयेत् ॥6॥

7. Work that is to be done should be thought out in mind and not expressed in words. It should be kept as a deep secret chant and then applied to work..

मन्त्रेण रक्षयेद् कार्ये च अपि नियोजयेत् ॥
कदाचित् कुपितम्मित्रं सर्वं गुह्यं प्रकाशयेत् ॥7॥

8. Ignorance is painful. Youth too is painful. But the worst pain is to live under someone else's roof.

कष्टं च खलु मूर्खत्वं कष्टं च खलु यौवनं ।
कष्टात् कष्टतरं चैव परगेहनिवासनम् ॥8॥

9. Not every mountain contains precious stones. Not every elephant has a pearl on its forehead. Not every forest has sandalwood trees. Not everywhere are there good men.

शैले शैले न माणिक्यं मौक्तिकं न गजे गजे ।
साधवो न हि सर्वत्र चन्दनं न वने वने ॥9॥

10. Wise men should put their sons into various ways of improving their minds. Principled and cultured sons are the ones revered in the family.

पुत्राश्च विविधैः शीलैर्नियोज्याः सततं बुधैः ।
नीतिज्ञाः शीलसम्पन्ना भवन्ति कुलपूजिताः ॥10॥

11. Parents who do not get their sons educated are, in fact, their enemies. In a gathering of enlightened men, an ignorant one is a crane among swans – a misfit.

माता शत्रुः पिता वैरी येन बालो न पाठित।
शोभते सभामध्ये हंसमध्ये बको यथा ॥11॥

12. Indulgence breeds many faults, reprimand many merits. So children are to be reprimanded rather than treated indulgently.

लालनात् बहवो दोषस्ताड़नात् बहवो गुणाः।
तस्मात्पुत्रं च शिष्यं च ताडयेन्न तु लालयेत् ॥12॥

13. The day should be made fruitful by an act of charity, by scholarly pursuit, by the recitation of a couplet, or a half of it, a line or even a letter from it.

श्लोकेन वा तदर्थेन पादेनै काक्षरेण वा।
अबंध्यं दिवसं कुर्यात् दानाध्ययन कर्मभिः ॥13॥

14. The following burn our bodies even though they are not actually fire: the loss of a wife, insult from one's own people, debt left outstanding , and service to be rendered to an unworthy ruler, condition of impoverishment and company of people not on par.

कान्ता वियोगः स्वजनापमानः ऋणस्य शेषं कुनृपस्य सेवा ।
दरिद्र भावो विषमा सभा च विना ग्निनैते प्रदहन्ति कायं ॥14॥

15. A tree on the riverside, a wife in another's household and a king without a minister are bound to go to a speedy ruin.

नदीतीरे च ये वृक्षाः परगेहेषु कामिनी ।
मंत्रिहीनाश्च राजानः शीघ्रं नश्यन्ति असंशयम् ॥15॥

16. The strength of *Brahmana*s is in learning, that of kings (*Kshatriya*s) is in their armies. The strength of the *Vaishya*s is in their wealth, that of *Shudra*s in their service.

बलं विद्या च विप्राणां रा ज्ञाम् सैन्यं बलं तथा ।
बलं वित्तं च वैश्यानां शूद्राणां परिचर्यिका ॥16॥

17. Courtesans should leave a man who has lost his wealth, subjects a king who has been defeated, birds a tree whose fruits are finished and guests a household where they have already eaten.

निर्धनम् पुरुषं वेश्या प्रजा भग्नं नृपं त्यजेत् ।
खगा बींतफलं वृक्षं भुक्त्वा च अभ्यागता गृहम् ॥17॥

18. Deer desert a burnt-out forest, students leave their teacher once they have got their lessons out of him, and the *Brahmana*s(priests) leave their *Yajamana*s (men on whose behalf they perform the sacrificial ceremonies) after collecting their fees.

गृहीत्वा दक्षिणाम् विप्रास्त्यजति यजमानकम् ।
प्राप्तविद्या गुरुं शिष्या दग्धाऽरणयम् मृगास्तथा ॥18॥

19. Good men too get ruined when befriended by bad men, i.e., people who perform evil deeds and have an evil outlook.

दुराचारी च दूरदृष्टि; दुरा आवासी च दुर्जनः ।
यन्मैत्री क्रियते पुम्भिर्नरः शीघ्रं विनश्यति॥19॥

20. Affectionate behaviour is befitting among equals, service is befitting towards rulers, exchange is befitting in practical situations, and a good wife is befitting at home.

समाने शोभते प्रीति राज्ञि सेवा च शोभते ।
वाणिज्यं व्यवहारेषु दिव्या स्त्री शोभते गृहे ॥20॥

## 3

1. Who has an entirely blameless family-line? Who has never suffered any illnesses? Who has never faced a calamity? Who has enjoyed unbroken companionship?

कास्य दोष: कुले नास्ति व्याधिना को न पीडित:।
व्यसनं् केन न प्राप्तं कस्य सौख्यं निरन्तरम्।।1।।

2. One's conduct shows what family one comes from and one's speech reveals what place he comes from. Respectful behaviour shows affection, physique reveals food-intake.

आचार: कुलमाख्याति देशमाख्याति भाषणम्।
सम्भ्रम: स्नेहमाख्याति वपुराख्याति भोजनम्।।2।।

3. One should put one's daughter into a good family, engage one's son in education. One should put one's enemy into trouble/danger and guide one's friend to what is right (*dharma*).

सुकुले योजयेत्कन्यां पुत्रं विद्यासु योजयेत्।
व्यसने योजयेच्छत्रुं मित्रं धर्मे नियोजयेत्।।3।।

4. Out of a snake and an evil man, it is the snake who is preferable. The snake bites once, at the time appointed for it by Kala (Time, also called the deity of Death). The evil man bites at every step.

दुर्जनस्य च सर्पस्य वरं सर्पो न दुर्जन:।
सर्पो दंशति कालेन दुर्जनस्तु पदे पदे।।4।।

5. Kings gather worthy men around them because they are loyal through and through, and do not desert either at the beginning, or at the middle or at the end.

एतदर्थं कुलीनानां नृपा: कुर्वन्ति संग्रहम्।
आदिमध्याऽवसानेषु न त्यजन्ति च ते नृपम्।।5।।

6. When the end of the world comes, the sea too changes its stand. The waters of the sea want change but worthy men do not.

प्रलये भिन्नमर्यादा भवन्ति किल सागरा:।
सागरा भेदमिच्छन्ति प्रलयेऽपि न साधव:।।6।।

7. Fools are biped beasts and to be rejected. They prick like unseen thorns.

मूर्खस्तु परिहर्तव्य: प्रत्यक्षो द्विपद: पशु:।
भिन्नति वाक्शल्येन अदृष्ट: कण्टको यथा।।7।।

8. Like flowers without fragrance are men without learning even if they have youth, good looks and noble birth.

रूपयौवनसम्पन्ना: विशालकुलसम्भवा:।
विद्याहीना न शोभन्ते निर्गन्धा इव किंशका:।।8।।

9. Sweet-singing voice is the beauty of blackbirds, loyalty to husband is the beauty of women, learning is the beauty of the ugly and a forgiving nature is the beauty of sages.

कोकिलानां स्वरो रूपं स्त्रीणां रूपं पतिव्रतम्।
विद्या रूपं कुरूपाणां क्षमा रूपं तपस्विनाम्।।9।।

10. For the welfare of the entire family-line, a single (unworthy) family-member should be given up, for the good of the whole village, a single (unworthy) family should be given up. For the betterment of the entire habitation/settlement, a single village should be given up, and for the improvement of the soul, the entire earth should be given up.

त्यजेदेकं कुलस्याऽर्थे कुलं त्यजेत् ।
ग्रामं जनपदस्याऽर्थे आत्माऽर्थे पृथिवीं त्यजेत् ।10।।

11. There is no poverty for the enterprising, no sin for the one constantly in prayer, no quarrel with one who is silent, no fear for one who is alert and awake.

उद्योगे नास्ति दारिद्रयं जपतो नास्ति पातकम्।
मौने च कलहो नास्ति नास्ति, जागरिते भयम्।।11।।

12. Too much of anything should be rejected. Sita was in trouble because she was too beautiful, Ravan because he was too proud, and Bali because he was over-generous.

अतिरूपेण वै सीता अतिगर्वेण रावण:।
अतिदानात् बलिर्दत्वा अति सर्वत्र वर्जयेत्।।12।।

13. For the able, nothing is too heavy. For those in business, no distance is too great. For the informed/learned one, no land is foreign. For the sweet-spoken, no one is alien/unrelated.

को हि भार: समर्थानां किं दूरं व्यवसायिनाम्।
को विदेश: सविद्यानां क: पर: प्रियवादिनाम्।।13।।

14. A single sweet-smelling flowering tree makes the entire forest fragrant, just as a single worthy son enhances/glorifies the entire family-line.

एकेनाऽपि सुवृक्षेण पुष्पितेन सुगन्धिना।
वासितं तद्वनं सर्वं सुपुत्रेण कुलं यथा।।14।।

15. A single dried-up tree, when it goes up in flames, makes the entire forest catch fire, just as an unworthy son ruins the entire family.

एकेन शुष्कवृक्षेण दह्यमानेन वह्निना।
दह्यते तद्वनं सर्वं कुपुत्रेण कुलं यथा।।15।।

16. A single moon lights up the entire night. So does a good son, honest and well-educated, illuminate entire family-line.

एकेनाऽपि सुपुत्रेण विद्यायुक्तेन साधुना ।
आह्लादितं कुलं सर्वं यथा चन्द्रेण शर्वरी।।16।।

17. What is the use of several sons who cause grief and regret? It is better to have a single one upon whose support the entire family can rest.

किं जातैर्बहुभि: पुत्रै: शोकसन्तापकारकै:।
वरमेक: कुलाऽऽलम्बी यत्र विश्राम्यते कुलम्।।17।।

18. Nurture a son for the first five years, admonish him for the next ten. Once he is sixteen years old, treat him like a friend.

लालयेत् पंच वर्षाणि दश वर्षाणि ताडयेत्।
प्राप्ते त षोडशे वर्षे पुत्रं मित्रवदाचरेत्।।18।।

19. In enemy-attacks, riots, terrible famines and cliques of dishonest men, it is the one running away who survives.

उपसर्गेऽन्यचक्रे च दुभिक्षे भयावहे।
असाधुजनसम्पर्केय: पलायति स जीवति।।19।।

20. He who has none of the four virtues of righteousness, material wealth, physical fulfillment and spirituality (*dharma, artha, kama* and *moksha*) is condemned to die again and again in one birth after another.

धर्मार्थकाममोक्षाणां यस्यैकोऽपि न विद्यते।
जन्म-जन्मनि मर्त्येषु मरणं तस्यं केवलम्।।20।।

21. Shri/Lakshmi, the goddess of prosperity, herself approached places where there is proper storage of grains, no domestic strife and no respect shown to fools

मूर्खा यत्र न पूज्यन्ते धान्यं यत्र सुसञ्चितम्।
दाम्पत्ये: कलहो नाऽस्ति तत्र श्री: स्वयमागता ।।21।।

## 4

1. Even in the mother's womb, one has the following five created for him: life expectation, occupation, wealth, skills and death.

आयु: कर्म च वित्तं च विद्या निधनमेव च।
पंचैतानि हि स्त्रज्यन्ते गर्भस्थस्यैव देहिन:।।1।।

2. Sons, friends and companions turn away from ascetics. But those who do go along with them bring credit to their families.

साधुभ्यस्ते निवर्तन्ते पुत्रा मित्राणि बान्धवा:।
ये च तै: सह गन्तारस्तद्धर्मात्सुकृतं कुलम्।।2।।

3. The company of good men is like the supervision, attention and contact by which mothers among fishes, tortoises and birds bring up their children.

दर्शनध्यानसंस्पर्शैर्मत्सी कूमी च पक्षिणी।
शिशुं पालयते नित्यं तथा सज्जनसंगति:।।3।।

4. As long as this body is healthy and death is far away, try for self-improvement. Once life is over, what is there to be done!

मावत्स्वस्थो ह्ययं देहो यावन्मृत्युश्च दूरत:।
तावदात्महितं कुर्यात् प्राणान्ते किं करिप्यति।।4।।

5. Skill/education is as useful as a wish-fulfilling celestial cow, yielding results in unlikely times. In an alien land it is like a mother, like the recollection of where some treasure is hidden.

कामधनुगुणा विद्या ह्यकाले फलदायिनी।
प्रवासे मात्सदृशी विद्या गुप्तं धन स्मृतम्।।5।।

6. A single virtuous son is better than a hundred sons with no virtues. A single moon dispels darkness, a thousand stars cannot.

वामेको गुणी पुत्रो निर्गुणैश्च शतैरयि।
एकश्चन्द्रस्तमो हन्ति न च तारा: सहस्रश:।।6।।

7. A son dead soon after birth is preferable to a dull and stupid son who has a long life. A dead son causes less pain than a dullard who is a torture for his parents all their lives.

मूर्खश्चिरायुर्जातोऽपि तस्माज्जातमृतो वर:।।
मृत: स चाऽल्पदु:खाय यावज्जीवं जडो दहेत्।।7।।

8. Even without a fire the following six burn the body: living in an uncongenial place, serving people without a worthy lineage, bad food, a cantankerous wife, an uneducated son and a widowed daughter.

कुग्रामवास: कुलहीनसेवा कुभोजनं कोधमुखी च भार्या।
पुत्रश्च मूर्खो विधवा च कन विनाऽग्निना पट् प्रदहन्ति कायम्।।8।।

9. What are you going to do with cattle which yield neither milk nor calves? What is the use of a son who is neither educated nor respectful?

किं तया क्रियते धेन्वा या न दोग्धी न च गुर्भिणी।
कोऽर्थ: पुत्रेण जातेन यो न विद्वान् न भक्तिमान्।।9।।

10. Three sources of rest and relief do they have whom life has burnt and scarred: a child, a wife and the company of the good.

संसारतापदग्धानां त्रयो विश्रान्तिहेतव:।
अपत्यं च कलत्रं च सतां संगतिरेव च।।10।।

11. Kings order just once, scholars pronounce just once, a father gives away his daughter's hand only once. These three actions are performed once for all and not again and again.

सकृज्जल्पन्ति राजान: सकृज्जल्पन्ति पण्डिता:।
सकृत् कन्या: प्रदीयन्ते त्रोण्येतानि सकृत्सकृत्।।11।।

12. Meditation /penance should be done by oneself. For studying, two people are needed, and for singing, three. For travel,

four people are best, for cultivating the field, five. When there are many, there is a battle.

एकाकिना तपो द्वाभ्यां पठनं गायनं त्रिभिः।
यतुर्भिर्गमनं क्षेत्रं पंचभिर्बहुभि रंणः।।12।।

13. She who is clean and pleasant of appearance, dedicated to her husband and content with him, she who is honest and truthful, is a worthy wife.

सा भार्या या शुचिर्दक्षा सा भार्या या पतिव्रता।
सा भार्या या पतिप्रीता सा भार्या सत्यवादिनी।।13।।

14. A home is empty without the son, all the quarters are empty without friends. The heart is empty without intelligence and everything is empty without wealth.

अपुत्रस्य गृहं शून्यं दिशः शून्यास्त्वबान्धवाः।
मूर्खस्य हृदयं शून्यं सर्वशून्या दरिद्रता।।14।।

15. Scriptures appear deadly when one is out of touch with them, food is deadly when there is dyspepsia, a social group (or community) is deadly when one is poverty-stricken and young men seem deadly when one is old.

अन्भ्यासे विषं शास्त्रमजीर्णे भोजनं विषम्।
दरिद्रस्य विषं गोष्ठी वृद्धस्य तरुणी विषम्।।15।।

16. One should abandon a *dharma* that is merciless, a guru who is without learning, a wife who is ill-tempered, and friends who are not affectionate.

त्यजेद्धर्मं दयाहीनं विद्याहीनं गुरुं त्यजेत्।
त्यजेत्क्रोधमुखीं भार्यां निःस्नेहान् बान्धवांस्त्यजेत।।16।।

17. Traversing long distances ages a man, being tied up long ages horses. Lack of intercourse ages a woman and sunshine ages clothes.

अध्वा जरा मनुष्याणांवाज्रिनां बंधनं जरा।
अमैथुनं जरा स्त्रीणां वस्त्राणामातपो जरा।।17।।

18. Reflect again and again on the sort of time one is passing through and the sort of friends one has, the situation the country is in , one's income and expenditure, one's worth and powers/abilities.

क: काल: कानि मित्राणि को देश: कौ व्ययऽऽगमौ ।
कश्चाऽहं का च मे शक्तिरिति चिन्त्यं मुहुर्मुहु:।।18।।

19. The parent who gives one birth, the priest who dons the sacred thread to a *Brahmana*, the teacher who imparts learning, the employer who feeds, and the patron who protects – these five are to be regarded as fathers.

जनिता चोपनेता च यस्तु विद्यां प्रयच्छति।
अन्नदाता भयत्राता पंचैते पितर: स्मृता:।।19।।

20. The king's wife, the teacher's wife, the friend's wife, the wife's mother and one's own mother – these five are to be regarded as mothers.

राजपत्नी गुरो: पत्नी मित्रपत्नी तथैव च।
पत्नीमाता स्वमाता च पंचैता मातर: स्मृता।।20।।

21. For the *Brahmana*s, the divine entity dwells in fire, for ascetics the divine dwells in the heart. For the less intelligent, divinity is in the image and for those who see everything as the same, divinity is everywhere.

अग्निर्देवो द्विजातीनां मुनीनां हृदि दैवतम्।
प्रतिमा स्वल्पबुद्धीनां सर्वत्र समदर्शिन: ।।21।।

## 5

1.The fire is preceptor to the *Brahmana*s, the *Brahmana* is preceptor to the various castes (*varna*).The husband is preceptor to a woman and to all, the guest is the preceptor.

गुरुरग्निर्द्विजातीनां वर्णानां ब्राह्मणो गुरु:।
पतिरेव गुरु: स्त्रीणां सर्वस्याऽभ्यागतो गुरु: ।।1।।

2. Just as gold is tested in four ways, by rubbing, cutting, heating and pressing, a man is tested by his sacrifice, conduct, qualities and deeds.

यथा चतुर्भि: कनकं परीक्ष्यते निघर्षणच्छेदनातापताडनै:।
तथा चतुर्भि पुरुष परीक्ष्यते त्यागेन शीलेन गुणेन कर्मणा।।2।।

3. Fear a calamity/danger only as long as it is yet to come. When it has already come upon you, attack it fearlessly.

तावद् भयेषु भेतव्यं यावद् भयमनागतम्।
आगते तु भयं दृष्टवा प्रहर्तव्यमशंकया।।3।।

4. Just as the thorns of Badarika berries are not identical, those born from the same womb and under the same stars are not the same.

एकोदरसमुद्भूता: एक नक्षत्रजातका:।
न भवन्ति समा: शीले यथा बदरिकण्टका:।।4।।

5. The disinterested ones do not occupy important posts, those without desire are not fond of decoration/ornamentation; the uncultured do not speak pleasantly and the outspoken are not cheats.

नि:स्पृहो नाऽधिकारी स्यान्नाकामी मण्डनप्रिय: ।
नाऽविदग्ध: प्रियं ब्रूयात: स्फुटवक्ता न वंचक:।।5।।

6. Learned men are disliked by the ignorant, wealthy men by the poor, women living outside the pales of home are disliked by women living in homes, and the unfortunate are disliked by the fortunate ones.

मूर्खाणां पण्डिता द्वेष्या अधनानां महाधना:।
वाराऽऽङ्गना: कुलस्त्रीणां सुभगानां च दुर्भगा: ।।6।।

7. A skill is gone if one is lazy, a wife is gone she falls into the hands of another, land is gone if too few seeds are sown in it, and an army is gone if it has no general.

आलस्योपहता विद्या परहस्तगता: स्त्रिय:।
अल्पबीजं हतं क्षेत्रं हतं सैन्यमनायकम्।।7।।

8. It is regular practice that maintains learning, it is good conduct that maintains the family-line. A worthy man (*Arya*) is known by his qualities and anger is known by the eye.

अभ्यासाद्धार्यते विद्या कुलं शीलेन धार्यते।
गुणेन ज्ञायते त्वार्य: कोपो नेत्रेण गम्यते।।8।।

9. Dharma has to be protected by wealth, learning has to be protected by Yoga, the ruler has to be protected by gentle words , and the household by a good wife.

वित्तेन रक्ष्यते धर्मो विद्या योगेन रक्ष्यते।
मृदुना रक्ष्यते भूप: सत्स्त्रिया रक्ष्यते गृहम:।।9।।

10. Those who counter the learning of the Vedas and the conduct recommended by the scriptures, and speak ill of men of quiet refinement, definitely come to grief.

अन्यथा वेदपाण्डित्यं शास्त्रमाचारमन्यथा।
अन्यथा कवच: शान्तं लोका: क्लिश्यन्ति चान्यथा।।10।।

11. A charitable act destroys poverty, good conduct destroys calamity, wisdom destroys ignorance and one's thought destroys fear.

दारिद्रयनाशनं दानं शीलं दुर्गतिनाशनम्।
अज्ञाननाशिनी प्रज्ञा भावना भयनाशिनी।।11।।

12. There is no disease like desire, no enemy like delusion. There is no fire like anger, no joy like that of learning.

नाऽस्ति कामसमो व्याधिर्नाऽस्ति मोहसमो रिपु: ।
नाऽस्ति कोपसमो वह्निर्नाऽस्ति ज्ञानात् परं सुखम: ।।12।।

13. One is born alone and dies alone and experiences the bad and good of life alone. One descends into hell while another ascends to heaven.

जन्ममृत्यु हि यात्येको भुनक्त्येक: शुभाऽशुभम् ।
नरकेषु पतत्येक एको याति परां गतिम्।।13।।

14. To one who has supreme knowledge, heaven is insignificant like a blade of grass. To one who is a brave warrior, life is insignificant. To one who has conquered the senses, a woman is insignificant. To one who has no material desire, the entire world is insignificant.

तृणं ब्रह्मविद: स्वर्गस्तृणं शूरस्य जीवितम्।
जिताऽशस्य तृणं नारी नि:स्पृहस्य तृणं जगत्।।14।।

15. In an alien country, a man's learning is his friend. At home, it is a man's wife who is his friend. For the sick, medicine is the friend, and Dharma is friend even to the dead.

विद्या मित्रं प्रवासेषु भार्या मित्रं गृहेषु च।
व्याधितस्यौषधं मित्रं धर्मो मित्रं मृतस्य च।।15।।

16. There is no water as good as that from the clouds, no strength like one's own self. There is no power like eyesight and nothing more dear than cereal.

नाऽस्ति मेघसमं तोयं नाऽस्ति चात्मसमं बलम् ।
नाऽस्ति चक्षु:समं तेजो नाऽस्ति धान्यसमं प्रियम् ।।16।।

17. Poor people want wealth, animals want the ability to speak, men want heaven and wise men want liberation.

अधना धनमिच्छन्ति वाचं चैव चतुष्पदा:।
मानवा: स्वर्गमिच्छन्ति मोक्षमिच्छन्ति देवता:।।17।।

18. It is truth that upholds the earth, makes the sun shine, and the wind blow. It is truth that upholds all.

सत्येन धार्यते पृथ्वी सत्येन तपते रवि:।
सत्येत वाति वायुश्च सर्वं सत्ये प्रतिष्ठितम्।।18।।

19. Chanchala (Lakshmi, the goddess of wealth) is always on the move. The length of life and indeed, life itself, is transient. One's place of stay is not fixed for ever. In this ever-changing world, the merit of being righteous is the only permanent element.

चला लक्ष्मीश्चला: प्राणाश्चलं जीवित-यौवनं।
चलाचले च संसारे धर्म एको हि निश्चल:।।20।।

20. Among men, the barber is known for his cunning, among birds the crow, among beasts the fox, and among women, the seller of flower-garlands.

नराणां नापितो धूर्त: पक्षिणां चैव वायस:।
चतुष्पदां श्रृगालस्तु स्त्रीणां धूर्ता च मालिनी।।1।।

## 6

1. The *Shrutishastras* (texts that are learnt by hearing rather than reading them) provide an understanding of *dharma*, remove malignancy, provide knowledge and liberate from material bonds.

श्रुत्वा धर्मं विजानाति श्रुत्वा त्यजति दुर्मतिम्।
श्रुत्वा ज्ञानमवाप्नोति श्रुत्वा मोक्षमवाप्नुयात्।।1।।

2. The crow is the vilest among birds, the dog among animals. The sinning ascetic is vile enough but the ascetic who defiles others is the vilest, no better than a low-born *Chandala*.

पक्षिणां काकश्चाण्डाल: पशूनां चैव कुक्कुर:।
मुनीनां कोपी चाण्डाल: सर्वेषां चैव निन्दक:॥2॥

3. Brass gets polished by ashes, copper by tamarind, a woman by her periods and a river by its flow.

भस्मना शुब्द्यते कांस्यं ताम्रमम्लेन शुध्यति।
रजसा शुध्यते नारी नदी वेगेन शुध्यति॥3॥

4. The king, the scholar, and the ascetic get respect for moving from place to place but a woman who does so is ruined.

भ्रमन् सम्पूज्यते राजा भ्रमन् सम्पूज्यते द्विज:।
भ्रमन सम्पूज्यते योगी स्त्री भ्रमती विनश्यति॥4॥

5. It is Providence or Divine Will which makes our intellect function, which controls our intellect, regulates our activities, and surrounds us with friends.

तादृशी जायते बुद्धिर्व्यवसायोऽपि तादृश: ।
सहायास्तादृशा एव यादृशी भवतिव्यता॥5॥

6. Time refines as well as destroys all living creatures. It is only Time which is awake when all others sleep. Time is above everything.

काल: पचति भूतानि काल: संहरते प्रजा:।
काल: सुप्तेषु जागर्ति कालो हि दुरतिक्रम:॥6॥

7. Those who are born blind cannot see. Neither can those possessed by desire. The arrogant do not see that they are doing any wrong. The avaricious do not see that they are committing any sin.

नैव पश्यति च जन्मान्ध: कामान्धो नैव पश्यति।
मदोन्मत्तो अर्थी दोषान: न पश्यति॥7॥

8. The *atman* or spirit goes through his own circuit of *karman* and suffers the consequences. On his own he gets entangled in the life of a householder and on his own he frees himself.

स्वयं कर्म करोत्यात्मा स्वयं तत्फलमश्नुते।
स्वयं भ्रमति संसारे स्वयं तस्माद्विमुच्यते॥8॥

9. The ruler of the land has to take upon himself the sins of his subjects. The royal priest has to take upon himself the sins of the

king. The husband has to take upon himself the sins of his wife. The guru has to do the same for his disciples.

राजा राष्ट्रकृतं पापं राज्ञ: पापं पुरोहित:।
भर्ता च स्वीकृतं पापं शिष्यपापं गुरुस्तथा।।9।।

10. A father who is perpetually in debt, a mother who is habitually an adulteress, a beautiful wife and an ignorant son are enemies in one's own home.

ऋणकर्ता पिता शत्रु: माता च व्यभिचारिणी।
भार्या रूपवती शत्रु: पुत्र: शत्रुर्नपण्डित:।।10।।

11. To conciliate an avaricious man, give him a gift. To conciliate a covetous man, approach him with folded palms. To conciliate a stupid man, humour him and to conciliate a learned man, speak the truth within.

लुब्धमर्थेन गृहणीयात्स्तब्धमंजलिकर्मणा।
मूर्खच्छन्दोऽनुवृत्तेन यथार्थत्वेन पण्डितम् ।।11।।

12. It is better to have no kingdom than to have an inconsequential one, to have no friend than to have an evil one, to have no disciple than to have a stupid one, and no wife than a bad one.

वरं न राज्यं न कुराजराज्यं वरं न मित्रं न कुमित्रमित्रम्।
वरं न शिष्यो न कुशिष्यशिष्यो वरं न दारा न कुदारदारा:।।12।।

13. How can people draw happiness from a small kingdom? How can one get peace from the friendship of a charlatan? How can a bad wife make the home happy? How can teaching an unworthy disciple lead to fame?

कुराजराज्येन कुत: प्रजासुखं कुमित्रमित्रेण कुतो निर्वृति:।
कुदारदारैश्च कुतो गृहे रति कुशिष्यमध्यापयत: कुतो यश:।।13।।

14-21. Learn one thing from a lion, two from a crane, three from a donkey, four from a cock, five from a crow and six from a dog. The one thing that can be learned from the lion is that whatever one does should be done with all one's energy. The two things to be learnt from the crane are restriction of sensory organs and knowledge of time, place and ability. The three things to be learnt from the donkey are to carry one's burden even when tired, not to mind heat and cold, and always be contented. The four things to be learnt from the cock are: to get up on time, to be ever ready for a fight, to give friends their fair share and to get one's food by grabbing it. The crow teaches us five good things: to be bold, to be private when mating, store away useful items, be watchful and be wary of others. The dog has six virtues: it is a voracious eater, yet contented with little. It sleeps well but is easily awakened. It is ever-devoted to the master and always brave. The man who acts according to these twenty qualities of the lion, the crane, the donkey, the crow and the dog becomes invincible in all situations.

सिंहादेकं बकादेकं शिक्षेच्चत्वारि कुक्कुटात्।
वायसात्पंच शिक्षेच्च षट् शनस्त्रीणि गर्दभात्।।14।।

प्रभूतं कार्यमल्पं वा यन्नर: कर्तुमिच्छति।
सर्वारम्भेण तत्कार्यं सिंहादेकं प्रचक्षते।।15।।

इन्द्रियाणि च संयम्य बकवत् पण्डितो नर:।
देशकालबलं ज्ञात्वा सर्वकार्याणि साधयेत।।16।।

प्रत्युत्थानं च युद्धं च संविभागं च बन्धुषु।
स्वयमाक्रम्य भुक्तं च शिक्षेच्चत्वारि कुक्कुटात्।।17।।

गूढमैथुनधाष्ट्र्य काले काले च संग्रहम्।
अप्रमत्तमविश्वासं पंच शिक्षेच्च वायसात्।।18।।

बह्वाशी स्वल्पसन्तुष्ट: सुनिद्रो लघुचेतन:।
स्वामिभक्तश्च शूरश्च षडेते श्वानतो गुणा:।।19।।

सुश्रान्तोऽपि वहेद् भारं शीतोष्णं न च पश्यति।
सन्तुष्टश्चरते नित्यं त्रीणि शिक्षेच्च गर्दभात्।।20।।

य एतान् विंशतिगुणानाचरिष्यति।
कार्याऽवस्थासु सर्वासु अजेय: स भविष्यति।।21।।

## 7

1. An intelligent person should not reveal the loss of wealth, mental turmoil, disloyalty at home (unfaithfulness of wives), deprivation and dishonour.

अर्थनाशं मनस्तापं गृहे दुश्चरितानि च।
वंचनं चाऽपमानं च मतिमान्न प्रकाशयेत्।।1।।

2. In monetary dealings, in acquiring learning, in eating and conducting oneself, to be unscrupulous is to be happy.

धन-धान्यप्रयोगेषु विद्यासंग्रहणेषु च।
आहारे व्यवहारे च त्यक्तलज्ज: सुखी भवेत:।।2।।

3. Avaricious people running here and there cannot have the happiness of quiet people satisfied with the nectar of contentment.

सन्तोषाऽमृततृप्तानां यत्सुखं शान्तचेतसाम्।
न च तद् धनलुब्धानामितश्चेतश्य धावताम्।।3।।

4. In three things - one's own wife, one's meals and one's wealth- one should have contentment. But one should never have a sense of contentment in respect of scholarly pursuits, practice of penance and acts of charity.

सन्तोषस्त्रिषु कर्तव्य: स्वदारे भोजने धने।
त्रिषु चैव न कर्तव्योऽध्ययने तपदानयो: ।।4।।

5. One should not get in between two *Brahmana*s, a *Brahmana* and his holy fire, a husband-and-wife couple, a master-and-servant duo and a bullock and its plough.

विप्रयोर्विप्रवह्नयोश्च दम्पत्यो: स्वामिभृत्ययो:।
अन्तरेण न गन्तव्यं हलस्य वृषभस्य च।।5।।

6. One should not touch the following with one's feet (i.e., show disrespect to): fire, one's teacher, a *Brahmana*, a cow, a virgin girl, an old man and a child.

पादाभ्यां न स्पृशेदग्निं गुरुं ब्राह्मणमेव च।
नैव गां न कुमारीं च न वृद्धं न शिशुं तथा।।6।।

7. Keep away from vehicles by about five *hasta*s (an ancient measure of distance), keep away from horses by about ten *hasta*s, and from elephants by a hundred. From evil men, keep your distance by leaving the country altogether.

शकटं पंचहस्तेन दशहस्तेन वाजिनम्।
हस्ती शतहस्तेन देशत्यागेन दुर्जनम्।।7।।

8. One should drive on an elephant by poking it with a goad, a horse by slapping it by the hand, a horned beast by hitting it with a

stick. But it is with sword in hand that one should drive away an evil man.

हस्ती अंकुशमात्रेण वाजी हस्तेन ताड्यते।
श्रृङ्गीं लगुडहस्तेन खड्गहस्तेन दुर्जन:।।8।।

9. *Brahmanas* are satisfied by feasting, peacocks by the sound of thunder, good men by the prosperity of others and deceitful men by others' adversities.

दुष्यन्ति भोजने विप्रा मयूरा घनगर्जिते।
साधव: परसम्पत्तौ खल: परविपत्तिषु।।9।।

10. The mighty should be treated in accordance with their nature (along the way their hair grows), the evil should be given a reverse treatment (against the way their hair grows). An enemy of comparable strength should be treated with either humility or strength. [Counter the mighty by being submissive and the evil by opposing them. Counter your equal either by civility or by force.]

अनुलोमेन बलिनं प्रतिलोमेन दुर्जनम्।
आत्मतुल्यबलं शत्रुं विनयेन बलेन वा।।10।।

11. Their physical and military forces are the strength of kings. Their knowledge of the Supreme (*Brahman*) is the strength of the *Brahmanas*. As for women, their youth, beauty and charm are their strength.

बाहुवीर्यं बलं राज्ञो ब्राह्मणो ब्रह्मविद् बली।
रूपयौवनमाधुर्य स्त्रीणां बलमुत्तमम्।।11।।

12. One should not be too straightforward and upright. Going to the forest, one can see that trees growing absolutely straight are axed down whereas the bent and bowed ones are left standing.

चाऽत्यन्तं सरलैर्भाव्यं गत्वा पश्य वनस्थलीम्।
छिद्यन्ते सरलास्तत्र कुब्जास्तिष्ठन्ति पादपा:।।12।।

13. Swans dwell where there is water and leave the place once its water dries up. Men should not be like that, coming and going again and again.

यत्रोदकं तत्र वसन्ति हंसा: तथैव शुष्कं परिवर्जयन्ति।
न हंसतुल्येन नरेण भाव्यं पुनस्त्यजन्ते पुनराश्रयन्ते।।13।।

14. To protect income that one is earning, one should spend off wealth that is already accumulated just as to take in fresh water into a lake, its standing waters should be made to flow out.

उपार्जिताना वित्तानां त्याग एव हि रक्षणम्।
तडागोदरसंस्थानां परीवाह इवाऽम्भसाम् ।।14।।

15. It is the one with money/wealth who has friends and allies, enjoys life and is considered an important man.

यस्याऽर्थास्तस्य मित्राणि यस्याऽर्थास्तस्य बान्धवा: ।
यस्याऽर्था: स पुमाँल्लोके यस्याऽर्था: स च जीवति ।।15।।

16. Four signs remain with those who have spent some time in heaven and now have come to the earth again: having charitable ways, being sweet-spoken, being worshipful to deities and being reverential to *Brahmana*s.

स्वर्गस्थितानामिह जीवलोके चत्वारि चिह्नानि वसन्ति देहे।
दानप्रसङ्गो मधुरा च वाणी देवाऽर्चनं ब्राह्मणतर्पणं च ।।16।।

17. Four signs remain with those who have had a stay in hell: being extremely bad-tempered, being caustic in speech, being poor, fighting with kinsmen, keeping evil company and serving lowly families.

अत्यन्तकोप: कटुका च वाणी दरिद्रता च स्वजनेषु वैरम्।
नीचप्रसङ्ग: कुलहीनसेवा चिह्नानि देहे नरकस्थितानाम्।।17।।

18. If one ventures into a shed where elephants live, one can find a pearl ornament. If you go into a cave of jackals, one will get only the tail of a calf or a piece of a donkey's skin.

मभ्यते यदि मृगेन्द्र-मन्दिरं लभ्यते करिकपोलमौक्तिकम्।
जम्बुकाऽऽलयगते च प्राप्यते वत्स-पुच्छ–खर-चर्म-खण्डनम्।।18।।

19. Without learning, life is futile like the tail of a dog – unable to either hide what should be hidden (the rectum) or drive away enemy attacks (mosquito bites).

शुन: पुच्छमिव व्यर्थं जीवितं विद्यया विना।
न गुह्यगोयने शक्तं न च दंशनिवारणे।।19।।

20. Spiritual aspirants should develop purity of speech, purity of mind, control of the senses and kindness to all creation.

वाच: शौचं च मनस: शौचमिन्द्रियनिग्रह:।
सर्वभते दया शौचं एतच्छौत्रं परार्थिनाम् ।।20।।

21. The fragrance is within the flower, the oil is within the oilseeds, jaggery is within the sugarcane-stalks, and ghee is within the milk. Hence, use your conscience to perceive the soul within the body.

पुष्पे गन्धं तिले तैलं काष्ठेऽग्निं पयसि घृतम् ।
दक्षौ गुडं तथा देहे पश्याऽऽत्मानं विवेकत: ।।21।।

## 8

1. The lowly want wealth, the middle-rankers want both wealth and respect. The noble ones want only respect. Respect is wealth to the noble ones.

अधमा धनमिच्छन्ति धनं मानं च मध्यमा:।
उत्तमा मानमिच्छन्ति मानो हि महतां धनम्।।1।।

2. Even after having sugarcane, water, milk, fruits and roots, betel-leaf and medicine, one can perform rituals like taking a holy dip and making donations.

इक्षुराप: पयो मूलं ताम्बूलं फलमौषधम्।
भक्षयित्वाऽपि कर्तव्या: स्नानदानाऽऽदिका: क्रिया: ।।2।।

3. The flame of a lamp devours darkness and produces decorative lamp-black for the eyes (*kohl/kajal*). Offspring are born as per their parents' intake.

दीपो भक्षयते ध्वान्तं कज्जलं च प्रसूयते।
यदन्नं भक्षयेन्नित्यं जायते तादृशी प्रजा।।3।।

4. O wise one! Give wealth to the qualified and hardly ever elsewhere. The water received by clouds from the sea is always sweet. Observe it reviving every creature and every movable and immovable object of the earth, going back to the sea, and getting multiplied a thousand times.

वित्तं देहि गुणान्वितेषु मतिमन्नान्यत्र देहि क्वचित्।
प्राप्तं वारिनिधेर्जलं घनमुखे माधुर्ययुक्तं सदा।।
जीवान्स्थावरजङ्गमांश्च सकलान् संजीव्य भूमण्डलम्।
भूय: पश्य तदेव कोटिगुणितं गच्छन्तमम्भोनिधिम्।।4।।

5. Wise men have pronounced a *Yavana* to be equivalent to a thousand *Chandalas* (the hunting tribes). There is no one more lowly than the *Yavana* (meat-eating foreigners).

चाण्डालानां सहस्त्रे च सूरिभिस्तत्त्वदर्शिभि:।
एको हि यवन: प्रोक्तो न नीचो यवनात् पर:।।5।।

6. Oil-massage, exposure to funereal fumes, and an intercourse or a shave makes one unclean like a *Chandala* until one has had a bath.

तैलाभ्यंगे चिताधूमे मैथुने क्षौरकर्मणि।
तावद्भवति चाण्डालो यावत्स्नानं न चाऽऽचरेत् ।।6।।

7. A drink of water is medicinal in dyspepsia, strength-giving once digestion is done, life-giving in course of the meal, and poison at the end of it.

अजीर्णे भेषजं वारि जीर्ण वारि बलप्रदम्।
भोजने चामतं वारि भोजनान्ते विषप्रदम।।7।।

8. The absence of knowledge and its application make a man as good as dead. The lack of an army-chief ruins soldiers, the lack of a husband ruins women.

हतं ज्ञानं क्रियाहीनं हतश्चाऽज्ञानतो नर:।
हतं निर्नायकं सैन्यं स्त्रियो नष्टा ह्यभर्तृका:।।8।।

9. Three are the misfortunes that men can have to face: the death of a wife in old age, the appropriation of wealth by a friend, the loss of independence in matters of eating.

वृद्धकाले मृता भार्या बन्धुहस्ते गतं धनम्।
भोजनं च पराधीनं तिस्त्र: पुंसां विडम्बना:।।9।।

10. Without rituals before the fire, the knowledge of the Vedas is incomplete. Without charity, a sacrificial ceremony is incomplete. Without genuine feelings, there is no success. Feelings are the basis of everything.

अग्निहोत्रं विना वेदा न च दानं विना क्रिया।
न भावेन विना सिद्धिस्तस्माद्भावो हि कारणम्।।10।।

11. If one serves any icon made of wood, stone or metal with genuine feelings, it is successful in pleasing Vishnu.

काष्ठपाषाणधतूनां कृत्वा भावेन सेवनम्।
श्रद्धया च तया सिद्धस्तस्य विष्णु: प्रसीदति।।11।।

12. The deity dwells in either wood nor stone nor earth. He dwells in genuine feelings and thus feelings are the basis of everything.

न देवो विद्यते काष्ठे न पाषाणे न मृन्मये।
भावे हि विद्यते देवस्तस्माद् भावो हि कारणम्।।12।।

13. There is no practice of penance superior to remaining at peace. There is no happiness more than contentment. There is no disease greater than lust and no Dharma superior to mercy.

शान्तितुल्यं तपो नास्ति न सन्तोषात् परंसुखम्।
न तृष्णाया: परो व्यार्धिन च धर्मो दयापर:।।13।।

14. Anger is like King Vaivasvata, lust like River Vaitarani (which lies before heaven and is very difficult to cross) . Learning is like celestial cows that fulfill all desires, and contentment is like Nandana, the garden of heaven.

क्रोधो वैवस्वतो राजा तृष्णा वैतरणी नदी।
विद्या कामदुघा धेनु: सन्तोषो नन्दनं वनम्।।14।।

15. Virtue enhances one's looks, conduct enhances one's family-line, successful application enhances learning and enjoyment enhances wealth.

गुणो भूषयते रूपं शीलं भूषयते कुलम्।
सिद्धिर्भूषयते विद्यां भोगो भूषयते धनम्।।15।।

16. Without virtue, one's good looks are gone. Without good conduct, family prestige is gone. Without successful application, learning is wasted. Without enjoyment, wealth is wasted.

निर्गुणस्य हतं रूपं दु:शीलस्य हतं कुलम्।
असिद्धस्य हता विद्या अयभोगेन हतं धनम्।।16।।

17. Pure is the water within the earth, and a woman devoted to her husband is pure. Pure is the king who looks after the welfare of his people, and so is a *Brahmana* who has contentment.

शुद्धंर्भूमिगतं तोयं शुद्धा नारी पतिव्रता।
शुचि: क्षेमकरो राजा सन्तोषी ब्राह्मण: शुचि:।।17।।

18. Discontented *Brahmana*s get ruined, so do kings who are contented and complacent. Shy courtesans get ruined, so do brash housewives.

असन्तुष्टा द्विजा नष्टा: सन्तुष्टाश्च महीभृत:।
सलज्जा गणिका नष्टा निर्लज्जाश्च कुलाङ्गना:।।18।।

19. What use to men are large families without any educated men in them! Educated men are respected by gods even when they come from tarnished family backgrounds.

किं कुलेन विशालेन विद्याहीनेन देहिनाम्।
दृष्कलीनोऽपि विद्वांश्च देवैरपि सुपूज्यते ।।19।।

20. It is the educated who are praised in the world, it is the educated who are honoured. Everything can be acquired through education. Education is worshipped everywhere.

विद्वान् प्रशस्यते लोके विद्वान् गच्छति गौरवम्।
विद्यया लभते सर्वं विद्या सर्वत्र पुज्यते।।20।।

21. Meat-eaters, drunkards, ignorant and illiterate persons are animals in the guise of men and a burden upon the earth.

मांसभक्षै: पुरापानैर्मूर्खैश्चाक्षरवर्जितै:।
पशुभि: पुरुषाकारैर्भाराऽऽक्रान्ता च मेदिनी ।।21।।

22. There is no enemy like a sacrificial ceremony. It burns up a nation deficient in food grains, a priest deficient in the knowledge of sacred chants, and a performer of sacrifice who is deficient in his donations.

अन्नहीनो दहेद् राष्ट्रं मन्त्रहीनश्च ऋत्विज:।
यजमानं दानहीनो नास्ति यज्ञसमो रिपु:।।22।।

## 9

1. If you want liberation, leave all these material possessions. Drink like nectar the virtues of mercy, rectitude, pity, purity and truth.

मुक्तिमिच्छसि चेत्तात! विषयान् विषवत् त्यज।
क्षमाऽऽर्जवं दया शौचं सत्यं पीयूषवद् पिब।।1।।

2. Like a snake that gets into a termite hill, is destroyed the man who lets out mutual secrets about each other's weak points.

वरस्परस्य मर्माणि ये भाषन्ते नराधमा:।
त एव विलयं यान्ति वल्मीकोदरसर्पवत्।।2।।

3. In ancient times there was no one who could advise Brahma, the Creator. That is why there is no fragrance in gold, no fruit upon the sugarcane-stalk, and no blossoms on the sandalwood tree.

गन्ध: सुवणे फलमिक्षुदण्डे नाऽकारि पुष्पं खलु चन्दनस्य।
विद्वान् धनाढ्यश्च नृपश्चिरायु: धातु: पुरा कोऽपि न बुद्धिदोऽभूत्।।3।।

4. Of all medicines, life-giving *amrita* is the best, of all pleasures, eating is the best. The eyes are the most important of all sense-organs and the head is the most important of all body-parts.

सर्वौषधीनाममृता प्रधाना सर्वेषु सौख्येष्वशनं प्रधानम्।
सर्वेन्द्रियाणां नयनं प्रधानं सर्वेषु गात्रेषु शिर: प्रधानम्।।4।।

5. No messenger moves across the sky and no information travels along it. No prior discussion or meeting has taken place with it. It is the excellent *Brahmana* who informs us about the eclipses of the sun and the moon in the sky. Why is he not to be regarded as the knowledgeable one?

दूतों न संचरति खे न चलेच्च वार्ता।
पूर्व न जल्पितमिदं न च सङ्गमोऽस्ति
व्योम्नि स्थितं रविशशिग्रहणं प्रशस्तं
जानाति यो द्विजवर: स कथं न विद्वान्।।5।।

6. Even if they are asleep, these seven should be awakened: a student, a servant, a traveler, a hungry man, a man who is troubled by fear, a store-keeper and a door-keeper.

विद्यार्थी सेवक: पान्थ: क्षुधाऽऽर्तो भयकातर:।
लम् भाण्डारी प्रतीहारी च सप्त सुप्तान् प्रबोधयेत्।।6।।

7. These seven should not be roused from their sleep: a snake, a king, a tiger, an insect that stings, a kid, a dog that belongs to another, and a fool.

अहिं नृपं च शार्दूलं किटिं च बालकं तथा।
परश्वानं च मूर्ख च सप्त सुप्तान् न बोधयेत्।।7।।

8. What are they to do, those who like snakes without poison, have only half-read the Vedas and partaken of food from *Shudra*s?

अर्थाऽधीताश्च यैर्वेदास्तथा शूद्रान्नभोजिनाः।
ते द्विजाः किं करिष्यन्ति निर्विषा इव पन्नगाः।।8।।

9. What is the use of satisfying one whose displeasure poses no threat and pleasure brings no income, one who can neither favour nor disfavour?

यस्मिन् रुष्टे भयं नास्ति तुष्टे नैव धनाऽऽगमः।
निग्नहोऽनुग्रहो नास्ति स रुष्टः किं करिष्यति।।9।।

10. Even a snake without poison should spread out a huge hood. Whether there is poison or not, the show of the hood is terrifying.

निर्विषेणाऽपि सर्पेण कर्तव्या महती फणा।
विषमस्तु न चाप्यस्तु घटाटोपो भयंकर।।10।।

11. Un-intelligent people while away their time thus: the morning in gambling, the mid-day in pleasuring with women and the night in thieving.

प्रातर्द्यूतप्रसंगेन मध्याह्ने स्त्रीप्रसङ्गतः।
रात्रौ चौर्यप्रसंगेन कालो गच्छत्ये धीमताम्।।11।।

12.A garland strung by oneself, sandalwood paste crushed by one's own hand and prayers written out by one's own hand lead to prosperity greater than that of Indra , the ruler of heaven.

स्वहस्तग्रथिता माला स्वहस्तघृष्टचन्दनम्।
स्वहस्तलिखितं स्तोत्रं शक्रस्यापि श्रियं हरेत्।।12।।

13. The more one crushes sugarcane, sesame, broken grains of rice, gold, women, sandalwood, curds and betel-leaves, the more their improvement.

इक्षुदण्डास्तिलाः क्षुद्राः कान्ता हेम च मेदिनी।
चन्दनं दधि ताम्बूलं मर्दनं गुणवर्धनम्।।13।।

14. One sets off one's poverty by displaying patience, poor clothing by keeping them clean, badly cooked meal of rice by serving it hot, and ugly looks by being well-behaved.

दरिद्रता धीरतया विराजते कुवस्त्रता शुभ्रतया विरातजे।
कदन्नता चोष्णतया विराजते कुरूपता शीलतया विराजते।।14।।

## 10

1. One who has no wealth is not really impoverished. If he has determination/conviction, he is a rich man. But one who is bereft of the gem that is learning, he is impoverished in every way.

धनहीनो न हीनश्च धनिक: स सुनिश्चय:।
विद्यारत्नेन यो ही न: स हीन: सर्ववस्तुषु।।1।।

2. One should take a step only after purifying (that is, scrutinizing, cleansing) the spot by a glance, one should drink water only after purifying it with a cloth (using it like a sieve), one should utter a sentence only after purifying it with the knowledge of scriptures (that is, getting it sanctioned) and one should interact with people only after purifying one's interaction with one's intellect (That is, one should not behave recklessly).

दृष्टिपूतं न्यसेत् पादं वस्त्रपूतं पिवेज्जलम्।
शास्त्रपूतं वदेद् वाक्यं मन: पूतं समाचरेत्।।2।।

3. Those seeking the pleasures of life should give up the pursuit of learning. Those seeking learning should give up the pursuit of pleasure. Where will the man seeking pleasure get learning, where will the man seeking learning get pleasure?

सुखार्थी वा त्यजेद्विद्यां विद्यार्थी वा त्यजेत् सुखम्।
सुखार्थिन: कुतो विद्या विद्यार्थिन: कुतो सुखम्।।3।।

4. What do the poets not observe? What do the women not do? What do the drunk not babble and what do the crows not eat?

कवय: किं न पश्यन्ति किं न कुर्वन्ति योषित:।
मद्यपा: किं न जल्पन्ति किं न भक्षन्ति वायसा:।।4।।

5. Fate makes a king of a wretched beggar and a beggar of a king, a poor man of a rich man and a rich man of a poor one.

रुड्क करोति राजानं राजानं रड्कमेव च।
धनिनं निर्धनं चैव निर्धनं धनिनं विधि:।।5।।

6. One who asks for alms is the enemy of the covetous man, the learned man that of the ignorant. Husbands are the enemy of amorous wives and moonlight is that of thieves.

लुब्धानां याचकः शत्रुर्मूर्खाणां बोधकः रिपुः।
जारस्त्रीणां पतिः शत्रुश्चोराणां चन्द्रमारिपुः॥6॥

7. Good advice does not benefit those who have no substance within. The bamboo does not become sandalwood even in association with the mountain Malaya (famous for its sandalwood trees).

अन्तः सारविहीनानामुपदेशो न जायते।
मलयाचलसंसर्गात् न वेणुश्चन्दनायते॥7॥

8. What will the scriptures do for someone who does not have wisdom of his own ? What can a mirror do for one who has no eyes?

यस्य नास्ति स्वयं प्रज्ञा शास्त्रं तस्य करोति किम्।
लोचनाभ्यां विहीनस्य दर्पणः किं करिष्यति॥8॥

9. There is no way to make a good man of an evil one. Even if washed a hundred times, the anus does not become the best sensory organ.

दुर्जनं सज्जनं कुर्तमुपायो न हि भूतले।
अपानं शतधा धौतं न श्रेष्ठमिन्द्रियं भवेत॥9॥

10. One will die by getting into conflict with trustworthy and able people. One will experience loss of wealth by getting into conflict with people who are not one's kinsfolk .One will get destroyed by conflict with the ruling power and one's entire family line will be destroyed by conflict with *Brahmana*s.

आत्मद्वेषात् भवेन्मृत्युः परद्वेषाद् धनक्षयः।
राजद्वेषात् भवेन्नाशो ब्रह्मद्वेषात्कुलक्षयः॥10॥

11. The forest, the abode of trees inhabited by tigers and elephants, where one feeds on fruits, leaves and water, and sleeps on a bed of grass, and dresses in barks and old tatters, is better than a life among friends when one has no wealth of one's own *Brahmana*s are the roots of trees whose branches are the Vedas and rituals like Sandhya and whose leaves are religious practices. Thus *Brahmana*s are to be preserved with care. Without the roots, there are no leaves or branches.

वरं वनं व्याघ्रगजेन्द्रसेवितं द्रुमालय: पत्रफलाम्बुभोजनम्।
तणेषु शय्या शतजीर्णवल्कलं न बन्धुमध्ये धनहीनजीवनम्।।
विप्रो वृक्षस्तस्य मूलं च सन्ध्या वेदा: शाखा धर्मकर्माणि पत्रम्।
तस्मान्मूलं यत्नतो रक्षणीयं छिन्ने मूले नैव शाखा न पत्रम्।।11।।

12. Three worlds become native land to the one who has Lakshmi (the consort of Vishnu) as his mother, Janardana (Vishnu) as his father and worshippers of Vishnu as his friends.

माता च कमलादेवी पिता देवा जनार्दन:।
बान्धवा विष्णुभक्ताश्च स्वदेशी भुवनत्रयम्।।12।।

13. Birds of feathers of many colours who perch on the same tree go away in ten directions when the day dawns. What is sad about it?

एकवृक्षसमारूढा नाना वर्णा विहङ्गमा:।
प्रभाते दशसु दिक्षु तत्र का परिदेवना।।13।।

14. Strength is his who has intelligence. Where will the stupid one get strength from? See, (in the *Panchatantra*) it is the rabbit which felled the power-intoxicated lion down.

बुद्धिर्यस्य बलं तस्य निर्बुद्धेश्च कुतो बलम्।
वने सिंहो मदोन्मत्त: शशकेन निपातित:।।14।।

15. What worry do I have in my life if I sing of Hari, the upholder of the world! Why else has the breasts of the mother been created for the life of the newborn? So, frequently thinking of Vishnu, the lord of the Yadu tribe and the consort of Lakshmi, I spend my time serving his lotus-feet.

का चिन्ता मम जीवने यदि हरिर्विश्वम्भरो गीयते,
नो चेदर्भकजीवनाय जननीस्तन्यं कथं निर्मयेत्।
इत्यालोच्य मुहुर्मुहुर्यदुपते लक्ष्मीपते केवलं,
त्वत्पादाम्बुजसेवनेन सततं कालो मया नीयते।।15।।

16. Although being distinguished by the knowledge of Sanskrit, the language of the gods, I am eager to know other languages, just as, even when there is amrita, the elixir of life, available in heaven, the gods still have a taste for the juicy lips of celestial maidens.

गीर्वाणवाणीषु विशिष्टबुद्धिस्तथापि भाषान्तरलोलुपोऽहम् ।
यथा सुराणाममृते स्थितेऽपि स्वर्गाङ्गनानामधरासवे रुचि:।।16।।

17. The pancake is ten times more nourishing than rice. Milk is ten times more strengthening than pancakes. Meat is eight times more nutritious than milk, and ghee is ten times more nutritious than meat.

अन्नाद् दशगुणं पिष्टं पिष्टाद्दशगुणं पय:।
पयसोऽष्टगुणं मांसं मांसाद्दशगुणं घृतम् ।।17।।

18. Herbal preparations increase ailments, milk increases body-size, ghee increases prowess and flesh increases flesh.

शाकेन रोगा वर्धन्ते पयसा वर्धते तनु:।
घृतेन वर्धते वीर्यं मांसान्मांसं प्रवर्धते।।18।।

## 11

1. It is through practice that these four inborn virtues are attained: generosity, sweetness of speech, patience and judiciousness.

दातृत्वं प्रियवक्तृत्वं धीरत्वमुचितज्ञता।
अभ्यासेन न लभ्यन्ते चत्वार: सहजा गुणा:।।1।।

2. As a king is ruined through acts contrary to Dharma, so is ruined the man who leaves his own tribe or community and resorts to others.

आत्मवर्गं परित्यज्य परवर्गं समाश्रयेत्।
स्वयमेव लयं याति यथा राजाऽन्यधर्मत: ।।2।।

3. The hefty elephant is controlled by the small probe (*ankusha*). The deep darkness is dispelled by the flame of a lamp. The mountain falls when hit by thunder. Is the elephant, the darkness or the mountain commensurate with the size of the probe, the flame or the thunder?He who has the fire of energy is the powerful one. How can one rely on mere size?

हस्ती स्थूलतनु: स चाङ्कुशवश: किं हस्तमात्रोऽङ्कुशो
दीपो प्रज्वलिते प्रणश्यति तम: किं दीपमात्रं तम:।
वज्रेणापि हता: पतन्ति गिरय: किं वज्रमात्रो गिरिमस्
तेजो यस्य विराजते स बलवान् स्थूलेषु क: प्रत्यय:।।3।।

4. Hari (Vishnu) leaves the earth when ten thousand years are left to the end of the Kali era. The river Ganga leaves the earth when half of that time (i.e., five thousand years) is left. Village

deities leave when half of that (two and a half thousand years) is left.

कलौ दशसहस्त्रेणु हरिस्त्यजति मेदिनीम्।
तदर्द्ध जाह्नवीतोयं तदर्द्ध ग्रामदेवता।।4।।

5. One over-attached to the household cannot acquire knowledge, the meat-eating one cannot experience pity, one covetous of material possessions cannot reach the truth, and one besotted with his wife cannot get a faithful one.

गृहाऽऽसक्तस्य नो विद्या नो दया मांसभोजिनः ।
द्रव्यलुब्धस्य नो सत्यं स्त्रैणस्य न पवित्रता।।5।।

6. A wicked person can never reach the status of a sage however many the ways he is taught in. The Neem tree does not attain sweetness even if watered to the roots by milk and ghee.

न दुर्जनः साधुदशामुपैति बहुप्रकारैरपि शिक्ष्यमाणः।
आमूलसिक्तः पयसा घृतेन न निम्बवृक्षो मधुरत्वमेति।।6।।

7. An evil person with dirt within him cannot get cleansed just like pots of wine cannot get purified even after being burnt.

अन्तर्गतमलो दुष्टस्तीर्थस्नानशतैरपि।
न शुध्यति यथा भाण्डं सुराया दाहितं च यत्।।7।।

8. No wonder one who does not know the true value of something constantly decries it, like a tribal woman who leaves pearls formed on an elephant's head and dons seeds of the wild Gunja plant.

न वेत्ति यो यस्य गुणप्रकर्षं स तं सदा निन्दति नाऽत्र चित्रम्।
यथा किराती करिकुम्भजाता मुक्ताः परित्यज्य बिभर्ति गुंजाः।।8।।

9. One who for a whole year takes his food in silence reigns in heaven for thousands of eras.

यस्तु सवत्सरं पूर्णं नित्य मौनेन भुंजत्ति।
युगकोटिसहस्त्रं तु स्वर्गलोके महीयते।।9।।

10. One seeking learning (that is, a student or *Brahmachari*) should give up desire, anger, avarice, going after tasty food, dressing-up, joking around, sleeping too much and taking too much care of his body.

कामं क्रोधं तथा लोभं स्वादं श्रृङ्गारकौतुके।
अतिनिद्राऽतिसेवे च विद्यार्थी ह्यष्ट वर्जयेत।।10।।

11. That *Brahmana* is called a *Rishi* (sage) who lives continuously in the forests eating uncultivated food (e.g., fruits and roots) and performing prayer ceremonies.

अकृष्टफलमूलेन वनवासरतः सदा।
कुरुतेऽहरहः श्राद्धमृषिर्विप्रः स उच्यते।।11।।

12. That *Brahmana* is called a *Dvija* (twice-born) who is satisfied with one meal a day, engaged all the time in the six *samskaras* (acts sanctioned by the scriptures), and performs the act of sex only in accordance with the wife's periods (that is, for procreation rather than for enjoyment).

एकाहारेण सन्तुष्टः षट्कर्मनिरतः सदा।
ऋतुकालाभिगामी च स विप्रो द्विज उच्यते।।12।।

13. That *Brahmana* who is engaged in worldly activities, takes care of animals, and practices trade and agriculture is called a *Vaishya.*

लौकिके कर्मणि रतः पशूनां परिपालकः।
वाणिज्यकृषिकर्ता यः स विप्रो वैश्य उच्यते।।13।।

14. That *Brahmana* who deals in lac, indigo, dyes, oil, honey, ghee, wine and flesh is called a *Shudra.*

परकार्यविहन्ता च दाम्भिकः स्वार्थसाधकः।
छली द्वेषी मृदुः क्रूरो विप्रो मार्जार उच्यते।।14।।

15. That *Brahmana* who spoils the good work of others, is selfish and haughty, devious, envious, soft-spoken and cruel, is called a *Marjara* (cat).

वापीकूपतडागानामारा मसुरवेश्मनाम्।
उच्छेदने निराऽऽशङ्क स विप्रो म्लेच्छ उच्यते।।15।।

16. That *Brahmana* who has no qualms about demolishing lakes, tanks, wells and temples of deities is called a *Mlechchha.*

लाक्षादितैलनीलानां कुसुम्भमधुर्पिषाम्।
विक्रेता मद्यमांसानां स विप्रः शूद्र उच्यते।।16।।

17. That *Brahmana* is who steals and uses the property of deities and teachers and the wives of others, and survives on food available anywhere and everywhere, is called a *Chandala*.

देवद्रव्यं गुरुद्रव्यं परदाराऽभिमर्शनम्।
निर्वाहः सर्वभूतेषु विप्रश्चाण्डाल उच्यते।।17।।

18. It is a good deed to give away wealth that is in the form of eatables, never to store it up. The achievements of Karna, Bali and Vikramaditya stand even today. The honeybees rubbing their hands and feet seem to say: Alas ! Lost is our honey that was stored-up for long without either consumption or donation.'

देयं भोज्यधनं सदा सुकृतिभिर्नो संचितव्यं कदा
श्रीकर्णस्य बलेश्च विक्रमपतेरद्याति कीर्तिः स्थिता।
अस्माकं मधु दानभोगरहितं नष्टं चिरात्संचितं
निर्वाणादिति पाणिपादयुगले धर्षन्त्यहो मक्षिकाः।।18।।

## 12

1. That home is praiseworthy where the environment is joyful, the sons are educated and the wife is sweet-spoken, where wealth is adequate to satisfy wishes, where there are good friends, marital fidelity, and obedience from servants, where every day there occur entertainment of guests, worship of Shiva, partaking of sweets and drinks, and constant reverence of sages and learned men.

सानन्दं सदनं सुताश्च सुधियः कान्ता प्रियालापिनी सुधनं।
सन्मित्रं स्वयोषितिरतिः स्वाऽऽज्ञापराः सेवकाः।
आतिथ्यं शिवपूजनं प्रतिदिनं मिष्टान्नपानं गृहे।
साधोः सङ्गमुपासते च सततं धन्यो गृहस्थाऽऽश्रमः।।1।।

2. O king! One does not get back the amount given to *Brahmanas* exactly as it was. Out of pity, if one respectfully gives even a small donation to a destitute or a *Brahmana*, it comes back infinitely multiplied.

आर्तेषु विप्रेषु दयान्वितश्च यत् श्रद्धया स्वल्पमुपैति दानम्।
अनन्तपारं समुपैति राजन् यद्दीयते तन्न लभेद द्विजेभ्यः।।2।।

3. O jackal! quickly throw down the damnable body whose hands have never performed acts of charity, whose ears have been against wise words , eyes have never beheld sages, whose feet have never gone on pilgrimage, whose belly is filled with ill-gotten gains

and whose head had been raised arrogantly high. Do not eat such a carcass lest it contaminates you.

हस्तौ दानविवर्जितौ श्रुतिपुटौ सारस्वतद्रोहिणौ
नेत्रे साधुविलोकनेन रहिते पादौ न तीर्थं गतौ।
अन्यायार्जितवित्तपूर्णमुदरं गर्वेण तुंगं शिरो
रे रे जम्बुक मुंच मुंच सहसा निन्द्यं सुनिन्द्यं वपु:।।3।।

4. Is it the spring's fault that the bamboo-shoot (Kareena) has no leaves? Is it the sun's fault that the owl cannot see in daylight? Is it the fault of the clouds that raindrops do not descend into the beaks of the Chataka bird? Who can wipe out the writings of the Creator on our foreheads?

पत्रं नैव यदा करीरविटपे दोषो वसन्तस्य किं
नालूकोऽप्यवलोकते यदि दिवा सूर्यस्य किं दूषणम्।
वर्षा नैव पतन्ति चातकमुखे मेघस्य किं दूषणं यत्पूर्वं
विधिना ललाटलिखितं तन्मार्जितुं क: क्षम:।।4।।

5. The wicked can become good in the company of the good but the good does not cease to be good in the company of the wicked. The earth is sweet-scented by the flower that drops on it but the flower does not pick up bad odour by falling upon the earth.

सत्सङ्गाद्भवति हि साधुता खलानां साधूना न हि खलसङ्गमात्खलत्वम्।
आमोदं कुसुम-भवं मृदेव धत्ते मृद्गन्धं न हि कुसुमानि धारयन्ति।।5।।

6. It is ennobling to see sages. Sages are born of pilgrimage spots. It takes time to reap the benefits of visiting pilgrimage spots. Visiting sages yields quick results. (Meeting a devotee is an instant cleanser whereas visiting a pilgrimage takes long to purify.)

साधूनां दर्शनं पुण्यं तीर्थभूता हि साधव:।
कालेन फलते तीर्थं ग्रसद्य: साधुसमागम:।।6।।

7. (A newcomer to a city asks of a *Brahmana*:) "O *Brahmana*! Who is great in this city?" "That clump of palm trees."(answers the *Brahmana*.)"Who is a generous donor?" "The washer man who gives back clothes every night after taking them in the morning." "Who is a man here with expertise?" "Everyone here is an expert at stealing the wealth and wives of others."(The newcomer asks, on learning that there are no noble, generous or skilled people in the

city:) "My friend! How do you manage to survive here ?" "Like the worm survives in the filth."

विप्राऽस्मिन्नगरे महान् कथय कस्तालद्रुमाणां गण: को ।
दाता रजको ददाति वसनं प्रातर्गृहीत्वा निशि।
को दक्ष: परदारवित्तहरणे सर्वोऽपि दक्षो जन:
कस्मांजीवसि हे सखे विषकृमिन्यायेन जीवाम्यहम्।।7।।

8. Like cremation-grounds are households where there is no mud from washing the feet of *Brahmanas* (i.e., where *Brahmanas* are not shown respect), there ring out no chanting of the Vedas and no Svaha and Swadha sounds (associated with sacrifices to the fire-god.)

न विप्रपादोदककर्दमानि न वेदशास्त्रध्वनिगर्जितानि।
स्वाहा स्वधाकार-विवर्जितानि श्मशानतुल्यानि गृहाणि तानि।।8।।

9. These six are our family-members. Truth-the mother, Knowledge-the father, Right Conduct (Dharma)-the brother, Mercy-the sister, Peace-the wife, Forgiveness-the son.

सत्यं माता पिता ज्ञानं धर्मो भ्राता दया स्वसा।
शान्ति: पत्नी क्षमा पुत्र: षडेते मम बान्धवा:।।9।।

10. One's body parts are temporary, wealth is not permanent. Death is all the time lurking around. Hence it is a must for one to acquire spiritual wealth.

अनित्यानि शरीराणि विभवो नैव शाश्वत:।
नित्यं सन्निहितो मृत्यु: कर्तव्यो धर्मसंग्रह:।।10।।

11. (Arjuna says to Krishna:)The Brahmanas are excited by invitations to feasts. Cows are excited by fresh grass. Women are excited by association with their husbands. O Krishna! I am excited by war.

आमन्त्रणोत्सवा विप्रा गावो नवतृणोत्सवा:।
पत्युत्साहयुता नार्य: अहं कृष्णरणोत्सव:।।11।।

12. He who looks upon the wife of another man as his mother, the property of another man as lumps of earth, and the pleasure and pain of all other people as his own, has the right perspectives on things and can be regarded as truly learned.

भ्रातृवत् परदारांश्च परद्रव्याणि लोष्ट्रवत्।
आत्मवत् सर्वभूतानि य: पश्यति स पश्यति।।12।।

13. (Sage Vashishttha, the royal priest of Ayodhya, had said to Rama, the descendant of Raghu and so, a Raghava): "O Raghava! In you exist eagerness for what is Right, sweetness of speech, enthusiasm in charity, loyalty to friends, humility towards the preceptor, sobriety in the mind, purity of conduct, appreciation of qualities (of others), knowledge of ancient scriptures, beauty of appearance, and reverence of all that is good (Shiva)."

धर्मे तत्परता मुखे मधुरता दाने समुत्साहता
मित्रेऽवंचकता गुरौ विनयता चित्तेऽति गम्भीरता।
आचारे शुचिता गुणे रसिकता शास्त्रेषु विज्ञानता
रूपे सुन्दरता शिवे भजनता स्वम्यस्ति भो राघव:।।13।।

14. "O king of the dynasty of Raghu! With what shall I compare these?" (said Vashishttha).The wish-fulfilling Kalpataru tree is just wood. The mountain Sumeru is immovable. The Chintamani (symbol of Vishnu) is just a rock, The sun is too piercing, the moon is subject to waning, the seas are full of acidic water, the deity of love is without body, the great king Bali is a demon and the wish-fulfilling celestial cow a mere animal. None of these are comparable to you."

काष्ठं कल्पतरु: सुमेरुरचलश्चिन्तामणि: प्रस्तर:
सुर्यस्तीव्रकर: शशी क्षयकर: क्षारो हि वारांनिधि:।
कामो नष्टतनुर्बलिदितिसुतो नित्यं पशु: कामगौ-नैतांस्ते
तुलयामि भो रघुपते कस्योपमा दीयते।।14।।

15. Courtesy is to be imbibed from princes, conversational skills from scholars. Gamblers can teach how to lie and women how to deceive.

विनयं राजपुत्रेभ्य: पण्डितेभ्य: सुभाषितम्।
अनतं द्यूतकारेभ्य: स्त्रीभ्य: शिक्षेत् कैतवम्।।15।।

16. One who spends unthinkingly, is without a guardian, quarrels without reason, and is overpowered by desire for all sorts of women, quickly goes to ruin.

अनालोक्य व्ययं कर्ता ह्यनाथ: कलहप्रिय:।
आतुर: सर्वक्षेत्रेषु नर: शीघ्रं विनश्यति।।16।।

17. The wise man does not worry about food but only about Dharma. Man's quota of food is decided with his birth. Drop by drop, the pot fills up gradually. This is the way it happens with all skills, wealth and Dharma.

नाहारं चिन्तयेत् प्राज्ञो धर्ममेकं हि चिन्तयेत्।
आहारो हि मनुष्याणां जन्मना सह जायते।।18।।

18. The Indra-Varun fruit does not become sweet even when it ripens. An evil (or idiotic) man does not become good (or wise) even when he grows old.

वयस: परिणामेऽपि य: खल: खल: एव स:।
सुपक्वमपि माधुर्य नोपयातीन्द्रवारुणम्।।19।।

19. In this world he only reaches a high position who is expert in the following arts: generosity to kinsfolk, kindness (even) to outsiders, constant shrewdness with evil men, affection for good people, wariness towards deceptive people, humility to learned people, boldness towards the enemy, deference to seniors and diplomacy with women.

दाक्षिण्यं स्वजने दया परजने शाठ्यं सदा दुर्जने
प्रीति: साधुजने स्मय: खलजने विद्वज्जने चार्जवम्।
शौर्यं शत्रुजने क्षमा गुरुजने नारीजने धृष्टता इत्थं ये पुरुषा:
कलासु कुशलास्तेष्वेवलोकस्थिति:।।20।।

## 13

1. It is better for a man to live a mere second by doing pure deeds than to live a whole era by suffering, sinning and having conflicts.

मुहूर्तमपि जीवेच्च नर: शुक्लेन चिन्तयेत्।
कल्पमपि कष्टेन लोकद्वयविरोधिना।।1।।

2. One should not lament the past or worry about the future. The wise move in the present times.

गते शोको न कर्त्तव्यो भविष्यं नैव चिन्तयेत्।
वर्तमानेन कालेन प्रवर्तन्ते विचक्षणा:।।2।।

3. One's goodness of nature is sufficient to please deities, good men and one's father. Relatives are pleased by hospitality and entertainment. Learned men are pleased by keeping one's word.

स्वभावेन हिं तुष्यन्ति देवा: सत्पुरुषा पिता।
ज्ञातय: स्वन्नपानाभ्यां वाक्यदानेन पण्डिता:।।3।।

4. Oh, strange is the character of great men! They regard prosperity as a mere blade of grass, yet when they get it, they bend under its weight.

अहो बत विचित्राणि चरितानि महाऽऽत्मनाम्।
लक्ष्मी तृणाय मन्यन्ते तद्धारेण नमन्ति च।।4।।

5. One's fear stems from the one for whom one has an affection. All the sorrows are due to attachment. One should drop all attachment and live happily.

यस्य स्नेहो भयं तस्य स्नेहो दु:खस्य भाजनम:।
स्नेहमूलानि दु:खानि तानि त्यक्त्वा वसेत्सुखम्।।5।।

6. Anagatavidhata (One who prepares for the unseen future, a fish in a famous Panchatantra tale) and Pratyutpannamati (One who is alert and quick to react, another fish from the same story) – these two enjoyed happiness – Yadbhavishya (One who believes in the future taking care of itself, a fatalist fish from the same story) died.

अनागतविधाता च प्रत्युत्पन्नमतिस्तथा।
द्वावेतौ सुखमेधेते यद्भविष्यो विनश्यति।।6।।

7. If the king is a righteous one following the path of Dharma, so are the subjects. If he is a sinner, so are the subjects. The people follow the ruler. They are as their ruler is.

रात्रि धर्मिणि धर्मिष्ठा: पापे पापा: समे समा:।
राजानमनुवर्तन्ते यथा राजा तथा प्रजा:।।7।।

8. Consider a living person who has rejected Dharma as good as dead. Consider a dead person long-living if while alive he has been associated with Dharma.

जीवन्तं मृतवन्मन्ये देहिनं धर्मवर्जितम्।
मृतो धर्मेण संयुक्तो दीर्घजीवी न संशय:।।8।।

9. Meaningless as the bust of a male goat is the life of one who has none of the four achievements of man - Dharma, Artha, Kama and Moksha – righteousness, wealth, satisfaction of desire and spiritual liberation.

धर्मार्थकाममोक्षाणां यस्यैकोऽपि न विद्यते।
अजागलस्तनस्येव तस्य जन्म निरर्थकम्।।9।।

10. Mean people burning with acute envy at the achievements of others decry them because they are unable to follow their path.

दह्यमाना: सुतीव्रेण नीचा: पर-यशोऽग्निना।
अशक्तास्तत्पदं गन्तुं ततो निन्दा प्रकुर्वते।।10।।

11. A mind engrossed in property matters contributes to bondage. A mind without material concerns contributes to spiritual liberation. The mind is the reason behind man's bondage as well as liberation.

बन्धाय विषयाऽऽसक्तं मुक्त्यै निर्विषयं मन:।
मन एव मनुष्याणां कारणं बन्धमोक्षयो:।।11।।

12. When pride in one's body gets melted, one gets to know the Supreme Soul. One gets into a state of trance (*samadhi*) wherever the mind goes.

देहाभिमाने गलिते विज्ञाते परमात्मनि।
यत्र यत्र मनो याति तत्र तत्र समाधय:।।12।।

13. Who gets all his mind's desires fulfilled? Everything is controlled by fate. Hence, resort to being content.

ईप्सितं मनस: सर्वं कस्य सम्पद्यते सुखम्।
दैवाऽऽयत्तं यत: सर्वं तस्मात्सन्तोषमाश्रयेत्।।13।।

14. Men's actions (*karma*) govern their achievements (*phala*) and lead their intelligence (*buddhi*). Even then, noble and wise men perform their deeds with due consideration.

कर्यायत्तं फलं पुंसां बुद्धि: कर्मानुसारिणी।
तथापि सुधियश्याऽऽर्या: सुविचार्यैव कुर्वते।।14।।

15. Even where there are a thousand cows in the herd, the calf follows its own mother. The result of the deed one has done follows the doer in the same way.

यथा धेनुसहस्त्रेषु वत्सो गच्छति मातरम्।
तथा यच्च कृतं कर्म कर्तारमनुगच्छति।।15।।

16. One whose deeds in life are unorganised finds no happiness either among men or in forests. Amongst men, it is their very

company that tortures him. In the forests, he gets tortured by the giving up of all company.

अनवस्थितकार्यस्य न जने न वने सुखम्।
जने दहति संसर्गो वने सङ्गविवर्जनम्।।16।।

17. One digging with a shovel finds water in the earth; so does one who is keen to listen acquire the learning that a guru has.

यथा खनित्वा खनित्रेण भूतले वारि विन्दति।
तथा गुरुगतां विद्यां शुश्रूषुरधिगच्छति।।17।।

18. The guru gives on the all-important single letter Aum. He who does not show respect to that guru suffers as a dog for a hundred lives and then gets reborn as a *Chandala* (the lowest Hindu class).

एकाक्षरप्रदातरं यो गुरुं नाभिवन्दति।
श्वानयोनिशतं भुक्त्वा चाण्डालेष्वभिजायते।।18।।

19. Even the mountain Meru (supposedly the centre of the earth, the pivot) moves at the end of an era (*yuga*).The seven seas shift at the end of a *kalpa* . But the sages do not ever change their decided/declared stand (*pratipanna artha*).

युगान्ते प्रचलते मेरु: कल्पान्ते, सप्त सागरा:।
साधव: प्रतिपन्नार्थान् न चलन्ति कदाचन्।।1।।

## 14

1. On this earth there are just three jewels: water, food grain and words of wisdom. Stupid people assign the status of jewels to bits and pieces of stone.

पृथिव्यां त्रीणि रत्नानि जलमन्नं सुभाषितम्।
मूढै: पाषाणखण्डेषु रत्नसंज्ञा विधीयते।।1।।

2. These are the fruits of the tree of one's misdeeds: poverty, disease, sorrow, bondage and trouble.

दारिद्रयरोगदु:खानि बन्धनव्यसनानि च।
आत्माऽपराधवृक्षस्य फलान्येतानि देहिनाम् ।।2।।

3. One can get wealth again, a friend again, a wife again, and land again. All these can be regained but the bodily life cannot be got again and again.

पुनर्वित्तं पुनर्मित्रं पुनर्भार्या पुनर्मही।
एतत्सर्वं पुनर्लभ्यं न शरीरं पुन: पुन:।।3।।

4. Co-operation of many separate identities can win over the enemy. A bed of grass can counter/check the force of rain clouds.

बहूनां चैव सत्त्वानां समवायो रिपुंजय:।
वष्ज्ञधाराधरो मेघस्तृणेरपि निवार्यते।।4।।

5. By the very nature of the following things, they spread out by themselves: oil on water, secret told to the devious, donation to a fit recipient and scriptures instructed to wise man.

जले तैलूं खले गुह्यं पात्रे दानं मनागपि।
प्राज्ञे शास्त्रं स्वयं याति विस्तारं वस्तुशक्तित:।।5।।

6. If the thoughts that sick people have on hearing religious discourses and visiting the cremation ground were long-lasting, who would not have been freed from all bonds!

धर्माऽऽख्याने श्मशाने च रोगिणां या मतिर्भवेत्।
सा सर्वदैव तिष्ठेच्चेत् को न मुच्येत बन्धनात्।।6।।

7. If the way a repentant person thinks had been there earlier, who would not have reached great heights!

उत्पन्नपश्चात्तापस्य बुद्धिर्भवति यादृशी।
तादृशो यदि पूर्व स्यात् कस्य न स्यान्महोदय:।।7।।

8. One should not marvel at one's own charity, penance, bravery, knowledge, humility and rectitude. The earth contains many gems and jewels.

दाने तपसि शौर्ये वा विज्ञाने विनये नये।
विस्मयो न हि कर्त्तव्यो बहुरत्ना वसुन्धरा।।8।।

9. He who is in one's thoughts, even if he is situated far away, is not far away. He who is not in one's heart, even if he is nearby, is far away.

दूरस्थऽपि न दूरस्थो यो यस्य मनसि स्थित:।
यो यस्य हृदये नास्ति समीपस्थोऽपि दूरत:।।9।।

10. One should speak pleasingly to one whom one wants to harm. To lure and kill a deer, the hunter has to sing in a pleasant voice.

यस्य चाप्रियमिच्छेत तस्य ब्रूयात् सदा प्रियम्।
व्याधो मृगवधं कर्तुं गीतं गायति सुस्वरम्।।10।।

11. To the following four, being too close is ruinous while being too distant is ineffective: the king, the fire, the preceptor (guru) and women. They are to be served from mid-distance.

अत्यासन्ना विनाशाय दूरस्था न फलप्रदा:।
सेवितव्यां मध्यमागेन राजा वहिर्गुरु स्त्रिय:।।11।।

12. These six are quick to take one's life: the fire, water, women, fools, snakes and members of the royal family. They are to be served constantly and with care.

अग्निरोप: स्त्रियो मूर्खा सर्पा राजकुलानि च।
नित्यं यत्नेन सेव्यानि सद्य: प्राणहराणि षट्।।12।।

13. He lives on who has good qualities. He lives on who follows Dharma. He has a futile existence who has neither good qualities nor Dharma in him.

स जीवति गुणा यस्य यस्य धर्म: स जीवति।
गुणधर्मविहीनस्य जीवितं निष्प्रयोजनम्।।13।।

14. If you want to bring the world under your control by any one particular activity, prevent your cattle from going into the crops of others, that is, do not blame and slander others.

यदीच्छसि वशीकर्तुं जगदेकेन कर्मणा।
परापवादसस्येभ्यो गां चरन्तीं निवारय।।14।।

15. The wise man knows how to speak as per the requirement (of the situation), favour as per one's ability (to grant favours) and display anger as per one's power (to reprimand).

प्रस्तावसदृशं वाक्यं प्रभावसदृशं प्रियम्।
आत्मशक्तिसमं कोपं यो जानाति स पण्डित:।।15।।

16. The same substance becomes three as perceived by different men. A woman's body is a smelly corpse to an ascetic (yogi), a desirable woman to a sensual man, and flesh to a dog.

एक एव पदार्थस्तु त्रिधा भवित वीक्षित:।
कुणप: कामिनी मांसं योगिभि: कामिभि: श्वभि:।।16।।

17. The intelligent man does not disclose the knowledge of an effective medicine, codes of righteousness, shortcomings of the household, physical enjoyment, bad food and bad talk.

सुसिद्धमौपधं धर्मं गृहच्छिद्रं च मैथुनेम्।
कंभुवतं कुश्रतं चैव मतिमात्र प्रकाशयेत्।।17।।

18. Till the arrival of the universally popular spring, the cuckoo bides its time in silence.

तावन्मौनेन नीयन्ते कोकिलैश्चैव वासराः।
यावत्सर्वजनानन्ददायिनी वाक्रवर्तते।।18।।

19. One should dutifully hold on to the principles of right conduct, wealth, food grains, medicines and the words of the guru. Otherwise, one perishes.

धर्मं धनं च धान्यं च गुरोर्वचनमौषधम्।
सुगृहीतं च कर्त्तव्यमन्यथा तृ न जीवति।।19।।

20. Leave the company of evil men, resort to the company of the good. All day and all night, do good deeds. Constantly keep in mind the impermanence/transience of life.

त्येज दुर्जनसंसर्गं भज साधुसमागमम्।
कुरु पुण्यमहोरात्रं स्मर नित्यमनित्यताम्।।20।।

21. If one mixes and mingles with evil people with no discipline, foresight or perception, one is quickly ruined.

दुराचारी च दुरदृष्टिर्दुराऽऽवासी च दुर्जनः ।
यन्मैत्री क्रियते पुम्भिर्नरः शीघ्रं विनश्यति।।21।।

22. Affection is best displayed among equals, service among royalty, business among traders and a wonderful wife, at home.

समाने शोभते प्रीति राज्ञि सेवा च शोभते।
वाणिज्यं व्यवहारेषु दिव्या स्त्री शोभते गृहे।।22।।

23. Those who have neither learning, nor powers of penance, nor knowledge, good conduct, virtues or righteousness, are burdens upon the earth, quadruples with human appearances.

येषां न विद्या न तपो न दानं न ज्ञानं न शीलं न गुणो न धर्मः।
ते मर्त्यलोके भुवि भारभूता मनुष्यरूपेण मृगाश्चरन्ति।।23।।

24. The pot gets filled gradually by the drops that fall is into it. This the way it happens with the acquisition of all learning, wealth and spiritual worth.

जलबिन्दुनिपातेन क्रमशः पूर्यते घटः।
स हेतुः सर्वविद्यानां धर्मस्य च धनस्य च।।24।।

25. Upon attaining fame, Chanakya said: "I have just lifted a small hillock upon my arms and its praises are being sung of as that of your lifting the Govardahana mountain.You bear the three worlds and I bear only you upon my heart. O Keshava! What is the use of saying a lot on this.Good deeds yield great merits. That is all."

उर्व्यां कोऽपि महीधरो लघुतरो दोर्भ्यां धृतौ लीलया तेन
त्वं दिवि भूतले च सततं गोवर्धनो गीयसे
त्वां त्रैलोक्यधरं वहायि कुचयोरग्रेण नो गणयते किं वा
केशव भाषणेन बहुना पुण्यं यशस लभ्यते।।25।।

## 15

1. One whose heart gets melted by pity for all men has no need to keep his hair matted and his body anointed with ashes in order to attain knowledge and salvation.

यस्य चित्तं द्रवीभूतं कृपया सर्वजन्तुषु।
तस्य ज्ञानेन मोक्षेण किं जटाभस्मलेपनैः।।1।।

2. There is just one letter (*Aum*) that the guru makes the disciple comprehend. There is no object in the world by giving which the disciple can replay his debt to the preceptor.

एकमेवाक्षरं यस्तु गुरुः शिष्यं प्रबोधयेत्।
पृथिव्यां नास्ति तद्द्रव्यं यद्दत्वा चाऽनृणी भवेत् ।।2।।

3. One can react to the deceptive person and the thorn in just two ways; crush its face/tip with the shoe or give it up from a distance.

खलानां कण्टकानां च द्विविधैव प्रतिक्रिया।
उपानन्मुखभङ्गों वा दूरतो वा विसर्जनम्।।3।।

4. Even if he is powerful like the discus-bearing Vishnu, one whose clothes are dirty and teeth unclean, one who is a rough-spoken glutton asleep at sunrise and sunset, gets forsaken by Lakshmi, the deity of prosperity.

कुचैलिन दन्तमलोपसृष्टं बह्वाशिनं निष्ठुरभाषिणं च।
सूर्योदये वास्तमिते शयानं विमुंचति श्रीर्यदि चक्रपाणि:।।4।।

5. Allies forsake one without wealth. So do wives, servants and well-wishers. The purport of this is that wealth is the true friend in this world.

त्यजन्ति मित्राणि धनैर्विहीनं दाराश्च भृत्याश्च सुहृज्जनाश्च।
तं चार्थवन्तं पुनराश्रयन्ते अर्थो हि लोके पुरुषस्य बन्धु:।।5।।

6. Wealth earnt through unfair means last only for ten years. As soon as the eleventh year is reached, it vanishes without a trace.

अन्यायोपार्जितं द्रव्यं दश वर्षाणि विष्ठति।
प्राप्ते चैकादशे वर्षे समूलं तद् विनश्यति।।6।।

7. Inappropriate action may be appropriate for the great while an appropriate action may be inappropriate for the mean. Amrit, the elixir of life, was death to the demon Rahu while the poison became an ornament of Shankara (Neelakanttha or blue-necked Shiva).

अयुक्तं स्वामिनो युक्तं युक्तं नीचस्य दूषणम्।
अमृतं राहवे मृत्युर्विषं शङ्कर भूषणम्।।7।।

8. The right food is that which is left after the *Brahmanas* have partaken of it. That is the true friendship which is done with people who are not kinsmen. That is wisdom which does not lead to sin. That is an act of *dharma* which is performed without arrogance.

तद्भोजनं यद् द्विजभुक्तशेषं तत्सौहृदं यत्क्रियते परस्मिन्।
सा प्राज्ञता या न करोति पापं दम्भं विना य: क्रियतेस धर्म:।।8।।

9. A gem may be rolling at one's feet and glass (beads) may be carried on the head. But when it comes to buying and selling, the gem is evaluated as a gem and the glass as glass.

मणिर्लुण्ठति पादाग्रे काच: शिरसि धार्यते।
क्रयविक्रयवेलायां काच: काचो मणिर्मणि:।।9।।

10. The scriptures are endless, the arts are numerous. Time is short and many are the impediments. Hence one should seek out the essence of available material like swans drink only the milk from water that has milk in it.

अनन्तशास्त्रं बहुलाश्च विद्याः अल्पश्च कालो बहुविघ्नता च।
यत्सारभूतं तदुपासनीयं हंसो यथा क्षीरमिवाम्बुमध्यात्॥10॥

11. He is called a *Chandala* who eats his own meal without showing respect to (that is, offering a meal) to one who has come to his door travelling a long distance, getting tired on the way or without having his purpose served.

दूरागतं पथि श्रान्तं वृथा च गृहमागतम्।
अनर्चयित्वा यो भुङ्क्ते स वै चाण्डाल उच्यते॥11॥

12. People may read all the four *Vedas*, and many holy scriptures, and yet have no realization of the Self, like the ladle has no idea of the taste of the curry it ladles out.

पठन्ति चतुरो वेदान् धर्मशास्त्राण्यनेकशः।
आत्मानं नैव जानन्ति दर्वी पाकरसं यथा॥12॥

13. In the ocean of life, the *Brahmana* is like a blessed ship that acts in a contrary way, saving people taking shelter under it and making people astride it (on it) fall down.

धन्या द्विजमयी नौका विपरीता भवार्णवे।
तरन्त्यधोगताः सर्वे उपरिस्थाः पतन्तयधः॥13॥

14. Even the bright moon whose body contains the immortalizing *Amrita*, and who lords over medicinal herbs loses its glow when it enters the orbit of the sun. Who does not lose importance on living in the house of another?

अयममृतनिधानं नायकोऽप्यौषणीनां अमृतमयशरीरः
कान्तियुक्तोऽपि चन्द्रः।
भवति विगतरश्मिर्मण्डलं प्राप्य भानोः
परसदननिविष्टः को लघुत्वं न याति॥14॥

15. The honeybee which used to enter the centre of lotuses and get replete and lazy with nectar forced by Fate to come to a different country considers the juice of Kutaja , blossoms growing on the rocks, to be great.

अलिरयं नलिनीदलमध्यगः कमलिनी-रन्दमदालसः।
विधिवशात्परदेशमुपागतः कुटजपुष्परसं बहु मन्यते॥15॥

16. "O lord!" (Lakshmi says to Vishnu) "I have left the abode of *Brahmanas* forever because I have been displeased by them. One

of them (Bhrigu) in his anger kicked my husband (Vishnu himself) on the chest. They carry within the cavity of their mouth (that is, constantly pray to) the deity Sarasvati who is my sister as well as my rival. Every day they tear up my home – the lotus - for the purpose of worshipping Umakanta (Shiva)."

पीत: क्रुद्धेन तातश्चरणतलहतो वल्लभो येन रोषाद्
आबाल्याद्विप्रवर्यैः स्ववदनविवरे धार्यते वैरिणी मे।
गेहं मे छेदयन्ति प्रतिदिवसमुमाकान्तपूजानिमित्तं तस्मात्खिन्न
सदाहं द्विजकलनिलयं नाथ युक्तं त्यजामि।।16।।

17. Indeed there are many forms of bonds. But the bond of love form the strongest ropes. Even though they are experts at piercing holes out of wood and coming out, bees become inactive in the cell formed by a lotus furled (at night).

बन्धनानि खलु सन्ति बहूनि प्रेमरज्जुदृढबन्धनमन्यत्।
दारुभेदनिपुणोऽपि षडंघ्रिर्निष्क्रियो भवति पङ्कजकोशे ।।17।।

18. Even when cut down, the sandalwood tree does not stop emitting fragrance. Even when aged the leader of an elephant herd does not stop its amorous play. Even when placed in the crusher the sugarcane does not stop giving out sweetness. Even though on the decline, one from a family of standing does not stop behaving according to the codes of good conduct.

छिन्नोऽपि चन्दन्तरुर्न जहाति गन्ध
वृद्धोऽपि वारणपतिर्न जहाति लीलाम्।
यन्त्रार्पितो मधुरतां न जहाति चेक्षुः क्षीणेऽपि
न त्यजति शीलगुणान् कुलीन:।।18।।

## 16

1. If we have not meditated upon the feet of God, lived worldly life as prescribed, not earned Dharma which is capable of opening the door to heaven nor embraced the woman's body even in dreams, we are only axes that have severed off our mothers' youth.

न ध्यातंपदमीश्वरस्य विधिवस्तंसारविच्छित्तये
स्वर्गद्वारकपाटपाटनपटुर्धर्मोऽपि नोपार्जित: ।
नारीपीनपयोधरोरुयुगलं स्वप्नेऽपि नालिङ्गितं
मातुः केवलमेव यौवनवनच्छेदे कुठारा वयम:।।1।।

2. Women have no consistency in matters of physical enjoyment. They chatter to someone, look enticingly at another and think of yet another in their hearts.

जल्पन्ति सार्धमन्येन पश्यन्त्यन्यं सविभ्रमा:।
हृदय चिन्तयन्त्यन्यं न स्त्रीणामेकतो रति:।।2।।

3. He who, out of delusion, thinks a woman to be devoted to him, goes under her control and dances to her tune like a bird kept as a pet for playing with.

यो मोहान्मन्यते मूढो रक्तेयं मथि कामिनी।
स तस्य वशगो भूत्वा नृत्येत् क्रीड़ा-शकुन्तवत्।।3।।

4. Who has not become arrogant on attaining wealth? Which man involved in worldly affairs has not run into trouble? Who in this world has not been smitten by women? Who has always remained in royal favour? Who has passed unnoticed by time? Who has attained glory by begging? Who has gone his way comfortably after falling into the snare/trap of evil men?

कोऽर्थान् प्राप्य न गर्वितो विषयिण: कस्यापदोऽतं गता:
स्त्रीभि: कस्य न खण्डितं भुवि मन: को नाम राज्ञां प्रिय:।
क: कालस्य न गोचरत्वमगमत्कोऽर्थी गतौ गौरवं को वा
दर्जनवागुरासु पतित: क्षेमेण यात: पथि।।4।।

5. No one has built a golden deer, no one has seen or heard of one. Yet Rama, the descendant of King Raghu, thirsted for it. That is how, at the time of destruction, one's intelligence works perversely.

न निर्मित: केन न दृष्टपूर्व: न श्रूयते हेममय: कुरुङ्ग।
तथाऽपि तृष्णा रघुनन्दनस्य विनाशकाले विपरीतबुद्धि।।5।।

6. One attains excellence by one's qualities, not by sitting on high positions. Even if the crow sits on top of a palace, does it become Garuda, the king of birds and carrier of Vishnu?

गुणेरुत्तमतां याति नोच्चैरासनसंस्थिता:।
प्रासादशिखरस्थोऽपि काक: किं गरुडायते।।6।।

7. Everywhere it is not the greatness of wealth that is revered, but good qualities. A thin sliver of the moon (say, the moon on the

second day of the bright fortnight) is worshipped (considered auspicious), rather than the full moon.

गुणा: सर्वत्र पूज्यन्ते न महत्योऽपि सम्पद:।
पूर्णेन्दु किं तथा वन्द्यो निष्कलङ्कों यता कृश:।।7।।

8. He whose virtues others proclaim is virtuous even without having any virtues. Even Indra, the king of gods, loses his weight and importance by himself proclaiming his own virtues.

पर-प्रोक्तगुणो यस्तु निर्गुणोऽपि गुणी भवेत्।
इन्द्रोऽपि लघुतां याति स्वयं प्रख्यापितैर्गुणै:।।8।।

9. Good qualities become more attractive in a man with a good conscience just as even priceless jewels await a setting in gold.

विवेकिनमनुप्राप्ता गुणा यान्ति मनोज्ञताम्।
सतरां रत्नमाभाति चामीकरनियोजितम्।।9।।

10. What is the use of wealth and prosperity (Lakshmi) which is only like a wife.That (wealth) is to be respected which is like the prostitute (*veshya*) who helps even the passer-by. (Wealth should be acquired for public good rather than private use.)

गुणै: सर्वज्ञतुल्योऽपि सीदत्येको निराश्रय:
अन्ध्यमपि माणिक्यं हेमाश्रयमपेक्षते।
किं तया क्रियते लक्ष्म्या या बधूरिव केवला।
या तु वेश्येव सा मान्या पथिकैरपि भुज्यते।।10।।

11. All living being have passed away, are passing away and will pass away without being fully satisfied with the wealth, the years of life, the women and the meals they have had.

अतिक्लेशेन य चार्था धर्मस्यातिक्रमेण तु।
शत्रूणां प्रणिपातेन ते ह्यर्था मा भवन्तु मे।।11।।

12. All the gifts of charity and all the acts of ceremonial sacrifices get eroded. But donations to the deserving and protection to all creatures never do so.

क्षीयन्तेसर्वदानानि यज्ञहोमबलिक्रिया:।
न क्षीयते पात्रदानमभयं सर्वदेहिनाम्।।12।।

13. A blade of grass is very light. Cotton is even lighter than grass. One who keeps on asking for charity is lighter even than

cotton. Why then does the wind not blow him away? (The wind answers:) "For, even of me he will ask something".

तृणंलघु तृणात्तूलं तूलादपि च याचकः।
वायना किं न नीतोऽसौ मामयं याचयिष्यति।।13।।

14. It is better to give up one's life rather than live on with one's pride/self-respect broken/hurt. It hurts for a moment to give up one's life. It hurts every instant if one's self-respect is hurt.

वरं प्राणपरित्यागी मानभङ्गेन जीवनात्।
प्राणतयागे क्षणं दुःखं मानभङ्गे दिने दिने।।14।।

15. All creatures get satisfied by gifts of sweet words. Such words only are therefore to be spoken. Why be stingy/ mean with words?

प्रियवाक्यप्रदानेन सर्वे तुष्यन्ति जन्तवः।
तस्मात्तदेव वक्तव्यं वचने का दरिद्रता।।15।।

16. The bitter tree of life has but two fruits: wise and well-spoken words and the company of wise and good men.

संसारकुटविषवक्षस्य द्वे फले अमतोपम।
सुभाषितं च सुस्वादु सङ्गतिः सुजने जने।।16।।

17. The practice of charity, study and meditation that one has been habitually doing in previous lives, they only are practiced again (in this life) by virtue of the connection of habit (*abhyasa-yoga*).

जन्म-जन्मन्यभ्यस्तं यद् दानमध्यवनं तपः।
तनैवाऽभ्यासयोगेन तदेवाभ्यस्यते पुनः।।17।।

18. When the time comes to apply them, both the learning confined to books and wealth in the possession of others are futile.

पुस्तकेषु च या विद्या परहस्तेषु यद्धनम्।
उत्पन्नेषु च कार्येषु न सा विद्या न तद्धनमः।।18।।

## 17

1. Learning acquired from books and not from the association of a guru/preceptor, even if acquired, is not true learning just as an illegitimate son is not one who can take his own place in a social gathering.

पुस्तकप्रत्ययाधीतं नाधीतं गुरुसन्निधौ।
सभामध्ये न शोभन्तेजारगर्भा इव स्त्रियः।।1।।

2. One should re-act to action and counter violence by violence. One should behave in a wicked way to the wicked. There is nothing wrong in that.

कृते प्रतिकृतं कुर्याद् हिंसने प्रतिहिंसनम्।
तत्र दोषो न पतति दुष्टे दुष्टं समाचरेत्।।2।।

3. The distant, the difficult, and the far-away can all be overcome by practice of austerity (*tapasya*). It is *tapasy*a which is difficult to overcome.

यद्दूरं यद्दुराराध्यं यच्च दूरे व्यवस्थितम्।
तत्सर्वं तपसा साध्यं तपो हि दुरतिक्रमम्।।3।।

4. If one is greedy, what need does he have of evil company? If there is slanderous tendency, what need is there for sin? If there is truth, what is the need for penance? If the heart is clean, what is the need of going on pilgrimage? If there is courtesy, what is the need for virtues? If there is glory, what is the need for decorations? If there are valuable skills, what is the need of wealth? If there is dis-honour/ill-repute, what is the need for death?

लोभश्चेदगुणेन किं पिशुनता यद्यस्ति किं पातकै:
सत्यं चेत्तपसा च किं शुचि मनो यद्यस्ति तीर्थेन किम्।
सौजन्यं यदि किं गुणै: सुमहिमा यद्यस्ति किं मण्डनै:
सद्विद्या यदि किं धनैरपयशो यद्यस्ति किं मृत्युना।।4।।

5. Shankha, the conch-shell (Shankha-chuda) has the sea for his father and the goddess Lakshmi for his own sister born of the same womb, the sea. But he goes begging with mendicants. A mean person never attains high status.

पिता रत्नाकरो यस्य लक्ष्मीर्यस्त सहोदरा।
शङ्खो भिक्षाटनं कुर्यान्नाऽदत्तमुपतिष्ठते ।।5।।

6. Incapacitated, one should become a *Sadhu* (mendicant). Bereft of wealth, one should become a *Brahmachari* (junior ascetic). A sick man should become a devotee of gods and an aged woman should become a faithful/loyal/ devoted wife.

अशक्तस्तु भवेत्साधुर्ब्रह्मचारी च निर्धनः।
व्याधिष्ठो देवभक्तश्च वृद्धा नारी पतिव्रता॥6॥

7. There is no act of charity greater than that of giving food and water. There is no day holier than *Dvadashi*, the twelfth day of the bright fortnight. There is no chanting superior to the *Gayatri-mantra*, and no deity superior than one's mother.

नाऽन्नोदकसमं दानं न तिथिर्द्वादशी समा ।
न गायत्र्याः परो मन्त्रो न मातुः परं दैवतमः॥7॥

8. Takshaka, the king of snakes, has his poison in his teeth. The bee has his poison in his head (from where the sting injects it).The scorpion has his poison at his tail. The evil man has his poison all over his body.

तक्षकस्य विषं दनते मक्षिकायास्तु मस्तके।
वृश्चिकस्य विषं पुच्छे सर्वाङ्गे दुर्जने विषम्॥8॥

9. If a wife practices rituals and goes on fasts without the approval of her husband, she takes away from the life of her husband and goes to hell.

पत्युराज्ञां विना नारी उपोष्य व्रतचारिणी।
आयुष्यं हरते भर्तुः सा नारी नरकं व्रजेत्॥9॥

10. A woman gets cleansed more by drinking the water in which her husband has washed his feet, than by acts of charity, ritual fasts or pilgrimage.

न दानैः शुध्यते नारी नोपवासशतैरपि।
न तीर्थसेवया तद्वद् भर्तुः पादोदकैर्यथा॥10॥

11. The hands are beautified by the act of giving in charity, not by bangles. The body is purified by bathing, not by sandalwood paste decoration. Satisfaction comes from being shown respect, not from mere eating. Liberation (from the world) comes from knowledge, not from decorating the body (with sandalwood markings).

दानेन पाणिर्न तु कङ्कणेन स्नाने शुद्धिर्न तु चन्दनेन।
मानेन तृप्तिर्न तु भोजनेन ज्ञानेन मुक्तिर्न तु मण्डनेन॥11॥

12. Going the barber's house to shave, anointing stone (images of deities) with fragrant paste, and looking at one's reflection in

water detract from prosperity on par with Shakra/Indra, the king of the gods.

नाषितस्य गृहे क्षौरं पाषाणे गन्धलेपनम्।
आत्मरूपं जले पश्यन् शक्रस्यापि श्रियं हरेत्।।12।।

13. The Tundi fruit robs one of his senses while the Vacha fruit quickly brings one to his senses. Women quickly take away men's strength while milk quickly builds it up.

सद्य: प्रज्ञाहरा तुण्डी सद्य: प्रज्ञाकरी वचा।
सद्य: शक्तिहरा नारी सद्य: शक्तिकरं पय:।।13।।

14. Those who constantly think of helping others have their troubles cleared and attain prosperity at every step.

परोपकरणं येषां जागर्ति हृदये सताम्।
नश्यन्ति विपदस्तेषां सम्पद: स्यु: पदे पदे।।14।।

15. If one has a wife both charming and virtuous, a son endowed with the quality of modesty, and the birth of a son through the son, what more does the abode of gods hold for him?

यदि रामा यदि च रमा यद्यपि तनयो विनयगुणोपेत:।
यदि तनये तनयोत्पत्ति: सुरवरननगरे किमोधिक्यम्।।15।।

16. Men and beasts are just the same in respect of the following: eating, sleeping, experiencing fear and getting physical pleasure. It is knowledge than man has as a special distinction. Without knowledge man is the same as a beast.

आहारनिद्राभयमैथुनंच सामान्यमेतत: पशुभिर्नराणाम:।
ज्ञान नराणामधिको विशेषो ज्ञानेन हीना: पशुभि: समाना:।।16।।

17. If the huge elephant with his intelligence dulled by intoxicating secretions from his decorated head flaps his ears to drive away the bees that come asking for it, he only harms the decorations on his cheeks. The bees go again and sit on the budding lotuses.

दानार्थिनो मधुकरा यदि कर्णतालैर्
दूरीकृता: करिवरेण मदान्धबुद्धया।
तस्यैव गण्डयुगमण्डनहानिरेषा भृड्गा:
पुनर्विकचपद्मवने वसन्ति।।17।।

18. The king, the prostitute, Yama (the deity of Death), the fire, the thief, the child, the and, eighth, the tax-collector who pesters the entire village –these do not understand the suffering of others.

राजा वेश्या यमो ह्यग्निस्तस्करो बालयाचकौ।
परदु:खं न जानन्ति श्रष्टमो ग्रामकण्टक:।।18।।

19. (Someone asks a maiden walking with eyes modestly cast down:) "O maiden! Why are you searching for, looking downwards? What possession of yours is it that has fallen down?" (The maiden replies:) "You fool! Don't you know that the pearl of my youth is gone?"

अध: पश्यसि किं बाले पतितं तव किं भुवि।
रे रे मूर्ख न जानासि गतं तारुण्यमौक्तिकम्।।19।।

20. O Ketaki (a fragrant white flower)! You are the resort of snakes, bear no fruits, have thorns, are crooked, muddy, and difficult to reach. Yet by your fragrance you befriend all creatures. One virtue can certainly kill all vices.

व्यालाश्रयाऽपि विफलापि सकण्टकाऽपि ।
वक्राऽपि पङ्किल-भवाऽपि दुरासदाऽपि।
गन्धेन बन्धुरसि केताकि सर्वजन्तोर्
एको गुण: खलु निहन्ति समस्तदोषान्।।20।।

21. Youth, wealth, power and lack of conscience…any one of these can singly destroy man, not to speak of when all four of them are together.

ग्रीयर्स वनसम्पत्ति: प्रभ्जुत्वमविवेकता।
एकैकमाषणर्क्षाय किमु यत्र चतुष्टयम्।।21।।

22. One whose heart constantly has the wish to help others finds all his troubles getting destroyed and wealth accruing to him at every step.

परोपकरणं येगां जागर्ति हृदये सताम्।
नश्यन्ति विपदस्तेषां सम्पद: स्यु पदे-पदे।।22।।

❒

# 5

# Chanakya Sutra

***This is in eight sections adding up to 636 tenets in the form of short sentences, sometimes even phrases. Again, the sections are neither thematic nor equal in length.***

**1**

1. It is righteousness (*Dharma*) which is at the root of happiness.

सुखस्य मूलं धर्मः।

2. It is material well-being (*Artha*) which is at the root of *dharma*.

धर्मस्य मूलमर्थः।

3. It is the governance of a kingdom (*rajya*) which is at the root of material well-being.

अर्थस्य मूलं राज्यम्

4. It is the conquest of the senses (*indriyajaya*) which is at the root of a kingdom.

राज्यस्य मूलमिन्द्रियजयः।

5. It is educated behaviour (*vinaya*) which is at the root of the conquest of senses.

इन्द्रियजयस्य मूलं विनयः।

6. It is the reverence of mature and elderly (*vriddha*) people that is at the root of education.

विनयस्य मूलं वृद्धोपसेवा।

7. Special learning (*vigyana*) comes from the reverence of mature, elderly people.

वृद्धोपसेवाया विज्ञानम्।

8. It is by this special learning that the king should govern/discharge his duties.

विज्ञानेनात्मानं संपादयेत्।

9. The king who discharges his duties is the one who can conquer his own self.

संपादितात्मा जितात्मा भवति।

10. It is the one who has conquered himself (is in command of himself) who acquires all material means of well-being (*sarvartha*).

जितात्मा सर्वार्थैस्संयुज्जयते।

11. It is material means of well-being which lead to the prosperity of the people.

अर्थसंपत् प्रकृतिसंपदं करोति।

12. The kingdom can run even without a leader or king if its people have prosperity.

प्रकृतिसंपदा ह्यनायकमपि राज्यं नीयते।

13. The wrath/anger of the people is more serious than all other types of wrath.

प्रकृतिकोपस्सर्वकोपेभ्यो गरीयान्।

14. To be without a king or leader is better than being with a king who does not have educated behaviour (*vinaya*).

अविनीतस्वामिलाभात् अस्वामिलाभः श्रेयान्।

15. Once he has made himself fit (for his duty), the king should seek advisors/ministers.

संपादद्यात्मानमन्विच्छेत् सहायान।

16. Without an advisor, one (the king) has no steady counsel/advice.

नासहायस्य मन्त्रनिश्चयः।

17. A single wheel cannot move (a vehicle).

नैकं चक्रं परिभ्रमति।

18. A respectable king should make a decision about an issue only after considering a second respectable person (who may have a counter-opinion).

मानी प्रतिमानिनमात्मनि द्वितीयं मन्त्रमुत्पादयेत्।

19. One who helps in happiness as well as sorrow is the true support.

सहायः समसुखदुःखः।

20. The king should not, out of affection/fondness, take the counsel/advice of one without educated conduct (*vinaya*).

अविनीतं स्नेहमात्रेण न मन्त्रे कुर्वीत।

21. Only the learned ones checked by tests (to be free from fraud) should be made ministers.

श्रुतवन्तमुपधाशुद्धं मन्त्रिणं कुर्वीत।

22. All jobs should begin with deliberation and consultation.

मन्त्रमूलास्सर्वारम्भाः।

23. The success of the job depends on keeping the deliberation/counseling secret.

मन्त्ररक्षणे कार्यसिद्धिर्भवति।

24. One who leaks out the deliberation ruins the job.

मन्त्रनिःस्रावी सर्वमपि कार्यं नाशयति।

25. Negligence or blunder leads to defection to the opponents.

प्रमादात् द्विषतां वशमुपयास्यति।

26. The deliberations should be kept secret from every outlet.

सर्वद्वारेभ्यो मन्त्रो रक्षितव्यः।

27. Good ministerial deliberations enhance the kingdom's prosperity.

मन्त्रसंपदा राज्यं वर्धते।

28. Secrecy of ministerial deliberation is most important.

श्रेष्ठतमां मन्त्रगुप्तिमाहुः।

29. Ministerial deliberation is a lamp that enlightens one who cannot see the right course of action.

कार्यान्धस्य प्रदीपो मन्त्र।

30. While consulting his ministers, the king should not quarrel with them.

मन्त्रकाले न मत्सर: कर्तव्य:।

31. Deliberations show up the defects of others .

मन्त्रचक्षुषा परच्छिद्राण्यवलोकयन्ति।

32. It is convincing when three people say the same thing.

त्रयाणामैकवाक्ये एवासम्प्रत्यय:।

33. It is the ministers who perceive what course of action is to be followed and what is not.

कार्याकार्यतत्वार्थदर्शिनो मन्त्रिण:।

34. The secrecy of the advice of ministers gets lost if it spreads to six ears, i.e., to several people.

षट्कर्णाद्भिद्यते मन्त्र:।

35. A friend is one who is affectionate even in situations of difficulty.

आपत्सु स्नेहसंयुक्तं मित्रम्।

36. Strength comes through the support of friends.

मित्रसङ्गहेण बलं सम्पद्यते।

37. The strong (*balavana*) king tries to acquire what is not already acquired (*alabdham*).

बलवानलब्धलाभे प्रयतते।

38. A lazy (*alasa*) king/person cannot acquire additional wealth that has yet not been earned (*alabdham*).

अलब्धलाभो नालसस्य।

39. A lazy king/person cannot even maintain/protect (*rakshana*) already acquired wealth (*labdham*).

अलसेन लब्धमपि रक्षितुं न शक्यते।

40. Nor can a lazy king/person increase (*vivardhana*) his already acquired wealth (*labdham*).

न चालसस्य रक्षितं विवर्धते।

41. He (a lazy one) nurtures neither servants and employees nor wise and expert people.

नासौ भृत्यान् पोषयति, न तीर्थं प्रतिपादयति च।

42. The principles of governance (*rajatantra*) consist of four tasks/activities: acquiring what has not yet been acquired (*alabdha labha*), protecting/guarding it (*labdha rakshanam*), expanding it (*labdha vivardhanam*) and distributing it (*bhritya preshanam*)

अलब्धलाभादिचतुष्टयं राज्यतन्त्रम्।

43. State policy (*rajya tantra*) comes within the scope of political principles (*Niti-shastra*).

तच्च राज्यतन्त्रमायत्तं नीतिशास्त्रेषु।

44. Internal administrative policy (*tantra*) and foreign policy (*avapa*) both are within the scope of State policy (*rajya tantra*).

राज्यतन्त्रेष्वायत्तौ तन्त्रावापौ।

45. Internal policy (*tantra*) is related only to administrative matters within the own country.

तन्त्रं स्वविषयकृत्येष्वायत्तम्।

46. Foreign policy (*avapa*) relates to the matters within the ring or circle (*mandala*) of adjoining/neighbouring countries

आवापो मण्डलनिविष्टः।

47. Treaties of war and peace (*sandhi-vigraha*) emanate from the ring of other countries, i.e., neighbouring countries.

सन्धिविग्रहयोनिर्मण्डलः।

48. The king should be well-versed in Political Principles (*Niti-shastra*).

नीतिशास्त्रानुगो राजा।

49. A king with whom there is constant conflict (because of the territories being adjoining) becomes an enemy or rival (*shatru*).

अनन्तरप्रकृतिश्शत्रुः।

50. A king who is the enemy of the enemy-king (because of having a kingdom adjoining that of the enemy-king) becomes an ally (*mitra*).

एकान्तरितं मित्रमिष्यते।

51. It is because of some reason that enmities and alliances get created.

हेतुतश्शत्रुमित्रे भविष्यतः।

52. A king who is getting weaker should make an alliance (i.e., go for a treaty of peace).

हीयमानस्सन्धिं कुर्वीत।

53. Strength/power is the reason for making alliances.

तेजो हि सन्धानहेतुस्तदर्थानाम्।

54. Unheated iron does not get fixed/forged with iron that is hot.

नातप्तलोहो लोहेन सन्धीयते।

55. The strong should have a war with the weak and not with a king who is equally strong or stronger.

बलवान् हीनेन विगृह्णीयात्, न ज्यायसा समेन वा।

56. To have a war with the powerful/strong is to have foot soldiers face the elephant brigade. It will get destroyed like an unbaked earthen pot striking another unbaked one.

गजेन पादयुद्धमिव बलवद्विग्रहः, आमपात्रमप्यामेन सह विनश्यति।

57. The king should observe and study the moves of the enemy.

अरि प्रयतनमभिसमीक्षेत ।

58. The king should study enemy movements even if he goes to one of them for an agreement of peace.

संध्यायैकतो वा यायात्

59. The king should keep oneself guarded from the attack of enemies.

अमित्रविरोधादात्मरक्षामावसेत्

60. The weak king should resort to the strong king.

शक्तिहीनो बलवंतमाश्रयेत्

61. Resorting to a weak king can only bring sorrow.

दुर्वलाश्रयो दुःखमावहति

62. After resorting to a (strong) king, the weak king should act as one does near a fire.

अग्निवद्राजानमाश्रयेत्

63. One should not act contrary to him (against his wishes).

राज्ञः प्रतिकुलं नाचरेत्

64. One should not appear before him in an insubordinate or arrogant guise.

उद्धतवेषधरो न भवेत् ।

65. One should not mimic the deities (or, copy the superior king's ways).

न देवचरितम् चरेत्

66. If the king has two enemies quarrelling with him, he should create an enmity/quarrel (*dvaidheebhava*) between them.

द्वयोरपीर्व्यतोः द्वैवीभावं कुर्वीत

67. Success does not come to the efforts of king addicted to vices.

न व्यसनपरस्य कार्यावाप्तिः

68. A king who is slave to his sensual pleasures perishes even if he has a vast army (with all its four divisions).

इंद्रिय वशवर्ती चतुरंगवानपि विनश्यति ।

69. A king addicted to gambling does not get any work done.

नास्ति कार्यम् द्युतप्रवृत्तस्य ।

70. A king addicted to hunting does not achieve either Dharma or Artha.

मृगयापरस्य धर्मार्थौ विनश्यतः ।

71. A king addicted to desire (full of lust) cannot perform any function.

न कामासक्तस्य कार्यानुष्ठानम् ।

72. (However) Pursuit of material welfare (Artha) is not a vice.

अर्थेषणा न व्यसनेषु गण्यते ।

73. The goddess of prosperity abandons a king who is complacent/ satisfied with his material well-being (Artha).

अर्थतोषिणम् हि राजानं श्रीः परित्यजति ।

74. The harshness of words burns more than fire.

अग्निदाहादपि विशिष्टम् वाक्पारुष्यम्।

75. A king who deals out very harsh punishment becomes disliked by all.

दण्डपारुष्यात् सर्वजनद्वेष्यो भवति ।

76. The enemy can be brought under control (only) by is *Dandaniti* (principles of using the ruling rod and imposing penalty).

अमित्रो दण्डनीत्यमायत्तम् ।

77. The king should firmly stand upon *Dandaniti* and so protect his subjects.

दण्डनीतिमधितिष्ठन् प्रजाससंरक्शति ।

78. It is the principles of *Danda* which augments the king's wealth.

दण्ड सम्पदा योजयति ।

79. Without the sceptre, there occurs the lack of *Dharma*, *Artha* and *Kama* (known as the *Trivarga*).

दण्डाभावे त्रिवर्गाभावः

80. It is because of (the fear of) the principles of *Danda* that people do not do what ought not to be done.

न दण्डादकार्याणि कुर्वन्ति

81. The king's own protection (self-defence) is dependent on *Dandaniti*.

दण्डनीत्यामायत्तमात्मरक्षणम्।

82. If oneself (the king) is protected, everyone is protected.

आत्मनि रक्षिते सर्व रक्षितं भवति।

83. One's prosperity and destruction are within one's control.

आत्मायत्तौ वृद्धिविनाशौ।

84. The *Dandaniti* principles should be applied judiciously/ knowledgably.

दण्डो हि विज्ञानेन प्रणीयते।

85. Even if weak, the king should never be insulted/belittled.

दुर्बलोऽपि राजा नावमन्तव्यः ।

86. Fire has no weakness.

नास्त्यग्नेर्दौर्बल्यमः।

87. It is the ruling rod which establishes all occupations/ livelihoods (*vritti*).

दण्डे प्रणीयते वृत्तिः।

88. Acquisition of material welfare is rooted in occupations.

वृत्तिमूलमर्थलाभः।

89. Righteousness and pleasure (*Dharma* and *Kama*) are rooted in the acquisition of material welfare (*Artha*).

अर्थमूलौ धर्मकामौ।

**2**

1. It is Material Welfare (*Artha*) which is the basis of all kinds of work, so that it is performed successfully with little effort.

अर्थमूलं सर्वं कार्यम्, यदल्पप्रयत्नात् कार्यसिद्धिर्भवति।

2. Work performed with a strategy is not difficult.

उपायपूर्वं कार्यं न दुष्करं स्यात्।

3. Work performed without any strategy, even if it is performed, gets destroyed.

अनुपायपूर्वं कार्यं कृतमपि विनश्यति।

4. For people who want work to be done, a strategy is the only help.

कार्यार्थिनामुपाय एव सहायः।

5. With a man's spiritedness (*purushakarena*), work can become a mission/objective.

कार्यं पुरुषकारेण लक्ष्यं संपद्यते।

6. Fortune/luck follows spiritedness.

पुरुषकारमनुवर्तते दैवम्।

7. Without fortune/luck, even work performed with great effort is fruitless.

दैवं विनाऽतिप्रयत्नं यत् करोतितद्विफलभ्।

8. One who is not calm and composed cannot perform any work.

असमाहितस्य कार्यं न विद्यते।

9. One should begin work only after deliberating and deciding upon it.

पूर्वनिश्चित्य पश्चात् कार्यमारभेत।

10. One should not procrastinate in between tasks.

कार्यान्तरे दीर्घसूत्रता न कर्तव्या।

11. One who is unsteady of purpose does not attain success.

न चलचित्तस्य कार्यावाप्तिः।

12. Disregarding the means at hand breaks the continuity of works.

हस्तगतावमाननात् कार्यव्यतिक्रमो भवति।

13. It is rare to find work that is faultless.

दोषवर्जितानि कार्याणि दुर्लभानि।

14. One should not begin a job encumbered with difficulties.

दुरनुबन्धं कार्य नारभेत।

15. He who knows the right time for a job succeeds at it.(In contemporary terms, this is Time Management.)

कालवित् कार्यं साधयेत्।

16. Exceeding the time for a task leads to time itself consuming up its results.

कालातिक्रमात् काल एव फलं पिबति।

17. Not for a moment should one waste time.

क्षणं प्रति कालविक्षेपं न कुर्यात् सर्वकृत्येषु।

18. One should begin a task after analyzing its appropriate place and possible consequences.

देशकालविभागौ ज्ञात्वा कार्यमारभेत।

19. A task which is not favoured by fortune, gets difficult even if it is easy.

दैवंहीनंकार्य सुसाधमपि दुससाधंभवति।

20. A learned man examines the time and the location.

नीतिज्ञो देशकालौ परीक्षेत।

21. The goddess of prosperity long favours the judicious man.

परीक्ष्यकारिणि श्रीश्चिरं तिष्ठति।

22. All kinds of riches should be collected by all kinds of means.

सर्वाश्च संपदः सर्वोपायेन परिगृह्णीयात्।

23. If he acts without due scrutiny/testing/analysis, even a lucky man loses the favour of Lakshmi, the goddess of prosperity.

भाग्यवन्तमप्यपरीक्ष्यकारिणं श्रीः परित्यजति।

24. One should scrutinize/test through knowledge as well as inference.

ज्ञात्वाऽनुमानैश्च परीक्षा कर्तव्या ।

25. In the very job in which one is skilled/efficient, should one be put. (This is Division of Labour in terms of Economics.)

यो यस्मिन् कर्मणि कुशलस्तं तस्मिन्नेव योजयेत्।

26. The one who knows strategy or the ways and means can make a difficult job easy.

दुस्साधमपि सुसाधं करोत्युपायज्ञः।

27. One should not make much of the work of an ignorant person even if it is indeed accomplished.

अज्ञानिना कृतमपि न बहुमन्तव्यम्, यादृच्छिकत्वात्।

28. Circumstances or fortunes can transform even a worm.

कृमयोऽपि हि कदाचित् रूपान्तराणि कुर्वन्ति।

29. Only when a task is accomplished should it be revealed.

सिद्धस्यैव कार्यस्य प्रकाशनं कर्तव्यम्।

30. Even the work of the learned get vitiated by disturbing factor, fortuitous or human.

ज्ञानवतामपि दैवमानुषदोषात् कार्याणि दुष्यन्ति।

31. One should counteract disturbances that are fortuitous by propitiating rituals.

दैवं दोषं शान्तिकर्मणा प्रतिषेधयेत्।

32. One should counteract human disturbing factors by strategy.

मानुषीं कार्यविपत्तिं कौशलेन विनिवारयेत्।

33. The stupid describe the problems of a task once it is (already) in trouble.

कार्यविपत्तौ दोषान् वर्णयन्ति बालिशाः।

34. One who wants to get the work done should not display charity/generosity (in the wrong place).

कार्यार्थिना दाक्षिण्यं न कर्तव्यम्।

35. A calf which wants milk hits at the under part (the udders) of its mother.

क्षीरार्थी वत्सो मातुरूधः प्रतिहन्ति।

36. Lack of effort ruins a task.

अप्रयत्नात् कार्यविपत्तिर्भवेत्।

37. One who trusts only in fortune cannot accomplish his task.

न दैवमात्रप्रमाणानांकार्यसिद्धि।

38. One who avoids (or runs away from) work cannot provide protection to others.

कार्यबाह्यो न पोषयत्याश्रितान्।

39. One who does not look to his work is blind.

यः कार्य न पश्यति सोऽन्धः।

40. One should examine a task directly, indirectly and through inference.

प्रत्यक्षपरोक्षानुमानैः कार्याणि परीक्षेत।

41. The deity of prosperity deserts those who do not examine a task (before taking it up).

अपरीक्ष्यकारिणं श्रीः परित्यजति।

42. Work trouble should be overcome by examining it. Those who examine/test their tasks (before taking them up) do not run into trouble.

परीक्ष्य तार्या विपत्ति।

43. One should begin a task only after knowing the extent of one's strength.

स्वशक्तिं ज्ञात्वा कार्यमारभेत।

44. One who satisfies his own people first and then partakes of the leftover, gets true satisfaction (the divine drink of amrita).

स्वजनं तर्पयित्वा यश्शेषभोजी सोऽमृतभोजी।

45. It is by the performance of all kinds of work that sources of income (*ayamukhani*) increases.

सम्यगनुष्ठानादाय मुखानि वर्धन्ते।

46. The cowardly has no worries about work.

नास्ति भीरो: कार्यचिन्ता।

47. One who wants to get a work done (through his master) first gets to learn the ways of his master.

स्वामिन: शीलं ज्ञात्वा कार्यार्थी कार्य साधयेत्।

48. The one who knows the ways of the cow gets to eat the preparation of thickened milk (*kshira*).

धेनोश्शीलज्ञो हि क्षीरं भुङ्क्ते।

49. A self-respecting person should not reveal oneself to petty people.

क्षुद्रे गुह्यप्रकाशनमात्मवान् न कुर्यात्।

50. A mild person gets disregarded even by his own dependents (or, by those whom he himself had given refuge).

आश्रितैरप्यवमन्यते मृदुस्वभाव:।

51. A person who rules by the sharp rod (i.e., metes out severe and strict punishment) causes distress to all.

तीक्ष्णदण्डस्सर्वेषामुद्वेजनीयो भवति।

52. One should be a just taskmaster. (The punishment that one deals out should ne appropriate).

यथार्हदण्डकारी स्यात्।

53. A shallow person, even if heard by people, does not get much importance.

अल्पसारं श्रुतवन्तमपि न बहुमन्यते लोक:।

54. Too heavy a burden makes a person exhausted.

अतिभार: पुरुषमवसादयति।

55. He who exposes others' faults in a public gathering, exposes his own faults.

यस्संसदि परदोषं शंसति स स्वदोषबहुत्वमेव प्रख्यापयति।

56. The anger of a person who loses self-possession is self-destructive.

आत्मानमेव नाशयत्यनात्मवता कोप:।

57. Nothing is unattainable for one who adheres to the truth.

नास्त्यप्राप्यं सत्यवताम्।

58. Simply being bold does not accomplish a task.

न केवलेन साहसेन कार्यसिद्धिर्भवति।

59. One troubled by calamity forgets necessary duties.

व्यसनार्तो विस्मरत्यवश्यकर्तव्यान्।

60. Wasting time does not bring any alternative route out of the problem.

नास्त्यनन्तराय: कालविक्षेपे।

61. A probable end is better than a certain end.

असंशयविनाशात् संशयविनाश: श्रेयान्।

62. Merely scattering away wealth is neither Beneficial to oneself, nor generosity or piousness.)

केवलं धनानि निक्षेप्तु: न स्वार्थं न दानं न धर्म:।

63. Material welfare coming from the uncultured (literally, non-Aryans) brings a contrary ill-feeling.

नार्या आगतोऽर्थ: तद्विपरीतमनर्थभावं भजते।

64. That which does not increase *Dharma* or Artha is Kama.It is the reverse and conducive to chaos.

यो धर्मार्थौ न व्यर्धयति स काम:, तद्विपरीतोऽनर्थसेवी।

65. A straight, upright and honest man is difficult to find.

ऋजुस्वभावपरो जनो दुर्लभः।

66. The honest person has a contempt from wealth that has come by some transgression or disrespect of norms.

अवमानेनागतमैश्वर्यमवमन्यत एव साधुः।

67. One vice eats up several virtues

बहूनपि हि गुणानेकदोषो ग्रसति।

68. With a strong and noble foe, one should not be defiant.

महात्मना परं साहसं न कर्तव्यम्।

69. The limits of good conduct should never be crossed.

कदाचिदपि चारित्रं न लङ्घयेत्।

70. However hungry, a lion does not wander about fields of grass.

क्षुधाऽऽर्तो न तृणं चरति सिंहः।

71. More than one's life, one's convictions should be protected. of one's convictions than of one's life.

प्राणादपि प्रत्ययो रक्षितव्यः।

72. A slanderer is abandoned even by his wife and son.

पिशुनो नेतापुत्रदारैरपि त्यज्यते।

**3**

1. Words of sense should be heeded even when they come from children.

बालादपि युक्तमर्थं श्रृणुयात्।

2. One should not speak words of disrespect even when they are words of truth.

सत्यमप्यश्रद्धेयं न वदेत्।

3. That which has many virtues should not be rejected because of a few vices/defects.

नाल्पदोषाद्बहुगुणास्त्यज्यन्ते।

4. Even among the learned, faults abound.

विपश्चित्स्वपि सुलभा दोषा:।

5. There is no precious stone that has no jagged/broken edge.

नास्ति रत्नमखण्डितम्।

6. Never trust a person who is too courteous.

मर्यादातीतं न कदाचिदपि विश्वसेत्।

7. Even a favour performed by someone who is disliked is a matter of dislike.

अप्रिये कृते प्रियमपि द्वेष्यं भवति।

8. Even while it bows to (dips into) to the well, the pitcher depletes its water.

नमन्त्यपि हि तुलाकोटि: कूपोदकक्षयं करोति।

9. One should not go against the opinion of good and wise men.

सतां मतं नातिक्रामेत्।

10. Even those who have no innate virtues develop them under the care of the virtuous.

गुणवदाश्रयन्निर्गुणोऽपि गुणी भवति ।
क्षीराश्रितं जलं क्षीरमेव भवति।

11. Water mixed with milk becomes milk itself.

गुणवदाश्रयन्निर्गुणोऽपि गुणी भवति ।

12. Even in the lump of earth (upon which it has fallen) the Patali (trumpet-flower) produces a sweet smell.

मृत्पिण्डेऽपि पाटलिपुष्पं स्वगन्धमुत्पादयति।

13. In contact with gold, even silver becomes gold.

रजतं कनकसङ्गात् कनकं भवति।

14. One without intelligence (*abudha*) wants to harm even the one who has helped him.

उपकर्तर्यपकर्तुमिच्छत्यबुध:।

15. The evil are not scared of the consequences of sin. Sinners have no fear of criticism

न पापकर्मणामाक्रोशभयम्।

16. Even enemies come under the control of enterprising and enthusiastic ones.

उत्साहवतां शत्रवोऽपि वशीभवन्ति।

17. Kings have the wealth of their valour.

विक्रमधना हि राजान:।

18. The lazy one has no happiness on earth or in heaven.

नास्त्यलसस्यैहिकमामुष्मिकं वा।

19. Even good fortune fails if there is lack of enthusiasm.

निरुत्साहाद्दैवं पतति।

20. Like the fisherman, one should take water and use it (as a resource for earning income).

मत्स्यार्थीव जालमुपयुज्यार्थं गृह्णीयात्।

21. One should not place one's trust upon the untrustworthy.

अविश्वस्तेषु विश्वासो न कर्तव्य:।

22. Poison is poisonous at all times.

विषं विषमेव सार्वकालम्।

23. While doing an income-earning activity, one should not keep company with enemies.

अर्थसमादाने वैरिणां सङ्ग एव न कर्तव्य:।

24. In income-earning activities, one should not trust one's enemies.

अर्थसिद्धौ वैरिणं न विश्वसेत्।

25. A regular relationship is dependent upon money.

अर्थाधीन एव नियतसंबन्ध:।

26. Keeping company with mean and lowly people should be done (only) for the sake of the king (i.e., to serve his purpose).

शत्रोरपि सुत: सखा रक्षितव्य:।

27. As long as one is observing the weaknesses of the enemy, one should press him by the hands or by the shoulders (i.e., keep an outward show of friendliness).

यावच्छत्रोश्छिद्रं पश्यति तावद्धस्तेन वा स्कन्धेन वा संवाह्य: छिद्रे तु प्रहरेत्।

28. One should not reveal one's own weak spot.

आत्मच्छिद्रं न प्रकाशयेत्।

29. One should (then) hit the enemy in his weak spot.

छिद्रप्रहारिणश्शत्रवोऽपि ।

30. One should not trust the enemy even the one who has come under one's control.

हस्तगतमपि शत्रुं न विश्वसेत्।

31. One should combat the enemies of one's friends (and not just one's own enemies)

स्वजनस्य दुर्वृत्तं निवारयेत्।

32. Noble-minded people feel sorry at any insult to their kinsmen, not just at themselves.

स्वजनावमानोऽपि मनस्विनां दु:खमावहति।

33. Even a partial defect in the body causes suffering to a man. (Concern about Disability)

एकाङ्गदोष: पुरुषमवसादयति।

34. Goodness in a man can conquer enemi

शत्रुं जयति सुवृत्तता।

35. Mean and lowly people are fond of making people suffer.

निकृतिप्रिया नीचा:।

36. Education/Enlightenment should not be given to the lean and lowly.

नीचस्य मतिर्न दातव्या।

37. Trust should not be reposed in mean, lowly people.

नीचेषु विश्वासो न कर्तव्य:।

38. Even if well-revered, evil men only cause trouble.

सुपूजितोऽपि दुर्जन: पीडयत्येव।

39. Forest fire burns even the sandalwood tree.

चन्दनादीनपि दावोऽग्निर्दहत्येव।

40. A man should never be insulted.

कदाऽपि कमपि पुरुषं नावमन्येत।

41. A man fit for forgiveness should not be tortured.

क्षन्तव्यमिति पुरुषं न बाधेत।

42. Stupid people want to speak out even the secret that the master has reposed in them.

भर्त्राऽधिकं रहस्युक्तं वक्तुमिच्छन्त्यबुद्धय:।

43. One's love/regard is indicated by its results/fruits.

अनुरागस्तु फलेन (हितेन सूच्यते)।

44. Prosperity results from (following/obeying) the king's command.

आज्ञाफलमैश्वर्यम्।

45. A stupid person makes even his donations with difficulty.

दातव्यमति बालिश: परिक्लेशेन दास्यति।

46. Even after getting great wealth, a stupid person destroys it

महदैश्वर्य प्राप्यापि अधृतिमान् विनश्यति।

47. The one without fortitude has neither present nor future.

नास्त्यधृतेरैहिकमामुष्मिकं वा।

48. The company of evil men should not be kept.

न दुर्जनैस्सह संसर्ग: कर्तव्य:।

49. Even milk in the hands of the drunkard should be considered unsuitable.

शौण्डहस्तगतं पयोऽप्यवमन्यते जनः।

50. In difficult situations it is intelligence that shows what is significant.

कार्यसङ्कटेष्वर्थव्यवसायिनी बुद्धिः।

51. It is healthy to eat in moderation.

मितभोजनं स्वास्थ्यम्।

52. Wholesome or otherwise, no food should be taken in case of indigestion.

पथ्यमप्यपथ्याजीसर्णे नाश्नीयात्।

53. The diseased person should take care of the food they digest.

जीर्णभोजिनं व्याधिर्नोपसर्पति।

54. Increasing disease in a worn-out body should not be neglected.

जीर्णशरीरे वर्धमानं व्याधिं नोपेक्षेत।

55. Eating is painful in case of dyspepsia.

अजीर्णे भोजनं दुःखम्।

56. Disease is even worse than an enemy.

शत्रोरपि विशिष्यते व्याधिः।

57. Donations should be according to one's capacity/ position.

दानं निधानमनुगामि।

58. Among clever and avaricious people, over-inquisitiveness or deceit is easy to find.

पटुतरेऽपि तुष्णापरे सुलभमतिसन्धानम्।

59. Avarice clouds/dulls one's judgement.

तृष्णया मतिश्छाद्यते।

60. When there are many jobs at hand, one should begin with the one likely to be more fruitful in future.

कार्यबहुत्वे बहुफलमायतिकं कुर्यात्।

61. One should oneself supervise work that has been already damaged (specifically, supervise repair work of one's own attacked and ravaged fort).

स्वयमेवावस्कन्नं कार्यं निरीक्षेत।

62. Boldness is always there among the foolish or ignorant.

मूर्खेषु साहसंनियतम्।

63. One should not quarrel with fools.

मूर्खेषु विवादो न कर्तव्यः।

64. With the ignorant, one should speak like the ignorant.

मूर्खेषु मूर्खवदेव कथयेत्।

65. Iron should be cut/pierced with iron itself.

आयसैरायसं छेद्यम्।

66. An unintelligent person has no friends.

नास्त्यधीमतस्सखा।

**4**

1. It is Dharma which bears a man up.

धर्मेण धार्यते लोकः।

2. Dharma and its violation follow even man even in death.

प्रेतमपि धर्माधर्मावनुगच्छतः।

3. Mercy is the motherland of Dharma.

दया धर्मस्य जन्मभूमिः।

4. *Dharma* is the root of Truth and Charity.

धर्ममूले सत्यदाने।

5. It is through *Dharma* that one the various worlds are conquered.

धर्मेण जयति लोकान्।

6. Even Death protects the adherent of Dharma.

मृत्युरपि धर्मिष्ठं रक्षति।

7. As opposed to this, wherever there is the spread of sin, there is the spread of a great violation of Dharma.

धर्माद्विपरीतं पापं रत्र यत्र प्रसज्यते तत्र तत्र धर्मावमतिरेव महती प्रसज्यते।

8. Impending danger can be observed in the appearance of nature.

उपस्थितविनाशानां प्रकृतिः आकारेण कार्येण च लक्ष्यते।

9. Evil thoughts portend self-destruction.

आत्मविनाशं सूचयत्यधर्मबुद्धिः।

10. Why tell secrets to slanderers ?

पिशुनवादिनो रसस्यं कुतः।

11. One should not hear rhe secrets of others.

पररहस्यं नैव श्रोतव्यम्।

12. For an agent, to pursue self-interest (rather than that of the person of whom he is agent of) is not right (*a-dharma*).

वल्लभस्य स्वार्थरत्वमधर्मयुक्तम्।

13. One should not transgress the limits set by one's own people.

स्वजनेष्वप्यतिक्रमो न कर्तव्यः।

14. Even a mother should be discarded if she is a contaminated or fallen woman.

माताऽपि दुष्टा त्याज्या ।

15. Even one's own head should be cut off if it is affected by poison.

स्वहस्तोऽपि विषदिग्धश्छेद्यः।

16. A well-wisher, even if he is not a kinsman, is a friend.

परोऽपि च हितो बन्धुः।

17. Medicine is to be culled even from grass (not just herbs).

कक्षादप्यौषधं गृह्यते।

18. Trust should not be reposed on thieves.

नास्ति चोरेषु विश्वासः।

19. What does not have to be remedied immediately (e.g., easy tasks, enemy inaction) should not be neglected either.

अप्रतीकारेष्वनादरो न कर्तव्यः।

20. A calamity, even if it is very small, makes one troubled.

व्यसनं मनागपि बाधते।

21. One should earn money as if one was immortal (for a long and gracious life).

अमरवदर्थजातमार्जयेत्।

22. A wealthy one is revered by all.

अर्थवान् सर्वलोकस्य बहुमतः।

23. Without wealth, even Indra, the king of gods, is not respected by many in the world.

महेन्द्रमप्यर्थहीनं न बहुमन्यते लोकः।

24. Poverty is living death for a man.

दारिद्रयं खलु पुरुषस्य सजीवितं मरणम्।

25. Even an ugly-looking man is good-looking if he is wealthy.

विरूपोऽप्यर्थवान् सुरूपः।

26. One seeking monetary aid does not let go of a rich man even if he is not generous.

अदातारमप्यर्थवन्तमर्थिनो न त्यजन्ति।

27. Even if low-born, a rich man will be considered superior to a high-born person who is not rich.

अकुलीनोऽपि धनवान् कुलीनाद्विशिष्टः।

28. A low-born (*anarya*) person has no fear of insult

नास्त्यवमानभयमनार्यस्य।

29. Alert and aware people have no worry for getting a livelihood (finding an occupation).

नोद्योगवतां वृत्तिभयम्।

30. People who have control over their senses have no fear for their property.

न जितेन्द्रियाणां विषयभयम्।

31. People who have fulfilled their tasks have no fear of their death.

न कृतार्थानां मरणभयम्।

32. The good man considers everyone else's property as his own (i.e. does not covet it).

कस्यचिदर्थं स्वमिव मन्यते साधुः।

33. One should not covet another's wealth.

परविभवेष्वादरो न कर्तव्यः।

34. Coveting the wealth of others leads to destruction.

परविभवेष्वादरोऽपि नाशमूलम्।

35. Even by an insignificant amount, comparable to a leafless plant (*palala*), the property of another should not be taken away.

पलालमपि परद्रव्यं न हर्तव्यम्।

36. Stealing others' property is the cause of destruction of one's own property.

परद्रव्यापहरणमात्मद्रव्यनाशहेतुः।

37. The noose of death is not worse than theft.

न चौर्यात् परं मृत्युपाशः।

38. In this world, people can survive merely by barley-gruel(*yavagu*).

यवागूरपि प्राणाधारणं करोति काले।

39. The dead has no need of medicines.

न मृतस्यौधषं प्रयोजनम्।

40. At all times equally, there is the need to have self-control.

समकाले प्रभुत्वस्य प्रयोजनं भवति।

41. The learning of the low-minded attaches them to sinful deeds.

नीचस्य विद्या: पापकर्मण्येव तं योजयन्ति।

42. Even to make the snake drink milk is to make it more poisonous; it has no immortalizing *amrita* in it.

पय:पानमपि विषवर्धनं भुजड्गस्य, न त्वमृतं स्यात्।

43. There is no wealth comparable to food grain.

न हि धान्यसमो ह्यर्थ:।

44. There is no enemy comparable to hunger.

न क्षुधासमश्शत्रु:।

45. People who do not do their work (or do not do the right work) constantly go hungry.

अकृतेर्नियता क्षुत्।

46. For one who is ravenously hungry, there is nothing that is inedible.

नास्त्यभक्ष्यं क्षुधितस्य।

47. The senses (i.e., sensual pleasures) are constantly bringing men under the control of old age.

इन्द्रियाणि प्रतिपदं नरान् जरावशान् कुर्वन्ति।

48. Women should live by their kindly husbands.

सानुक्रोशं भर्तारमाजीवेत्।

49. One serving an avaricious master is blowing on a firefly for fire.

लुब्धसेवी पावकेच्छया खद्योतं धमति।

50. One should resort to a learned master,

विशेषज्ञं स्वामिनमाश्रयेत्।

51. Physical union (*maithuna*) brings old age to men. Lack of physical union brings old age to men.

पुरुषस्य मैथुनं जरा।

52. One should resort to a learned master.

स्त्रीणाममैथुनं जरा।

53. There should be no marriage between the lowly and the high-born.

न नीचोत्तमयोर्वैवाहः।

54. By visiting prohibited places, one loses longevity, reputation and merit.

अगम्यागमनादायुर्यशःपुण्यानि क्षीयन्ते।

55. There is no enemy like arrogance.

नास्त्यहङ्कारसमश्शत्रुः।

56. One should not chastise one's enemy in a public gathering.

संसदि शत्रुं न परिक्रोशेत्।

57. It is pleasant to hear of any danger that had befallen the enemy.

शत्रुव्यसनं श्रवणसुखम्।

58. The penniless has no brains.

अधनस्य बुद्धिर्न विद्यते।

59. Even good advice is not heeded if it comes from the penniless.

हितमप्यधनस्य वाक्यं न गृह्यते।

60. The penniless man is insulted even by his wife.

अधनः स्वभार्ययाऽप्यवमन्यते।

61. Even a mango tree is not visited by bees if it bears no mango-blossoms.

पुष्पहीनं सहकारमपि नोपासते भ्रमराः।

## 5

1. Learning is the wealth of the poor and penniless.

विद्या धनमधनानाम्।

2. Learning cannot be grabbed even by a thief.

विद्या चोरैरपि न ग्राह्या।

3. Fame is easy to come by means of learning.

विद्यया सुलभा ख्याति:।

4. One's body of fame is never destroyed.

यशश्शरीरं न विनश्यति।

5. One who goes forward for the welfare of others is a good man,

य: परार्थमन्यमुपसर्पति स सत्पुरुष:।

6. It is sacred texts that calm down the senses.

इन्द्रियाणां प्रशमं शास्त्रम्।

7. The sacred texts act as elephant's prods to pull back ones who have turned to prohibited acts.

अकार्यप्रवृत्ते: शास्त्राङ्कुशं निवारयति।

8. One should not take lessons (learn) from the lowly.

नीचस्य विद्या नोपेतव्या।

9. One should not learn the language of foreigners/aliens (*mlechchha*).

म्लेच्छभाषणं न शिक्षेत।

10. Worthy activities should be learnt/collected/accepted even from foreigners.

म्लेच्छानामपि सुवृत्तं ग्राह्यम्।

11. One should not degrade/deny good qualities even when they are found in men one dislikes.

गुणे न मत्सर: कर्तव्य:।

12. Good qualities are to be acknowledged/accepted even from enemies.

शत्रोरपि सुगुणो ग्राह्यः।

13. Nectar is to be extracted/culled even from poison.

विषादप्यमृतं ग्राह्यम्।

14. A man gets respected because of his status/position.

अवस्थया पुरुषस्संमान्यते।

15. Only in their positions/office are men shown respect.

स्थान एव नराः पूज्यन्ते।

16. One should stay in positions befitting Aryans (i.e., noble positions).

आर्यवृत्तमनुतिष्ठेत्।

17. One should never cross the limits of decorum.

कदापि मर्यादां नातिक्रामेत्।

18. A gem-of-a-man is priceless.

नास्त्यर्घः पुरुषरत्नस्य।

19. There is no gem like a gem-of-a-woman.

न स्त्रीरत्नसमं रत्नम्।

20. Gems are most rare.

सुदुर्लभं हि रत्नम्।

21. Discredit/dishonour is the greatest of fears

अयशो भयं भयेषु।

22. It is not possible for the lazy to master the sacred texts.

नास्त्यलसस्य शास्त्राधिगमः।

23. Men who are over-attached to their wives cannot attain heaven and perform dharma.

न स्त्रैणस्य स्वर्गाप्तिर्धर्मकृत्यं च।

24. Even the wife disregards a man over-attached to his wife.

स्त्रियोऽपि स्त्रैणमवमन्यन्ते।

25. A man who wants flowers (i.e., wants to be an achiever) does not water a dried-up plant.

न पुष्पार्थी सिज्जति शुष्कतरुम्।

26. To begin a work without equipment and resources is to try to extract oil from sand.

अद्रव्यप्रयत्नो वालुकाककाथनादनन्य:।

27. Jokes at great men should not be made.

न महाजनहास: कर्तव्य।

28. The worth of the work indicates its merit.

कार्यसंपदं निमित्तानि सूचयन्ति।

29. Omens too indicate the merit of a task undertaken.

नक्षत्रादपि निमित्तानि विशेषयन्ति।

30. One who wants to get his work done quickly has no need of astrological observations.

न त्वरितस्य नक्षत्रपरीक्षा।

31. As one gets acquainted with others, one's own faults do not remain hidden.

परिचये दोषा न छाद्यन्ते।

32. One who is impure himself fears others.

स्वयमशुद्ध: परानाशङ्कते।

33. Habits are hard to overcome.

स्वभावो दुरतिक्रम:।

34. Punishment should be according to the offence committed.

अपराधानुरुपो दण्ड:।

35. The reply should be according to the query.

प्रश्नानुरूपं प्रतिवचनम्।

36. The ornament should be according to one's status/wealth.

विभवानुरूपमाभरणम्।

37. The occupation/profession should be according to the family-line.

कुलानुरूपं वृत्तम्।

38. The effort should be in accordance with the task.

कार्यानुरूप: प्रयत्न।

39. The donation should be according to the recipient.

पात्रानुरूपं दानम्।

40. The dress should be according to the age.

वयोऽनुरूपो वेष: ।

41. The servant should behave in conformity with the master.

स्वाम्यनुकूलो भृत्य:।

42. The wife should be under the control of the husband.

भर्तृवशवर्तिनी भार्या।

43. The disciple should follow the guru/preceptor.

गुरुवशानुवर्ती शिष्य:।

44. The son should be under the control of the father.

पितृवशानुवर्ती पुत्र:।

45. One should be wary of too much of courtesy.

अत्युपचारश्शङ्कितव्य:।

46. When the husband/master is angry, it is he who should be followed.

स्वामिनि कुपिते स्वामिन मेवानुवर्तेत।

47. A child scolded by the mother goes following the mother alone.

मातृताडितो वत्सो मातरमेवानुरोदिति।

48. The anger of the affectionate elders is of short duration.

स्नेहवतस्स्वल्पो हि रोष:।

49. The stupid does not see the faults of his own but sees only those of others.

बालिश: आत्मच्छिद्रं न पश्यति, अपितु परच्छिद्रमेव पश्यति।

50. One who makes much external display of courtesy is a cunning rogue.

सदोपचार: कितव:।

51. Serving someone with his favourite objects is being excessively courteous to him and so, being cunning.

काम्यैर्विशेषैरुपचारणमुपचार:।

52. Excessive courtesy from old acquaintances is a matter of concern.

चिरपरिचितानामत्युपचारश्शङ्कितव्य:।

53. A cow, even if ill-behaved, is better than a thousand dogs.

श्वसहस्रादेकाकिनी गौ: श्रेयसी।

54. A pigeon today is better than a peacock yesterday.

श्वो मयूरादद्य कपोतो वर:।

55. Too close a contact/connection produces defects/faults.

अतिसङ्गो दोषमुत्पादयति।

56. The one without anger conquers everything.

सर्वं जयत्यक्रोध:।

57. If it is a duty to display anger to those that harm, it is also a duty to display anger at one's own anger.

यद्यपकारिणि कोप: कर्तव्य:, तर्हि स्वकोपे एव कोप: कर्तव्य:।

58. Conflict is not advisable with the intelligent, the stupid, a friend, a guru, and the husband.

मतिमत्सु मूर्खमित्रगुरुवल्लभेषु विवादो न कर्तव्य:।

59. Riches are not without evil influences (*a-pishacha*).

नास्त्यपिशाचमैश्वर्यम्।

60. The rich do not have to make much effort to do good work.

नास्ति धनवतां सुकर्मसु श्रमः।

61. Those having vehicles to carry them along do not have to make the effort of movement.

नास्ति गतिश्रमो यानवताम्।

62. The wife is a chain that is not made of iron.

अलोहमयं निगडं कलत्रम्।

63. One should be employed/engaged in work for which he is most efficient/skilled.

यो यस्मिन् कर्मणि कुशलः स तस्मिनः योक्तव्यः।

64. Bad wives wear down the bodies of intellectual men.

दुष्कलत्रं मनस्विनां शरीरकर्शनम्।

65. One should observe one's wife in a sober (un-intoxicated) condition.

अप्रमत्तो दारान् निरीक्षेत।

66. Women should not be trusted at all.

स्त्रीषु किंचिदपि न विश्वसेत्।

67. Women do not have either composure or knowledge of how to behave in public. (This is Gender Bias, in today's terminology.)

न समाधिः स्त्रीषु लोकज्ञता च।

68. Among gurus, the mother is the greatest.

गुरूणांमाता गरीयसी।

69. The mother is to be maintained/ looked after at every stage of life.

सर्वावस्थासु माता भर्तव्या।

70. One's physical defects can be covered up by ornaments.

वैरूप्यमलङ्कारेणाच्छाद्यते।

71. The ornament of women is modest, decorous behaviour.

स्त्रीणां भूषणं लज्जा।

72. The ornament of the *Brahmanas* is knowledge of the Vedas.

विप्राणां भूषणं वेदः।

73. *Dharma* is the ornament of all.

सर्वेषां भूषणं धर्मः।

74. Learning with humility (*vinaya*) is the best ornament of all.

भूषणानां भूषणं सविनया विद्या।

**6**

1. One should live in a safe and secure, trouble-free country.

अनुपद्रवं देशमावसेत्।

2. A country prolific in good men is the right country to take shelter in.

साधुजनबहुलो देशः आश्रयणीयः।

3. The king is to be feared at all times.

राज्ञो भेतव्यं सार्वकालम्।

4. There is no deity higher than the king.

न राज्ञः परं दैवतम्।

5. Royal rage flows a long distance.

सुदूरमपि दहति राजवह्निः।

6. One should not approach the king empty-handed, nor the preceptor and the deity.

रिक्तहस्तो न राजानमभिगच्छेत् गुरुं दैवंच।

7. One should be wary of members of the royal family.

कुटुम्बिनो भेतव्यम्।

8. One should regularly go and visit the royal family.

गन्तव्यं च सदा राजकुलम्।

9. One should develop ties with royal officers.

राजपुरुषैस्संबन्धं कुर्यात्।

10. One should not court royal maids.

राजदासी न सेवितव्या।

11. One should not look the king straight in the eyes.

न चक्षुषाऽपि राजानं निरीक्षेत ।

12. When sons are virtuous, that is heaven for relatives.

पुत्रे गुणवति कुटुम्बिन: स्वर्ग:।

13. One should make one's sons reach the utmost limits of education.

पुत्रा विद्यानां पारं गमयितव्या:।

14. One should leave the village for the sake of the (entire) habitation.

जनपदार्थं ग्रामं त्यजेत:।

15. One should leave the kinsfolk for the sake of the village.

ग्रामार्थं कुटुम्बस्त्यज्यते।

16. Getting a son is an extreme gain.

अतिलाभ: पुत्रलाभ:।

17. The one who protects/saves one's parents in trouble is a (true) son.

दुर्गतेर्य: पितरौ रक्षति स पुत्र:।

18. The one who proclaims the family-line is the son.

य: कुलं प्रख्यापयति स पुत्र:।

19. There is no prospect of heaven for those who do not have a son. (In Sociology, this is called Son Preference.)

नानपत्यस्य स्वर्ग:।

20. One who bears (a son) is the wife.

या प्रसूते सा भार्या।

21. In a gathering at a pilgrimage, follow in the wake of a woman who has a son.

तीर्थसमवाये पुत्रवतीमनुगच्छेत।

22. Physical relation with a woman having her periods destroys the *brahmacharya* stage (of scholarship and abstention).

न तीर्थाभिगमनाद्ब्रह्मचर्यं नश्यति।

23. Do not throw your seeds into another's field. (Do not cohabit with a woman who is not your wife and generate sons for another family).

न परक्षेत्रे बीजंविनिक्षिपेत्।

24. Wives are there for (the purpose of having) sons.

पुत्रार्था हि स्त्रिय:।

25. Having physical relation with one's own maid-servant is behaving like a servant oneself.

स्वदासीपरिग्रहो हि स्वस्यैव दासभावापादनम्।

26. The dying one does not listen to advice that could have acted as a curative diet.

उपस्थितविनाश: पथ्यवाक्यं न शृणोति।

27. There is no lack of joys and sorrows for living beings.

नास्ति देहिनां सुखदु:खाभाव।

28. Joys and sorrows follow man, the do-er of activities, like a child follows its mother.

मातरमिव वत्सा: सुखदु:खानि कर्तारमेवानुगच्छन्ति।

29. A saintly person considers the slightest favour done to him as huge as a mountain.

तिलमात्रमप्युपकारं शैलमात्रं मन्यते साधु:।

30. One should not do a favour to someone who is ignoble (lit. not an Aryan).

उपकारोऽनार्येष्वकर्तव्य:।

31. Out of fear of having to return the favour, the ignoble becomes an enemy of the one who has done him the favour).

प्रत्युपकारभयादनार्यश्शत्रुर्भवति।

32. The noble one dreams of returning the favour to someone who has done him a small favour.

स्वल्पोपकारकृतेऽपि प्रत्युपकारं कर्तुमार्यो जागर्त्ति।

33. The deities are never to be insulted.

न कदाऽपि देवताऽमन्तव्या।

34. There is no light like that of eyesight.

न चक्षुष: समं ज्योतिरस्ति।

35. To living beings, the eyes are the leader.

चक्षुर्हि शरीरिणां नेता।

36. What is the use of the body if it is without eyes ? (This is a comment on the issue of Disability.)

अपचक्षुष: किं शरीरेण?

37. One should not urinate into water (This is an observation on Health and Hygiene).

नाप्सु मूत्रं कुर्यात्।

38. One should not enter the waters in a naked state.

न नग्नो जलं प्रविशेत्।

39. One acquires knowledge as per one's physical capacity.

यथा शरीरं तथा ज्ञानम्।

40. One acquires riches as per as one's intelligence.

यथा बुद्धिस्तथा विभव:।

41. One should not throw fire into fire.

अग्नावग्निं न निक्षिपेत।

42. Ascetics should be worshipped.

तपस्विन: पूजनीया:।

43. One should not approach/seek the wives of others.

परदारान् न गच्छेत्।

44. Donation of rice atones even for the sin of abortion.

अन्नदानं भ्रूणहत्यामपि मार्ष्टि।

45. Dharma is not external to the Vedas.

न वेदबाह्यो धर्मः।

46. Somehow, to some extent at least, one should serve Dharma.

कथंचिदपि धर्म निषेवेत।

47. Honest conduct takes one to heaven.

स्वर्गं नयति सूनृतम्।

48. There is no penance greater than keeping to truthful and honest ways.

नास्ति सत्यात् परं तपः।

49. Truth is the means/way to heaven.

सत्यं स्वर्गस्य साधनम्।

50. It is truth by means of which the world is held up (borne).

सत्येन धार्यते लोकः।

51. It is truth through which the gods shower their blessings.

सत्याद्देवो वर्षति।

52. There is no sin worse than untruth.

नानृतात् पातकं परम्।

53. Gurus (elders) should not be analyzed and criticized.

न मीमांस्या गुरवः।

54. One should not adopt deceptiveness.

खलत्वं नोपेयात्।

55. No one befriends the deceptive (Or, A deceiver has no friends).

नास्ति खलस्य मित्रं।

56. Leading a social life (*lokayatra*) is a strain for the poor.

लोकयात्रा दरिद्रं बाधते।

57. A person generous in charity is the truly brave man.

अतिशूरो दानशूरः।

58. Devotion towards the gurus, the gods and towards *Brahmanas* is the true ornament.

गुरुदेवब्राह्मणेषु भक्तिर्भूषणम्।

59. Humility, born of education, is the true ornament for all.

सर्वस्य भूषणं विनयः।

60. An educated and humble person with a good way of conducting himself distinguishes himself even if he does not come from a noble family.

अकुलीनोऽपि विनीतः कुलीनाद्विशिष्ट।

61. It is from correct conduct that longevity and achievement come.

आचारादायुर्वर्धते कीर्तिः श्रेयश्च।

62. One should not speak evil even if it sounds sweet.

प्रियमप्यहितं न वक्तव्यम्।

63. One should not follow someone whom everyone opposes.

बहुजनविरुद्धमेकं नानुवर्तेत।

64. One should not link one's fate with evil men.

न कृतार्थस्य नीचेषु संबन्धः।

65. Evil men are to be rejected even when they are endowed with good thoughts and intentions.

ऋणशत्रुव्याधयो निःशेषाः कर्तव्याः।

66. The elixir of life for a man is to follow excellence.

भृत्यनुवर्तनं पुरुषस्य रसायनम्।

67. One should not ignore or humiliate seekers of aid.

नार्थिष्ववज्ञा कार्या।

68. Lowly men insult the masters after making them perform very difficult favours for them.

दुष्करं कर्म कारयित्वा कर्तारमवमन्यते नीचः।

69. There is no return from hell for ungrateful people.

नाकृतज्ञस्य नरकान्निवर्तनम्।

70. The tongue is the container of both development and destruction.

जिह्वायत्तौ वृद्धिविनाशौ।

71. The tongue is the container of both poison and nectar.

विषामृतयोराकरी जिह्वा।

72. Those who speak sweetly have no enemies.

प्रियवादिनो न शत्रुः।

73. On being praised, even the gods are pleased.

स्तुता अपि देवतास्तुष्यन्ति।

74. Even if untrue, ill-spoken words live on/endure for ever.

अनृतमपि दुर्वचनं चिरं तिष्टति।

75. One should not say anything against royalty.

राजद्विष्टं न वक्तव्यम्।

76. Because it is pleasant to hear, people get satisfied with the cuckoo's calls.

श्रुतिसुखात् कोकिलालापादपि तुष्यन्ति जनाः।

77. A good man exists for the purpose of being true to his prescribed way of life (*swadharma*).

स्वधर्महेतुस्सत्पुरुषः।

78. There is no pride in asking for favours. (One who is always asking for things gets no respect.)

नास्त्यर्थिनो गौरवम्।

79. The ornament of a woman is her good fortune (that of having a husband who is alive).

स्त्रीणां भूषणं सौभाग्यम्।

80. Even an enemy should not be deprived of his livelihood.

शत्रोरपि न पातनीया वृत्तिः।

81. The right field is where one does not have to make much effort for getting water.

अप्रयत्नोदकं क्षेत्रम्।

82. With (only) the support of a small Eranda (Castor) tree, one should not anger an elephant.

एरण्डमवलम्ब्य कुंजरं न कोपयेत्।

83. A very aged Shalmali (silk-cotton) tree cannot be the column to tie a huge elephant to.

अतिप्रवृद्धापि शाल्मली वारणस्तम्भो न भवति।

84. Even if very old, the Karnikara tree does not become fit for making clubs.

अतिदीर्घोऽपि कर्णिकारो न मुसली भवति।

85. However bright, a glow-worm is not fire.

अतिदीप्तोऽपि खद्योतो न पावकः।

86. Merely getting old does not make a man virtuous.

न प्रवृद्धत्वं गुणहेतुः।

87. Even when very old, the Neem tree does not become the Shankula.

सुजीर्णोऽपि पिचुमन्दो न शङ्कुलायते।

88. The fruit is according to the seed. (As you sow, so you shall reap.)

यथा बीजं तथा निष्पत्तिः।

89. As the education is, so is the intelligence.

यथा श्रुतं तथा बुद्धिः।

90. As the family is, so is the conduct.

यथा कुलं तथाऽऽचारः।

91. Even after processing/culturing, the Pichumanda or Neem tree does not become a Sahakara or mango tree.

संस्कृत: पिचुमन्दो न सहकारो भवति।

92. One should not reject happiness that has arrived.

न चागतं सुखं त्यजेत्।

93. People approach unhappiness themselves.

स्वयमेव दुःखमधिगच्छति।

94. One should not roam about at night.

रात्रिचारणं न कुर्यात्।

95. One should not go to sleep at midnight (i.e., keep awake till midnight.)

न चार्धरात्रं स्वपेत्।

96. One should get everything examined by the learned ones (who know *tat* or the Brahman.)

तद्विद्वद्भिः परीक्षेत।

97. One should not enter the house of another without due reason.

परगृहमकारणतो न प्रविशेत्।

98. People commit offences knowingly.

ज्ञात्वाऽपि दोषमेव करोति लोकः।

99. The occupations of people are largely based on the scriptures.

शास्त्रप्रधाना लोकवृत्ति।

100. In the absence of scriptures, one should follow the codes of conduct.

शास्त्राभावे शिष्टाचारमनुगच्छेत् ।

101. There is no scripture superior to (good) conduct.

नाचरिताच्छास्त्रं गरीयः।

102. A king takes note even of distant people and events through his second set of eyes – the spies .

दूरस्थमपि चारचक्षुः पश्यति राजा।

103. People follow the usual track (i.e., are custom-bound).

गतानुगतिको लोकः।

104. One should not speak ill of the person on whom one depends for livelihood.

यमनुजीवेत् तं नापवदेत्।

## 7

1. To subjugate the senses is the best way of performing *tapasya.* (Punishing the senses is the crux of penance).

तपस्सार इन्द्रियनिग्रहः।

2. It is difficult to be freed from attachment to women.

दुर्लभः स्त्रीबन्धनान्मोक्षः।

3. Women are the breeding-ground of all evil.

स्त्री नाम सर्वाशुभानां क्षेत्रम्।

4. There is no test of manhood for women.

न च स्त्रीणां पुरुषपरीक्षा।

5. Women are fickle-minded. (Or, Women's minds are not steady).

स्त्रीणां मनः क्षणिकमः।

6. Those who hate evil should not get embroiled in women.

अशुभद्वेषिणः स्त्रीषु न प्रसक्ता भवेयुः।

7. Those who are learned in the three Vedas are the ones who know about the results of respective sacrificial ceremonies.

यज्ञफलज्ञास्त्रिवेदविदः।

8. A stay in heaven is not permanent but only up to the limit of merits acquired through one's good deeds (*punyaphala*).

स्वर्गस्थानं न शाश्वतं, अपितु यावत्पुण्यफलम:।

9. There is no greater sorrow than falling down from heaven.

न च स्वर्गपतनात् परं दु:खम्।

10. A living person does not want to be the lord of heaven by giving up his life.

देही देहं त्यक्त्वा ऐन्द्रपदं न वांछति।

11. The antidote for sorrow is Nirvana (an ultimate stage beyond the cycle of re-birth).

दु:खानामौषधं निर्वाणाम्।

12. Hostility with the noble (lit. Aryan) is better than friendship with the ignoble (Non-Aryan).

अनार्यसंबन्धाद्वरमार्यशत्रुता।

13. A foul-mouthed person destroys his family.

निहन्ति दुर्वचनं कुलम्।

14. There is no happiness greater than contact with one's son.

न पुत्रसंस्पर्शात् परं सुखम्।

15. In the matter of any judgment, one must follow one's Dharma.

विवादे धर्ममनुस्मरेत्।

16. One should get up early. It is at night-end that one should think of what to do, what the right course of action is.

निशान्ते कार्य चिन्तयेत्।

17. One should not have intercourse in the evening (the first part of the night).

प्रदोषे न संयोग: कर्तव्य:।

18. When destruction is imminent, a good outcome is considered to be difficult.

उपस्थितविनाश: दुर्नयं शुभं मन्यते।

19. What is the use of elephants to someone who wants thickened milk?

क्षीरार्थिन: किं करिण्या।

20. Nothing brings people under control as charity does.

न दानसमं वश्यम्।

21. One should not be tense about matters which are not in one's own control.

परायत्तेषूत्कण्ठां न कुर्यात:।

22. The prosperity of evil men is enjoyed only by evil men. Good people cannot enjoy it.

असत्समृद्धिरसद्भिरेव भुज्यते।

23. The bitter fruits of Neem are eaten only by crows.

निम्बफलं काकैर्हि भुज्यते।

24. The vast ocean cannot quench one's thirst,

नाम्भोधिस्तृष्णामपोहति।

25. Even sand resorts to its own nature.

वालुका अपि स्वगुणमाश्रयन्ते।

26. Saintly people do not enjoy the company of evil men.

सन्तोऽसत्सु न रमन्ते।

27. Swans do not roam about in the garden of ghosts (i.e., cremation ground).

हंस: प्रेतवने न रमते।

28. People function for the sake of material welfare, i.e., work for their livelihood.

अर्थार्थं प्रवर्तते लोक:।

29. The world is held together by hope.

आशया बध्यते लोक:।

30. Prosperity does not stay long with people who depend only on hope.

न चाशापरैश्श्रीस्सह तिष्ठति।

31. Those depending primarily upon hope do not have patience.

आशापरे न धैर्यम्।

32. Death is better than poverty.

दैन्यान्मरणमुत्तमम्।

33. Hope removes the sense of shame.

आशा लज्जां व्यपोहति।

34. One should not live with one's own mother.

न मात्रा सह वास: कर्तव्य:।

35. One should not indulge in self-laudation.

आत्मा नस्तोतव्य:।

36. One should not indulge in day-dreaming.

न दिवा स्वप्नं कुर्यात्।

37. One blinded by his prosperity does not foresee the future or listen to good advice.

न चासन्नमपि पश्यत्यैश्वर्यान्ध:, नापि श्रृणोतीष्टं वाक्यम्।

38. For women there is no deity superior to the husband.In the wife's following the husband lies happiness for both.

स्त्रीणां न भर्तु: परं दैवतम:, तदनुवर्तनं तासामुभयसौख्यम्।

39. The guest who has arrived should be revered as per custom.

अतिथिमभ्यागतं च पूजयेद्यथाविधि।

40. There should be no disturbance or problem in the distribution process.One should regularly share earnings (among those who had helped in the process).

नास्ति हव्यस्य व्याघात:।

41. Sometimes the enemy appears like a friend.

शत्रुर्मित्रवत् प्रतिभाति।

42. A mirage appears like water.

मृगतृष्णा जलवद्भाति हि।

**8**

1. Evil scriptures delude the evil-minded.

दुर्मेधसोऽसच्छास्त्रं मोहयति।

2. Having the company of good people is living in heaven.

सत्सङ्ग स्वर्गवास:।

3. A noble man (lit. an Aryan) has the same regard for another as for himself.

आर्या: स्वमिव परं मन्वते।

4. Virtues are according to appearances.

रूपानुवर्ती गुण:।

5. The right place is where one can live happily.

यत्र सुखेन वर्तते तदेव स्थानम्।

6. The unfaithful/treacherous ones have no release/salvation.

विश्वासघातिनो न निष्कृति:।

7. One should not lament over what is in the control of deities.

दैवायत्तं न शोचेत्।

8. A saintly person considers the sorrows of his dependents as his own.

आश्रितदु: खमात्मन इव मन्यते साधु:।

9. An unworthy (*an-arya*) hides what is in his heart and says something else. He has no mercy.

हृद्गतमाच्छाद्यान्यद्वदत्यनार्य:।

10. A stupid person is like a demon.

बुद्धिहीन: पिशाचतुल्य:।

11. One should not proceed on one's way without any help or support.

असहायः पथि न गच्छेत्।

12. A son is not to be revered or lauded (by the father).

पुत्रो न स्तोतव्यः।

13. The master is to be revered by the servants/followers (whose livelihood depends on him).

स्वामी स्तोतव्योऽनुजीविभिः।

14. In rituals of *Dharma* as well, one (the servant) should declare the virtues of the master (or, proclaim the master).

धर्मकृत्यानिसर्वाणि स्वामिन इत्येव घोषयेत्।

15. One should not delay in executing the king's order.

राजाज्ञां नातिलङ्घयेत्।

16. Doing, as the master says, is for the servants an act of *Dharma*. One should do as one is told to do, in every detail.

यथाऽऽज्ञप्तं तथा कुर्यात्।

17. The intelligent have no enemies.

नास्ति बुद्धिमतां शत्रुः।

18. One's own weaknesses should not be revealed.

आत्मच्छिद्रं न प्रकाशयेतः।

19. Only the forgiving person can accomplish all.

क्षमावानेव सर्वं साधयति।

20. Keep your wealth protected for some adverse occurrence.

आपदर्थं धनं रक्षेत्।

21. The courageous should do things which are nice and pleasant.

साहसवतां प्रियं कर्तव्यम्।

22. Work due tomorrow should be done today itself.

श्वः कार्यमद्य कुर्वीत।

23. Work due in the afternoon should be done in the forenoon itself.

आपराह्णिकं पूर्वाह्ण एव कर्तव्यम्।

24. Behaviour or conduct is superior to the principles of *Dharma.*

व्यवहारानुलोमो धर्मः।

25. To be all-knowing, one has to know about the ways of men.

सर्वज्ञता लोकज्ञता।

26. A scholar is a fool if he does not know about the ways of men.

शास्त्रज्ञोऽप्यलोकज्ञो मूर्खतुल्यः।

27. Theory and philosophy are needed for knowledge of the scriptures.

शास्त्रप्रयोजनं तत्वदर्शनम्।

28. Theories are for throwing light on practices.

तत्वज्ञानं कार्यमेव प्रकाशयति।

29. One should not be partial in one's behaviour.

व्यवहारे पक्षपातो न कार्यः।

30. One's behaviour is superior even to *Dharma*.

धर्मादपि व्यवहारो गरीयान्।

31. The soul is the witness of behaviour.

आत्मा हि व्यवहारस्य साक्षी।

32. The soul is witness to all.

सर्वसाक्षी ह्यात्मा।

33. One should not be a false witness (*kootasakshi*).

न स्यात् कूटसाक्षी।

34. A false witness goes to hell.

कूटसाक्षिणो नरके पतन्ति।

35. The great elements bear witness to sins done in secrecy

प्रच्छन्नपापानां साक्षिणो महाभूतानि।

36. It is one's own soul that leads to one's sins being revealed.

आत्मन: पापमात्मैव प्रकाशयति।

37. Outward behaviour indicates inward behaviour.

व्यवहारेऽन्तर्गतमाकारस्सूचति।

38. Even the gods cannot disguise/control their forms.

आकारसंवरणंदेवानामप्यशक्यम्।

39. Wealth needs protection from thieves as well as government officers.

चोरराजपुरुषेभ्यो वित्तं रक्षेत्।

40. It is inaccessibility that destroys a king's subjects.

दुर्दर्शना हि राजान: प्रजा रक्षन्ति।

41. Easily accessible/visible kings please their subjects.

सुदर्शना राजान: प्रजा रक्षन्ति।

42. A just king is considered to be a mother by his subjects.

न्याययुक्तं राजानं मातरंमन्यन्ते प्रजा:।

43. A king like that (i.e., a just king) gets happiness in this world as well as access to heaven.

तादृश: स राजा इह सुखं ततस्स्वर्गं चाप्नोति।

44. Non-violence is the characteristic of *Dharma*.

अहिंसालक्षणो धर्म:।

45. A saintly man considers even his own body to be another's (i.e., for another's benefit).

स्वशरीरमति परशरीरं मन्यते साधु:।

46. Eating meat(non-vegetarianism) is unsuitable for all.

मांसभक्षणमप्ययुक्तं सर्वेषाम्।

47. For one who has true knowledge, there is no fear of the troubles of earthly life.

न संसारभयं ज्ञानवताम्।

48. The lamp of science dispels the fear of worldly life.

विज्ञानदीपेन संसारभयं निवर्तयति।

49. Everything is transient.

सर्वमनित्यं भवति।

50. It is the body - a container for stool, urine, and worms - that generates virtue and vice.

कृमिशकृन्मूत्रभाजनं शरीरं पुण्यपापजन्महेतुः।

51. There is only sorrow in life and death; one should try to go beyond them.

जन्ममरणादिषु तु दुःखमेव।

52. Heaven is attained through penance (*tapasya*).

तपसा स्वर्गमाप्नोति।

53. The forgiving/merciful have their powers of penance enhanced.

क्षमायुक्तस्य तपो विवर्धते।

54. It is through penance that everybody attains his objective.

तस्मात् सर्वेषां सर्वकार्यसिद्धिर्भवति।

❐

# 6

# Chanakya Encapsulated:
## *Concluding Lines*

As we come to the end of Chanakya's works, we bow our heads in acknowledgment of his great prowess. Chanakya was a super statesman and a super scholar built into one.

But personally, in our own small individual ways, as ordinary people going about our everyday business of life, what can we learn from him?

Out of the numerous tenets of Chanakya's, let us select and put 25 in a curative capsule.

1. Chanakya believed in people, whose habitation he considered to be the essence of the kingdom that the king was governing.
2. He wanted people to acquire wealth. He valued enterprise.
3. He was a big one for personal cleanliness and hygiene, discipline and organization.
4. He wanted people to have happy family lives, respect their marriages and not indulge in extra-marital relationships.
5. He felt very strongly about ignorant fools and lazy louts in the family. He emphasized education and skill-formation. He urged young people to read and write and generally to develop.
6. He wanted parents and teachers to be shown respect.
7. Chanakya believed that people should keep their thoughts to themselves and not blab about their plans till they were accomplished.
8. He wanted people to have self-respect and not live lives of humiliation. It was important, he felt, to have one's own home and independent livelihood.
9. Chanakya also felt that it was important to have sons but more so to educate the ones that are there rather than go in for a number too large to educate and bring up properly.

10. Father and son should have mutual respect.
11. Life-partners should be chosen carefully.
12. Wives of others are to be respected and not coveted.
13. Family life is most precious but one must not get too attached to it.
14. Chanakya is rather emphatic on the choice of friends and associates. They must be chosen with care, and from equals. Dishonest ones are to be avoided.
15. One should not associate too much with depressed people either.
16. Servants and advisors too should be chosen carefully.
17. There is no strength like one's own.
18. One should be honest and upright but not rigid and inflexible. One must bend occasionally. Power lies in using intelligence rather than brute strength.
19. One should not be ritualistic and rigid but adjust diplomatically.
20. One should not just gather and hoard but spend judiciously and well.
21. One should not take insults lying down. One should protest and even take revenge.
22. But Chanakya believed that one should take revenge or retribution intelligently, planning it, and taking co-operation from those who, for reasons of their own, happen to be inimical to one's enemy.
23. Chanakya wanted the king to govern well and see that his officers were protective yet fair to his people.
24. He wanted the king to keep himself fully informed about his subjects and make full use of espionage for the purpose.
25. Chanakya's seminal work is on *Artha* or Material well-being. Material well-being should not be neglected, he emphasized, but he also put in that it should be combined with spiritual well-being, honesty and other moral values.

What is so new about these points that Chanakya makes, one may ask. We have all heard such advice before, at home, at educational institutes, at courts of law and numerous other contexts.

Well, that is not surprising, is it? Chanakya's principles have emerged out of Indian wisdom and traditions and been passed on to countless generations. In tune with the philosophy of the *Veda*s and *Upanishad*s, the lore of the *Ramayana* and the *Mahabharata*, they have fed the Indian psyche and, in turn, been nourished by it. They are golden words of advice, because they are old, and gold. Open to various interpretations and applications, from Business Management to Home Economics, International Relations to Family Relations, Chanakya's tenets are part of what Indians have lived by, right from 2300 years ago.

But we need to take a fresh look at them, re-discover and re-invent them for the years ahead. So let us meet Chanakya in this book and begin an interface.

❐

# References


1. *Kautaliyarthashastra of Sri Vishnugupta*, Oriental Research Institute, University of Mysore, Mysore; Sanskrit Series 103,General Editor Deveerappa, Editor Viswan N.S.Venkatanathacharya, 1960
2. *Arthasastra of Kautilya and The Chanakya Sutra*, Editor: Shri Vachaspati Gairola; Chowkhamba Vidyabhawan Varanasi 221001; 4th edn, 1991
3. *Arthashastra of Kautilya*, R. Shama Shastri, Mysore, 1923, reprinted 1924 and 1951
4. *Kautilya's Political Ideas and Institutions*, Radhakrishna Chaudhari, Chowkhamba Publication, Varanasi, 1971, p 15
5. *Arthashastra of Kautilya*, Editor:T.Ganapati,Trivandrum, 1924-25
6. *Arthashastra*, J. Jolly and R Schmidt, Lahore,1924
7. *Arthashastra of Kautilya,* J.J.Meyer, Leipzig, 1926
8. *Arthashastra* (Russian translation), by Kaliyanov, Moscow, 1959
9. *Arthashastra,* R.P.Kangle, Bombay, 1960-65
10. *Kautilya The Arthashastra*, L.N. Rangarajan, Penguin Classics, Penguin Books India Pvt Ltd 1992, New Delhi, 1992
11. *A Military History of Ancient India,* Major General G. S. Sandhu, Vision Books, Delhi, 2000
12. *Chanakya's New Manifesto To Resolve The Crisis Within India*, Pavan Verma, Aleph Book Company, Rupa Publications India, 2013. p 9 (available in DCMS)
13. http://www.silashruparell.com/1/post/2012/02/amartya-sen-the-idea-of-justice-2009.html
14. The world according to Gita: Millennia before European thinkers, Gita and Arthashastra embodied Indian tradition of realpolitik, November 21, 2014, 12:04 am IST Henry Kissinger in TOI Edit Page | Edit Page, India | *TOI*
15. *Discovery of India* , Jawaharlal Nehru

16. *Chanakya*, Series Editor: M.H.Syed, Editors: R.K.Singh & P.K. Choudhry, Himalaya Publishing House Pvt Ltd, New Delhi 110002,2011
17. Foundation of the Mauryan Empire, R.R. Mukherjee
18. `Chandragupta'(Bengali play), D.L..Roy, Dwijendra Rachanabali, Vol.I, pp 603-662, Haraph Prakashani, Calcutta 12,1974
19. CHANDRAGUPTA Path of a Fallen Demigod, The untold version of his life story, Rajat Pillai published by Cedar Books An Imprint of Pustak Mahal Delhi, 2012
20. CHANAKYA The Master Statesman, by Roopa Pai; cover and illustrations by Moonis Ijlal, Charitavali series, Rupa & Co, New Delhi;2003
21. `Economic Diplomacy-The Making and Un-making of India', World Focus Special Edition, India's Economic Diplomacy, No 424,April 2015, Dipavali Sen
22. Chanakyasootra (Hindi), by Dr Bhawan Simha Rana, Anil Prakashan, Delhi 110006, 1989
23. Sampurna Chanakya Niti, Tulsi Sahitya Publication, Meerut
24. Studies in Kautilya, M.V.Krishna Rao, Munshiram Manoharlal Publishers Pvt. Ltd.
25. *Aspects of Political Ideas and Institutions in Ancient India*, Ram Sharan Sharma, Motilal Banarasidass Publishers Pvt Ltd, Delhi
26. Nobel Prize-Winning Economist Amartya Sen: Social Choice And Social Welfare,http://jewishbusinessnews.com/2014/12/06 /nobel-prize-winning-economist-amartya-sen-social-choice-and-social-welfare/
27. `Kautilya',G.Harihar Sastri, *Social Philosophers*, General Editor: V.Raghavan, Publications Division, GOI, 1980
28. *Indian Political Thinkers*, Dr Vishnoo Bhagwan, Atma Ram & Sons, Delhi 110006, pp 30-66
29. *The Idea of Justice,* Amartya Sen
30. *`Jhelum Nodir Teere'* and *`Tumi Sandhyar Megh'*, Saradindu Bandopadhyaya, *Saradindu Omnibus,*Ananda Publishers, Kolkata, 1974
31. *Corporate Chanakya: Successful Management: The Chanakya Way*, RadhakrishnanPillai, http://www.crossword.in/books/

corporate-chanakya-successful- management-chanakya-way-radhakrishnan-pillai/p-books-8184951337.html

32. Jaideep Prabhu and Sourav Roy http://souravroy.com/2012/03/09/the-indian-machiavelli/#comments
33. http://www.tirunarayana.in/res/Chanakya_VVS_070309.pdf
34. On November 09, 2010 Article: http://EzineArticles.com/?expert=Challa_S.S.J._Ram_Phani
35. The Tradition of Himalayan Yoga Meditation, Swami Yoga Bharati, Full Circle, 2015, p 206-17, specifically p 206, chapter 'Yoga, Polity, Economy and Family'
36. R. Trautmann, referred to in Namita Sanjay Sugandhi (2008), Between the Patterns of History: Rethinking Mauryan Imperial Interaction in the Southern Deccan. ProQuest. pp. 88–89. ISBN 978-0-549-74441-2. Retrieved 2012-06-06)

❐

# Glossary

## A

**Abaliyasa:** 9th section of *Arthashastra*, about the weak king
**Adhikarana**: sections or themes of the *Arthashastra* text
**Adhyakshavichara:** 2nd section of *Arthashastra*, about officers
**Amatya:** courtier, minister
**Artha:** material well-being
**Arthashastra:** treatise on material well-being by Kautilya

## C

**Chanaka:** scholar who was Chanakya's father
**Chanakya:** son of Chanaka, also called Kautilya., teacher and minister of Chandragupta, expert who authored *Arthashastra, Niti* and *Sutra*
**Chandragupta:** king of Magadha groomed by Chanakya to overthrow reigning king Dhana Nanda and set up a new empire
**Chandanadasa:** friend of Amatya Rakshasa

## D

**Danda:** penalty, punishment
**Dandaniti:** rules of meting out punishment
**Dhana:** wealth, riches
**Dhana:** Nanda king of Nanda dynasty, slain by Chandragupta
**Dharma:** righteousness, rules of right conduct
**Dharmasthiya:** 3rd section of *Arthashastra*, on Civil Law
**Durga-lambhopaya:** 13th section of *Arthashastra*, about conquest of forts

## G

**Gandhara:** ancient Indian kingdom upto present Pakistan and Afghanistan and including Takshashila

## K

**Kama:** desire, physical pleasure
**Kamboja:** ancient Indian kingdom

**Kantaka:** people who pester ; craftsmen( in Tamil)
**Kantaka-shodhana:** 4th section of *Arthashastra*, on Penal Law
**Kautilya:** Chanakya, name referring to his diplomacy
**Koota:** devious
**Krodha:** anger

## M

**Magadha:** ancient kingdom of India, in present Bihar
**Mandala-yoni:** 6th section of *Arthashastra*, about circle of kings
**Mantri:** minister, advisor
**Moksha:** spiritual well-being
**Moora:** mother of Chandragupta
***Mudrarakshasa*:** old Sanskrit play, figuring Chanakya

## N

**Nanda:** a dynasty of northern India
**Niti:** rules, principles, maxims
**Nyaya:** justice, rules of justice

## O

**Oupanishadika:** 14th section of the *Arthashastra*, on secret advice

## P

**Pataliputra:** ancient city of India, near modern Patna
**Prakarana:** a part of an Adhikarana

## R

**Rajaniti:** principles of governance/politics
**Rakshasa:** demon, here chief minister of Dhana Nanda

## S

**Samghavritta:** 11th section of *Arthashastra*, about groups
**Sangramika:** 10th section of the *Arthashastra* dealing with war
**Seleucus:** a general in Alexander's army, later governor
**Shadgunya:** 7th section of *Arthashastra*, on foreign policy
**Shastra:** ancient texts
**Sutra:** short tenets
**Swami:** king, lord

## T

**Takshashila:** ancient city now, in Rawalpindi, Punjab, Pakistan
**Tantrayukti:** logistics, the last section of *Arthashastra*

## U

**Upajapa:** psychological warfare
**Upangshuvadha:** secret assassination

## V

**Varna:** castes
**Vijigeeshu:** a king who aspires to conquer other territories
**Vinayadhikarika:** 1st section of *Arthashastra*, on disciplined conduct
**Vishnugupta:** original name of Chanakya /Kautilya
**Vyasana:** 8th section of *Arthashastra*, relating to calamities

## Y

**Yogavritta:** 5th section of *Arthashastra*, on retainers

❑❑❑